D1713301

VISIONS OF DEVELOPMENT

For the writers of the stories
and for all the people about whose life, work and faith they tell us.
With grateful thanks.

Visions of Development

Faith-based Initiatives

WENDY R. TYNDALE

ASHGATE

HD
82
V57
2006

© Wendy R. Tyndale 2006

All rights reserved. No part of this publication may be reproduced, stored in a retrieval system or transmitted in any form or by any means, electronic, mechanical, photocopying, recording or otherwise without the prior permission of the publisher.

Wendy R. Tyndale has asserted her moral right under the Copyright, Designs and Patents Act, 1988, to be identified as the editor of this work.

Published by
Ashgate Publishing Limited
Gower House
Croft Road
Aldershot
Hampshire GU11 3HR
England

Ashgate Publishing Company
Suite 420
101 Cherry Street
Burlington, VT 05401-4405
USA

Ashgate website: http://www.ashgate.com

British Library Cataloguing in Publication Data
Visions of development : faith-based initiatives
    1. Community development – Religious aspects
    I. Tyndale, Wendy
    307.1'4

Library of Congress Cataloging-in-Publication Data
Visions of development : faith-based initiatives / [edited by] Wendy R. Tyndale.
        p. cm.
    Includes bibliographical references and index.
    ISBN 0-7546-5623-3 (hardback : alk. paper)
    1. Economic development – Religious aspects – Case studies. 2. Rural development – Religious aspects – Case studies. I. Tyndale, Wendy.

    HD82.V55 2006
    201'.73–dc22

                                                    2005034564

ISBN-13: 978-0-7546-5623-4
ISBN-10: 0-7546-5623-3

Printed and bound in Great Britain by TJ International Ltd, Padstow, Cornwall.

Contents

List of Plates and Table   vii
List of Contributors   ix
Foreword by Arvind Sharma   xiii
Preface   xv
Acknowledgements   xxi

1   **Transformation through Self-Knowledge and 'Awakening'**   1
    Swadhyaya: A Movement Experience in India   1
    R.K. Srivastava (Hindu: India)
    The Sarvodaya Shramadana Movement   9
    Kamla Chowdhry with Wendy Tyndale (Buddhist: Sri Lanka)
    What Kind of 'Development'?   17

2   **Filling State Deficiencies at the Grass Roots**   29
    Association for Environmental Conservation and Social Progress:
    Sarkan Zoumountsi (Chain of Solidarity)   29
    Ibrahim Salissou (Muslim: Cameroon)
    Generosity Comes from the Strength of the Waters:
    The Socio-Educational Activity of the 'Terreiro' Ilê Axé Omin Funkó   37
    Jussara Rêgo (Candomblé: Brazil)
    An Experience of Development with a Christian and Mayan Focus:
    The Case of Awakatán   44
    Antonio Otzoy (Christian/Mayan: Guatemala)
    Viable Work?   50

3   **Tribal People Take Development into Their Own Hands**   61
    Vivekananda Girijana Kalyana Kendra   61
    K.R. Usha (Hindu: India)
    Tokombéré: A Project for Human Development Founded on Faith   69
    Etienne Zikra (Christian: Cameroon)
    Faith in Ourselves   77

4   **Working with Women**   87
    Addis Ababa Muslim Women's Council   87
    Bedria Mohammed (Muslim: Ethiopia)
    Women's Empowerment through Islamic Organizations: The Role of
    'Nahdlatul Ulama' in Transforming the Government's
    Birth Control Programme into a Family Welfare Programme   94
    Christopher Candland and Siti Nurjanah (Muslim: Indonesia)

Empowering Women to Improve Rural Lives:
The Story of the Barli Development Institute for Rural Women   102
The Bahá'í International Community (Bahá'í: India)
Rights and the Bargaining Power to Claim Them   110

5   **Action for Justice and Freedom**   121
    Engaged Buddhism in Siam and South-East Asia   121
    Pracha Hutanuwatr and Jane Rasbash (Buddhist: South-East Asia)
    National Fish Workers Forum: A Spiritually Inspired Movement for
    Alternative Development   130
    Wendy Tyndale (Christian: India)
    Sebastián Acevedo Movement against Torture: A Project for the
    Dignity of Life   137
    Rosa Parissi (Christian: Chile)
    Signs of the Times: Courage to Take Action   145

6   **Some Final Reflections**   153
    Religion and Spirituality   153
    Development   156
    Contributions of Religion and Spirituality to Development   160
    Views of Development Agencies   166
    Challenges for Working Together   170
    Dialogue Must Take Place, But How?   175
    Beyond Pragmatism   177

References and Further Reading   179
Index   185

List of Plates and Table

Plates

1   Sarvodaya: pre-school
    With kind permission of Sarvodaya
2   Sarkan Zoumountsi: footbridge linking two communities
    Wendy Tyndale
3   Awakatán: strawberry picking
    Wendy Tyndale
4   VGKK: Dr Sudarshan examines a Soliga woman
    With kind permission of the Vivekananda Girijana Kalyana Kendra
5   Tokombéré: Peasant's House meeting
    With kind permission of Tokombéré
6   Sebastián Acevedo Movement against Torture: 'Secret Police Continue
    Torturing'
    With kind permission of the Sebastián Acevedo Movement against Torture

Table

5.1   Traditional Buddhist precepts and contemporary considerations   127

List of Contributors

Christopher Candland has worked for Church World Service and the United Nations. He taught South Asian politics and development studies for three years at the University of California Berkeley before taking up his present post as Assistant Professor in the Department of Political Science at Wellesley College. His stay in India in the early 1980s, his work with refugees in India and Sri Lanka in the mid 1980s, and the language study and research he has been doing since the late 1980s in Bangladesh, India, Pakistan and Sri Lanka, as well as in Thailand and Indonesia, have made him keenly aware of the centrality of faith to life in South and South-East Asia and to any full understanding of community development dynamics in the area.

Kamla Chowdhry worked with many organizations, including the Ford Foundation and the National Wastelands Development Board. The long list of institutions she helped to establish include the Indian Institute of Management in Ahmedabad, the Institute of Rural Management in Anand, the Centre for Women's Development Studies and the Vikram Sarabhai Foundation, of which she was the Founder-Director. Her interest in strategies for environmental protection and the involvement of rural people in counteracting poverty was reflected in her membership of the World Commission on Forestry and Sustainable Development, the Earth Charter Commission, the Panel of Eminent Persons for the World Summit for Sustainable Development and the Group of Trustees of the World Faiths Development Dialogue. She wrote extensively on the ethics of development, Gandhian economics and ecological survival. Kamla remained ceaselessly active until she died in January 2006, at the age of 85.

Pracha Hutanuwatr is a Thai activist and intellectual, a former Buddhist monk with a socialist background. He has worked under the guidance of Buddhadasa Bhikku – a renowned Buddhist monk and philosopher who developed the concept of Dhammic Socialism – and Sulak Sivaraksa, an influential, independent thinker. In 1988 Sulak and Pracha founded the International Network of Engaged Buddhists. His present positions include Director of the Wongsanit Ashram and Director of the Spirit in Education Movement, an NGO organizing Grassroots Leadership Training in South East Asia. He has published several major books in Thai and recently, with Ramu Mannivan, he published *The Asian Future: Dialogues for Change*, which contains intensive interviews (in English) with 14 prominent Asian thinkers.

Bedria Mohammed has a long history of defending the rights of Muslim women in Ethiopia. She is a founding member and, since 2000, has been Chairperson and Executive Director of the Addis Ababa Muslim Women's Council. Before this, she had gathered wide experience and promoted awareness of civic education and development issues through various jobs that included Project Co-ordinator for Women's Political Participation with the Ethiopian Women Lawyers' Association, Researcher on Muslim Women and Development Action for the Royal Tropical Institute (KIT) of the Netherlands and Researcher in the Gender and Civil Society Department of the Canadian government's development agency (CIDA). She has also worked with the Ethiopian National Democratic Institute for International Affairs (NDI) and with the Inter-Africa Group, where she focused on preparing the contribution of religious institutions to the new Constitution of Ethiopia.

Siti Nurjanah was born and raised in rural East Java. She is a member of the Muslim Association Nahdlatul Ulama (NU). In 1997, with fellow students from Airlangga University, she founded the Institute for Religion and Democracy, which developed programmes for the students of the NU's schools ('pesantren') and presented 'pesantren' thinking to a wider audience. She has developed programmes and resources on gender empowerment through Islamic teaching. Nurjanah is an avid writer and has worked for five years as a print and radio journalist in Indonesia and the United States. She has also conducted research for Petra Christian University and the United Nations Development Programme in Indonesia and Timor Leste. Nurjanah is now pursuing a masters degree in Social Policy at Brandeis University in Massachusetts.

José Antonio Otzoy Sotz is a Guatemalan Kaqchikel Maya and a pastor in the Kaqchikel Presbytery of the Presbyterian Church. Having studied theology at the Panamerican University of Guatemala, he worked as Co-ordinator of the Biblical Theological Unit of the Conference of Evangelical Churches of Guatemala (CIEDEG), of which he was a co-founder. He has collaborated as a consultant on education and indigenous cultures in the Latin American Biblical University based in San José, Costa Rica. His publications include: *La Espiritualidad y La Vida Cotidiana* [Spirituality and Daily Life] and *De Colores, Olores y Melodías Diferentes* [Of different Colours, Scents and Melodies]. While working with the indigenous presbyteries, he was one of the founders of the Brotherhood of Mayan Presbyteries of Guatemala.

Rosa Parissi graduated as a journalist from the University of Chile just before the military coup in 1973. Since 1964, she had been carrying out governmental social development programmes in areas of extreme poverty in Chile. After the coup she started working with human rights movements and was a founding member of the Sebastián Acevedo Movement against Torture. In 1978 her expertise in social development led to her appointment as Manager of the co-ordinated Chilean programmes of three British agencies: Christian Aid, OXFAM and CAFOD and she is still CAFOD's representative. Parissi has written many articles on social development, mainly for teaching purposes, one of which was recently published in *Le Monde Diplomatique*. She has also taught mathematics and biology in secondary schools.

Jane Rasbash lives in Scotland and works in sustainable development and Engaged Buddhism with the Spirit in Education Movement, with extensive involvement in South East Asia. She also assists with fundraising and project management of the Kitezh Children's Village in Russia. In the past she served as Co-Director of the Grassroots Leadership Training programme in Burma and as Executive Secretary to the Alternatives to Consumerism conferences in Thailand. She has written several papers on various aspects of Engaged Buddhism jointly with Pracha Hutanuwatr.

Jussara Cristina Vasconcelos Rêgo is a biologist and also holds a master's degree in Geography from the State University of Bahia, Brazil. She has been a researcher at the federal government's National Research Council and has co-ordinated ethnobotanic projects in Candomblé 'terreiros'. At present she co-ordinates the field activities of the Egbé Traditional Black Territories programme of the ecumenical organization, KOINONIA Presença Ecumênica e Serviço, which works in defence of the land and cultural rights of the Candomblé communities.

Ibrahim Mahama Salissou was born in 1956 into an impoverished Muslim family in Yaoundé, Cameroon. His parents could not read or write in French or English. They lived in a milieu marked by its cultural, ethnic and linguistic diversity but they held fast to their Muslim identity and were determined that their son should first go to a Muslim school to learn to read the Qur'an. Ibrahim was thus already 11 years old when he went to a French-speaking primary school that most children entered at the age of seven. He progressed to secondary school but for financial reasons he had to leave without passing the highest level examinations in order to get a job in the National Social Security Office. In 1995 he co-founded Sarkan Zoumountsi and is now the General Co-ordinator.

Arvind Sharma is the Birks Professor of Comparative Religion in the Faculty of Religious Studies at McGill University in Montreal, Canada. He has also taught in Australia (University of Queensland; Sydney University) and the United States (Northeastern University; Temple University; Boston University; Harvard University), and has published over 50 books and 500 articles in the fields of Indian religions and comparative religion. Two books edited by him – *Our Religions* (Harper, 1993) and *Women in World Religions* (Suny, 1987) – are widely used in teaching world religions. He is currently engaged in promoting the adoption of a Universal Declaration of Human Rights by the world's religions.

Raj Srivastava was formerly Director of the Centre for the Study of Developing Societies, Delhi, of which he is now a Senior Fellow. He has worked in the area of international politics, urban affairs, development praxis, civil society issues and socio-religious movements in India. He has served on the Faculty of the Indian School of International Studies, Delhi University, in the Shriram Centre for Human Relations and more recently at Yokohama National University. He has also been associated with the Human and Social Development Programme of the United Nations University, Tokyo and the Fundación Bariloche, Argentina. He has authored three books, including an edited volume on Swadhyaya: *Vital Connections* (2000).

Wendy Tyndale began a life-long connection with Latin America in the early 1960s, when she went to work as a volunteer teacher in Peru. She lived in a village in Chile during the government of Salvador Allende and then, in the 1990s, in Guatemala. Since 1974, when she co-founded the Chile Committee for Human Rights in London, she has worked with human rights groups, as a freelance journalist and as a development practitioner, both in the UK and Germany. After 11 years in the Latin America department of Christian Aid, she joined the World Faiths Development Dialogue. This gave her the opportunity to travel extensively in Asia and Africa, and to engage with people from many different religious traditions beyond her own. She is at present in Guatemala working in rural development with the Catholic Diocese of San Marcos.

K.R. Usha's field of work has been teaching, writing and editing. With an MPhil in history, she has taught the subject at school and undergraduate level. Presently, she is Associate Editor of *IIMB Management Review*, a quarterly journal in management studies. She is primarily a writer of fiction and is the author of two novels: *Sojourn* (Manas, 1998) and *The Chosen* (Penguin India, 2003). Her short stories have been published in various newspapers and magazines in India, and one of her short stories, *Sepia Tones*, won the Katha Award for Fiction in 1995.

Etienne Zikra Malla grew up with and in the Project for Human Promotion in Tokombéré, Cameroon, where his father started working in the early days as a nurse and Itinerant Agent. He graduated in law at Yaoundé University in 1994, and thereafter began working with the international organization Action of Christians for the Abolition of Torture (ACAT), most recently as a human rights trainer. He has written several articles and also a play on the theme of human rights. In 1998, he started work in the Tokombére Project as a teacher at the Baba Simon College and Administrator of the Youth Project. He was appointed Principal of the College in 2005. He is married and has two young children.

Foreword

Arvind Sharma
McGill University

This is an important book. Perhaps it is even more than that, on account of its revolutionary potential, for it compels one to fundamentally reassess the role of non-economic factors in economic development. The importance of the book consists in the concrete way it documents the role non-economic factors have actually played in promoting not merely economic growth but also economic development in the field. It is true that these are micro-examples and it could well be that, in economics, the scale creates the phenomenon. It could also be true that what works at the micro-level may not work at the macro-level – in fact the division of the study of economics into micro-economics and macro-economics is based on this very insight. But this is a point to be settled by evidence rather than speculation. After all, non-violent resistance on a local, personal level had been tried successfully before Mahatma Gandhi in the private sphere; it was the Gandhian experiment which demonstrated the viability of the idea that such a movement on a massive scale could even challenge the might of empires in the public sphere. It is also true that the examples are limited in number, but just when do isolated examples begin to form a pattern?

The evidence provided in this book is potentially revolutionary in no less than three ways: it demonstrates (1) that spiritual and moral development might contribute or even lead to material development; (2) that, to up the ante, the relationship of the material to the spiritual realm may not be a one-way street, as fellow travellers might insist and as much of both formal capitalist and Marxist thought has dogmatically presupposed; and (3) that, to up the ante still further, a holistic view of the world promoted by the spiritualities associated with the various religions of the world may offer a more comprehensive concept of human flourishing, including economic well-being, than the reductionistic view of the world promoted by modernity and modern economics; and that a spiritual efflorescence might simultaneously contribute equally to a spiritual as well as a material flowering. This last perspective also makes the following phenomenon less puzzling: that even the fundamentalist movements in the world often succeed in empowering their followers more than their secular counterparts.

This book deals with 13 faith and interfaith movements which have walked their talk. These movements have actually tried to organize the socio-economic life of communities along idealistic and spiritual lines, and, in doing so, have succeeded in lifting them up by their bootstraps economically as well. This is surely a phenomenon which deserves serious notice in a world in which religion is coming to play an increasingly significant role in the public sphere, irrespective of whether it dispirits us with its fundamentalism or uplifts us with its spirituality.

The larger message of the book seems to be that we should be wary of thinking homeopathically – namely, that the cure of the disease must share the nature of the cause of the disease, and that therefore economic development can only be brought about by manipulating economic variables. But whether there is a car in the garage is not decided in the garage, any more than whether there is meat in the kitchen is decided in the kitchen. Maybe the time has come to abandon the monolithic thinking that if actions have consequences, then material actions alone have real material consequences and spiritual actions have only immaterial spiritual consequences.

The evidence of this book forces one to rethink not only modern but even traditional cultural assumptions. To provide an illustration from the tradition I am most familiar with: Hindu classical thought identifies four legitimate goals of human endeavour: 'dharma' [righteousness], 'artha' [economic prosperity and political well-being], 'kāma' [the pursuit of happiness] and 'mokṣa' [liberation or salvation]. This standard view looks upon 'dharma' as regulating the pursuit of prosperity and happiness. The case studies in this book provide convincing evidence that 'dharma' can also further it, an insight which would immensely enrich modern Hindu thought.

One wonders whether the disenchantment of the world, brought about in the modern West by emphasizing the transcendent dimension of ultimate reality at the expense of the immanent, explains not only the heavy focus on economic indices of progress per se as the only indices of progress, but also the neglect of the role of non-economic and especially religious factors in the discourse on economic development. Modern spirituality implicitly recognizes the immanent dimension of the ultimate reality. Marxism perhaps went too far in denying the transcendent while imbuing the immanent with a *telos* of its own. In doing so it may have thrown the baby away with the bathwater. Modern spirituality may be less apocalyptic but is more pragmatic in viewing transcendence and immanence in mutual apposition rather than opposition.

When the shortcomings of religion were brought to the notice of the Hindu mystic Ramakrishna (1836–86) he remarked: 'Religion is like a cow. It kicks, but it also gives milk.' Modern scholars have only dealt with the kicks; this book highlights that it might also give milk, and, in a more utopian vision, may even make the land flow with milk and honey.

Preface

*For me the different religions are beautiful flowers from the same garden, or they
are branches of the same majestic tree. Therefore they are equally true, though
being received and interpreted through human instruments, equally imperfect.*
Mahatma Ghandi [1]

*The sustained commitment to just and humane developmental change is not founded
on any rational calculus of necessary or probable success. Rather it is based on a
hope-laden belief that every effort is worth making to create new possibilities.*
Denis Goulet [2]

'Until lions have their historians, tales of hunting will always glorify the hunter', says
an old African adage. This book is an attempt to listen to the roar of the lions, or more
specifically to the voice of those who, inspired by their religion or spiritual tradition,
are engaged in work with materially poor communities. It is based on a collection of
stories gathered while I was working with the World Faiths Development Dialogue
(WFDD), an initiative set up in 1998, sponsored by Rt Revd George Carey, at that
time Archbishop of Canterbury, and James D. Wolfensohn, who was then President
of the World Bank. The aim was to try to bring about a rapprochement between
the development agencies and religiously inspired organizations working with the
poor.

No collation of material is disinterested. The evident political significance of the
circumstances out of which this collection of stories arose influenced the criteria
on the basis of which they were chosen. On the one hand it was crucial to address
the characteristics of faith-based groups and movements that made them different
from other non-governmental organizations (NGOs) with which the World Bank had
hitherto engaged. The stories were thus commissioned with the intention of recording
how the religious beliefs and practice of people involved in particular examples of
faith-based work with grassroots communities influence both their vision of what
development is about as well as the way in which they try to carry it out.

On the other hand, for fruitful interaction between two parties to emerge there
must be some common ground between them. The choice of the movements and
organizations was therefore based on a set of criteria which not only included a
spread of countries and religions, but also criteria about the kind of work that was
being done. The search was for work that aimed to improve the physical as well as

---

1   M.K Ghandi, *Hindu Dharma*, Bharatan Kumarappa (ed.) (Ahmedabad, 1950),
pp. 231–2, quoted in Arvind Sharma, *Hinduism and Human Rights* (Oxford, 2004), p. 100.

2   Denis Goulet, 'Confronting Social Upheaval', in Thomas. M. McFadden (ed.),
Theology Confronts a Changing World, (West Mystic, CT, 1977), p. 35.

the spiritual well-being of people in marginalized communities – work that did not consist largely of 'handouts' (which, though essential in particular contexts, can be made with an attitude of pity that patronizes the receivers) and work that was not linked to any intention of religious conversion among the beneficiaries. I sought out examples of work that had changed people's lives for the better or had the potential to do so, while explicitly being grounded in a religious tradition. However, resources were limited so that, within the framework of these criteria, the collection is an anthology and makes no claim to being a systematic or 'representative' series.

A further choice had to be made, this time about how the stories were to be written. One alternative would have been to look for writers among development experts coming from outside the organizations. Whereas this might have produced a more conventionally 'objective' and critical account of the work being done, it would have meant once again hearing the stories at second hand rather than from the protagonists themselves, and a lot of the immediacy of the insiders' view of the relationship between their religion and their work would have inevitably been lost. As this was the most important aspect of the research, it was decided, wherever possible, to ask people who belonged to the movements or were very close to them to write their own stories.

In most cases, this has resulted in largely unproblematized narratives. Rather than aiming to 'evaluate' their activities, the writers tell of their vision, their values and the way they work against the background of their spiritual beliefs and practice. They do so with a degree of authenticity concerning the emotions and motives of the people involved that an outsider would have been at pains to capture. This is a valuable element, since it is precisely the feelings and motivation of materially poor people – as well as of development workers themselves – that development literature has up to now been very prone to ignore.

The book does not, therefore, claim to be a 'neutral' study, made at a distance from the issues and people concerned. It is founded on the assumption that there is a contribution to be made to intellectual argument from the standpoint of committed involvement and that there is no particular prime value in 'objectivity'.

The limitations of the study are obvious in its particularity. Nevertheless there is a conviction inherent in it that the prioritization of theory and its application to particular contexts that is the characteristic of most academic studies is by no means the only way of understanding what is happening. Too quickly we resort to theoretical abstractions when the need is patiently to accumulate the evidence and to accept the possibility that a theoretical framework may well not be forthcoming. Thus the starting point was not a hypothesis which the book has sought to prove. The method has been to begin with real-life stories and to draw conclusions from them that it is hoped are valid not only for these specific stories but in some cases more widely.

With the juxtaposition of even this small number of different groups and movements I have tried to give a glimpse of the range of faith-based work being carried out. However we must be careful not to suppose that what might bring good results in Guatemala will necessarily apply in India. Indeed, the differences we encounter among these examples of faith-based development seem to corroborate the often-expressed belief that generalizations across different geographical, cultural, economic and political contexts are hard to make and that 'one size fits all' development policies are unlikely to bear much fruit.

Although there has been no attempt to make a rigorous evaluation of the effectiveness of the work done in terms of economic development, the focus on the spiritual insights and resulting practice of these groups and movements has given rise to some deep and critical questioning. Issues raised include how the work described here complies with or diverges from more conventional development work, and above all what the real meaning of 'development' for the protagonists of the stories might be.

Despite genuine efforts to remain as faithful as possible to the contributors' accounts, and especially to the ideas embedded in them, some filtering has inevitably gone on through my translations of several of the stories as well as through my editing of them. Almost all the stories have been cut in length, for instance, and my choice of what to leave out might not have been the same as the writers', had they had first go. Nevertheless, the book has been written in close collaboration both with the stories' writers and with participants of the movements portrayed. In February 2004 the WFDD, together with the Vikram Sarabhai Foundation (VSF), held a workshop in Delhi for the writers and some of the protagonists of the stories.[3] This and subsequent correspondence and meetings with individuals over almost two years has ensured that everyone has had the chance to make any desired amendments through an open process, though I accept sole responsibility for the parts that I wrote myself.

Many of the points of view of the protagonists of the stories are neither unique nor necessarily unchallengeable. Some are shared and others are hotly disputed by people who would consider themselves well-rooted in the secular world but who are as wholeheartedly committed as any others to improving the lives of those whom the globalized economy ignores or victimizes. It is these shared or disputed visions that can provide the starting point for a dialogue, as long as there is a willingness to bridge the gigantic chasm that stretches ever wider between even the largest of these grassroots movements and the powerful forces that dictate how the world is ordered. A pre-requisite for such willingness is the belief that the visions of these grass-roots groups have their own validity, however limited their influence might be as yet at a global level.

Challenges to their visions do not, of course, come only from the world of secular development workers. Indeed, the most painful divergence of viewpoints can often be found among organizations and individuals that belong to the same faith traditions as the ones featured in this book, but whose vision of development is very different from theirs or who even reject the idea that religious communities should be involved in the practical affairs of this world at all.

It is also true that groups or movements working for any sort of social change sometimes find themselves at variance with their own religious institutions and hierarchies. This may be because they perceive these as having accumulated habits

---

3   See Taylor, Michael, *Eat, Drink and Be Merry for Tomorrow We Live* (London: Continuum, 2005), Chapter 7.

and beliefs over the ages that have more to do with cultural traditions than the original spirit of their faith, particularly with regard to the position of women. They may also consider that through their accommodation to the current economic system, their religious institutions have become blunt instruments when it comes to standing up for the rights of the poor or doing anything real to change their situation for the better. But all individual followers of a faith are themselves part of their institutions; hence the efforts we see in the stories to transform them from within, be this by the training of monks (Sarvodaya and the International Network of Engaged Buddhists) or by allying with religious scholars to build up a body of consensus about the meaning of their scriptures (Addis Ababa Muslim Women's Council and the Nahdlatul Ulama women's movements).

Religious involvement in matters that are now broadly described as 'development' – health, education, agriculture and so on – is as old as the hills. The dichotomy we now experience between religion and development, spirit and matter was unknown before the dualistic ways of thinking brought in by the European thinkers of the Enlightenment. The cycle of agriculture, for example, was always filled with spiritual practices and prayers for each season, and temples, mosques and churches were traditionally centres of learning and communal activities. We are thus not experiencing a new phenomenon.

The groups and movements portrayed here are carrying on these traditions, but with the added insights that their experience of internal armed conflict, religious strife, social discrimination on the grounds of class, race and caste and the misuse of secular and religious power has afforded them. Many, too, are trying to learn from their experience of both missionaries and development workers who have arrived with the best of intentions but with their own ideas of what the poor might need. But perhaps the greatest challenges they are facing now come from certain values and practices of modernity (consumerism, competition, material opulence and spiritual poverty, as well as the overriding value placed on scientific, rational thought and the devaluation of the intuitive). Each in their own way, they are wrestling with the question of what the most truly human way of living might be in the context of our age.

None of these movements is likely to come up with a blueprint for alternative development plans for the world, but they can and do provide signposts to direct us towards a different way of ordering life based on different values and a different quality of relationships among human beings and between them and their natural environment. Development practitioners around the world are faced with adverse contexts of increasing violence: structural violence and widening rather than narrowing gaps between the rich and the poor, political violence, drug-trafficking, common crime, youth gangs, gender violence in its different shades and grades, and the violence of environmental destruction. Development work in these conditions can seem overwhelming or simply a hopeless enterprise. The call, therefore, to promote spiritual and human values such as generosity, kindness, compassion, honesty, respect, justice, restraint and humility makes a lot of sense not only for faith-based organizations but for development work – and development workers – in general.

I hope this book will make a contribution towards creating a greater understanding among development agencies of the views and practice of some of the spiritually inspired groups that work most faithfully alongside the poor. I believe that these should be taken into account when any development plans are drawn up and, above all, if the intention of building broad alliances between religious and secular organizations is to bear fruit. I hope, too, that the stories show that spiritual insights and experiences are not the prerogative of the people of any single religion but, in their multifarious forms, can become integral to the daily life of all who seek their inspiration.

Wendy Tyndale
Guatemala, 2006

Acknowledgements

Visions of Development is the result of a truly collective effort in which the writers and many of the protagonists of the stories have played a major part by contributing information, insights, ideas and a great deal of personal support. The book belongs to all of us!

I have been helped along the way by many other people, too, all of whom it is impossible to name here. But I should first acknowledge the role of those who worked with me in the World Faiths Development Dialogue (WFDD). Without the Dialogue – and that means without the vision and courage of its founders and patrons George Carey and Jim Wolfensohn – I might never have had the opportunity to enter the world of so many faith traditions beyond my own. Nor would I have had the chance to meet the many staff members of the World Bank, from whose commitment and clarity I have learnt so much – Katherine Marshall must receive a special mention here.

It was Kamla Chowdhry who, with her characteristic determination and energy, originally encouraged me to embark upon a collection of 'case studies' and she supported me all the way through. We travelled to Kerala and Sri Lanka together and in 2005 Kamla had her own collection of Indian studies published.[1] It is a great sorrow to me that Kamla is no longer with us to see this book. Michael Taylor, as Director of WFDD during my last two years as researcher, was the person who bore the brunt of the ups and downs caused by the challenging task of collecting the stories. His kindness, patience and unfailing sense of humour kept me going, and I greatly appreciate his help in doing the index for me. I would like to say a special thank you, too, to Sunil Wijesiriwardena, Lapapan Supamanta, Hanumappa Sudarshan, Rajesh Parikh and Janak and Jimmy McGilligan for their help with these stories, and Abdus Sabur, Jenny Marcus, Venerable Nhem Kim Teng, Mr Yi Thon and the Aga Khan Development Network, who wrote the remaining stories from our collection which I have not been able to include in this book but which also provided the inspiration for it. Many people have, I hope, been able to read their stories on the WFDD website.[2]

Then there are all the people from many different countries and many different religious traditions who have acted as my teachers and guides over the last eight years or, in many cases, far longer. Some whose books or articles I have read are not even aware of the extent to which they have influenced me, and this may apply as well to many others who generously spent time with me at conferences (Chandra Muzaffar was among these), in villages, in urban settings or in their offices, sharing

---

1   Makarand Paranjape (ed.), Dharma and Development: The Future of Survival (New Delhi, 2005).

2   www.wfdd.org.uk.

their ideas with me about how they see development from the perspective of their religious tradition. One such conversation, on a bus in Malaysia, was with Arvind Sharma, who has been kind enough to write the foreword to the book.

Hard though it is to make such choices, I want particularly to acknowledge the help of several people who have made a very direct contribution to the book as well as, over many years, to my own ideas. Countless breakfasts with Chris Rowland at The Queen's College in Oxford have been memorable for Chris's excellent home-made bread, but especially for our deeply interesting and inspiring conversations that have given me so much orientation and encouragement. Chris's thoughts have left their mark on many parts of the book. Thierry Verhelst's perspectives more than any other's have influenced my own views on culture and development, and he helped me greatly when the book was staggering through its first phases. Morna Macleod has been at a greater distance in Mexico, but with her knowledge of Mayan culture and spirituality and her extensive experience of development practice she has given me constant support and creative advice by email. And so, from Canada, has Bill Ryan, to whose wisdom and insights the book owes a great deal. I will always remember with gratitude, too, the help that the late Maurice Wiles gave me right at the beginning with the outline of the book.

Others whom I would also like to thank for their comments and/or practical help are Jack Hogan for his very important initial encouragement, Duncan Forrester, Jean-Blaise Kenmogne, Mirabelle Damtse, Deudonné Tambe, Mother Rosemary, Paul Spray, the late Fr Dominic George, Hans Ucco, Anivaldo Padilha, Rafael Soares de Oliveira, Daleep Mukarjee, Mary Evelyn Tucker, Somboon Chungprampree, Kenneth Cragg, Hazel Johnson, Alok Mukhopadhyay, Hugo Garrido, Sandy and Jael Bharat, Roger Riddell, Sue Brandford, Deborah Eade, Francisco Alvarez, Suresh Kumar, Joel Callow, Jim Mackie, Maggie Clay, Clare Dixon, Emilio Bermejo, Dee Andrews and Imogen Mark, whose advice from her home in Chile to 'get on and write it!' started me off.

Finally I want to express my gratitude to Simon and Celia Gibbs who through the Ms C.F. Gibbs Trust gave me some generous financial assistance which greatly helped to cover costs that have arisen while I have been writing.

Chapter 1

Transformation Through Self-Knowledge and 'Awakening'

We begin with the stories of two very large grassroots movements in India and Sri Lanka whose spirituality has given them their own particular vision of 'development', though it is unlikely that Swadhyaya would even use the term in relation to its work. 'Inner transformation' – a theme which is to run through the entire book – emerges at once as an integral part of social change. Although there are many overlaps between the work described in these stories and that of more conventional development programmes, we see how certain concepts such as 'poverty' and 'empowerment' are broadened and deepened. Questions are raised about the relationship of donors to the organizations they fund, about patterns of organization and leadership and about the political engagement of such movements as these. Finally their role within their own religious traditions is considered.

Swadhyaya: A Movement Experience in India

R.K. Srivastava, August 2003

The Beginnings

It is difficult to pinpoint any particular date or year when Swadhyaya began its journey. In the early and middle forties of the twentieth century, one Pandurang Vaijnath Athavale Shastri (affectionately and popularly addressed as Dada, or Elder Brother), a young scholar in his early twenties, began to debate with his listeners in Bombay (now Mumbai) about the true import of 'bhakti' [devotion]. Within the framework of traditional religious discourses, Dada raised uncomfortable questions about the dilemmas of modern humanity and the problems of material life, individual and social. He argued that neither liberal welfarism nor socialism was capable of bridging the gulf between the haves and the have-nots, and that private charity or government hand-outs only managed to erode human dignity and a sense of self-worth. Rejecting materialism as well as fatalism, he posited that ideas expounded in the Bhagavad Gita were capable of eliminating differences between human beings, and he was determined to implement his ideas at the grassroots level in India. So began Swadhyaya.

What is Swadhyaya?

Swadhyaya is frequently and formally described as a movement of social regeneration in the Indian context. 'Swadhyaya', a Sanskrit word, means 'self-study', but it is more than this. Active as a process of self-transformation and self-empowerment, for the adherents of the movement – Swadhyayees – it is a life-changing experience that gives dignity, self-respect and self-esteem. It is a network of interacting individuals and communities. They have different identities and orientations but they come forward to share a system of belief and a sense of belonging. Such integration unleashes certain impulses at the individual and social level that facilitate community regeneration and healing.

The germinal idea of Swadhyaya is to develop an awareness of an in-dwelling God – the divine presence in every human being. Another basic idea of Swadhyaya is that 'bhakti' [devotion] is not an introverted activity; rather it is a social force. 'Bhakti' is an understanding of the relationship of human beings with the divine and with each other. For 'bhakti' to be a social force and move beyond ritualism, temple worship, scriptural learning and attending religious discourses, it has to be transformed into action – selfless, righteous action based on devotion. Self-perfection channelled through constructive work towards collective good is seen as 'krutibhakti' [devotional activism] that promotes the 'we-ness' of the human family under 'the fatherhood of God'.

Simply put, for Swadhyayees it is an experience called Swadhyaya. For them it has dramatically changed the way God is understood. It is not some kind of millennial kingdom that they are after. Swadhyaya reinterprets the received wisdom of doctrinal creed and theological traditions. It offers practical ways of drawing closer to God and others through activities that may seem far from spiritual pursuits. The signs of the sacred are all pragmatic. It works. It helps people to do better in their businesses and jobs, behave better with their families, and feel better about themselves. It is a commitment that manifests itself as an ongoing process of self-study.

Swadhyaya is an everyday experience which Swadhyayees find edifying because they feel they have entered a special community graced by God. It is a 'parivar' [family], which does not acknowledge a dichotomy between the spiritual and material, and where self-achievement gets a new meaning by working through family processes. It endows the individual with a new kind of integrity and a sense of responsibility; it means returning the best you have to the collective good. It is a celebration of life. It is a context in which everyone has their own skill and efficiency or capital in the broad sense and no one is poor. Belonging to such a 'parivar' gives a sense of security and equality. The status of the individual no longer depends on wealth but comes from a commitment to a lived idea of the divine presence. It is what Swadhyayees term a 'divine brotherhood'.

Swadhyaya in Action

Swadhyaya is non-political and maintains a low profile. Its approach is primarily (but neither exclusively nor dogmatically) inspired by insights culled from India's classical wisdom as found in the Bhagavad Gita and the Upanishads, adumbrating the common divinity dwelling within everyone. Emphasis is placed on using personal efficiency and time as a devotional offering, generating what is called 'apaurusheya laxmi' [impersonal wealth]. These insights are used to give rise to and sustain self-esteem and to counteract conventional ills (alcoholism, domestic violence, the practice of untouchability, gambling, petty crime, ethnic violence and so on).

The activities of Swadhyaya are based on a range of original economic and social 'experiments', many designed to generate 'impersonal wealth' and self-esteem in participating villages. The idea of impersonal wealth is not the end of Swadhyaya but rather perhaps its starting point. It is regulated neither by need nor by expediency. It is not about equity; it is about culture. Its appeal is based on the belief that unless cultural barriers between human beings are removed through the idea of divine brotherhood and experiments promoting ego-moderation, equality in other realms is almost impossible to achieve.

Swadhyaya, then, is the great accommodation of the material with the spiritual and the individual with the social. This cohesion is achieved and its continuity maintained by relating small concrete programmes to the larger frame of ideas and beliefs that is reflected in each of its activities. These include the following.

'Bhaktipheri' [devotional tour]

Swadhyaya places a very high value on face-to-face personal contacts in contrast to impersonal, formal contacts. Over 200,000 volunteers travel far and near on their own initiative at least two days a month, spending their own money to establish living contacts and intimate caring ties with other people and to utilize these contacts for spreading God's love. Such a Swadhyayee activist, whatever their station in life may be, carries their own food, refuses all hospitality other than simple shelter and travels with unfailing regularity. It is strictly a self-imposed obligation. Proselytizing is strictly discouraged; no effort is made to impose any pattern of activity or belief.

'Teerthyatra' [pilgrimage]

Within this framework, Swadhyaya encourages its adherents to undertake a novel kind of pilgrimage to supplement the usual 'bhaktipheris'. Small groups, mostly couples, visit various parts of the village for a longer duration, say one week, and discuss the message of Swadhyaya with individuals and groups. At the end of it all, these pilgrims assemble at a pre-designated place to show their gratitude to God. The reiterative nature of 'bhaktipheri' and 'teerthyatra' is crucial for integrating a myriad of local communities into the Swadhyaya family.

'Loknath Amritalayams' [eternal abode of the Lord of the World]

To restore the temples to their original role as socio-economic centres of the village, Swadhyaya has taken on a new initiative of non-sectarian temple-building called 'Loknath Amritalayam'. Built from locally available material and with voluntary labour of the Swadhyayees, 'Amritalayams' are simple, semi-permanent structures without walls, but mostly with gardens around them.

Each village couple, irrespective of caste origin, gets a chance to work as 'pujari' [priest] for a few days in the year. Villagers gather in the 'Amritalayam' every morning and evening for prayers. A Hindu can recite the Gita with the same freedom as a Muslim the Qu'ran or a Christian the Bible. After the evening community prayer, the assembly discusses individual and collective problems and attempts to sort them out informally. It reviews the progress of Swadhyaya activities running in the village. At regular intervals the Swadhyayee villagers offer to God a portion of their earnings; they do so anonymously and voluntarily. The collections so received are distributed to the needy as a benediction of the temple and the surplus is spent on infrastructural needs of the village as a whole.

Even more than a place for remembering God, the 'Amritalayam' becomes the focus of an alternative world of learning and culture, of personal and social renewal, and of community life independent of state institutions and processes. A spirit of mutual help is reinforced and initiatives are taken for innovations and reforms. The first 'Amritalayam' was built in 1980. Villages where 90 per cent of the people are committed Swadhyayees are allowed to build them. There are now about 150 of them.

'Yogeshwar Krishi' [divine farming]

This is the collective farming of a single field (normally of 3–5 acres) by the villagers who give their labour possibly for one or two days per cropping season as an offering to God. The resulting crop belongs to no one except God. The wealth generated by the sale of the output is thus 'impersonal'.

One-third of the benefits of the harvest is used to meet short-term needs of individual indigents, not as a loan or charity, but as 'prasad' [divine grace]. The recipient is under no obligation to repay it, and there is certainly no interest to be paid. The giving and receiving of these sums is done so discreetly and with such subtle grace that it obviates any sense of inferiority on the part of recipients. The remaining two-thirds of the income is kept in a trust fund to meet the long-term needs of the local community and to buy agricultural inputs needed for 'yogeshwar krishi' from time to time. Currently there are some 3,500 such devotional farming experiments.

Swadhyaya is not involved in questions of property relations and peasant rights but it tries to create a common ground where disinterested action aimed at the good of all is possible. The very opening up of this space projects the possibility of deepening its impact to transform traditionally anchored mindsets. Its initial effort is to rid the farmers of docility and the lower strata of servility and to instil in them a feeling of self-respect. The farming community also learns self-reliance and escapes dependence on the state or anybody else.

'Shree Darshanam' [divine communes]

Swadhyaya believes that since egalitarian divisions of property or wealth do not necessarily eradicate avarice and acquisitiveness, the socialization of ownership is no answer to people's economic predicament. The answer lies in selfless collective action grounded in the belief that God is with me and is my co-partner in my daily life. Collective efforts are organized not in the framework of competition and fear but in the framework of devotional offering, brotherhood, harmony and selfless action.

To confirm this belief, in recent years Swadhyaya has introduced the idea of 'shree darshanam', where Swadhyayees from about 20 villages come together to work on a single large farm of 20 acres or more. The produce of such divine communes, now about two dozen in number, is redistributed for the larger good of the community, even outside the villages involved in the experiment. But the principle aim is not economic. It is to build selfless relations among the neighbouring villages, inspire the people to sublimate their egos, and extend the inclusiveness of community, cutting across deeply rooted primordial affiliations.

'Matsyagandha'

In a similar manner, Swadhyaya has brought cultural and socio-economic transformation to the fishing communities living in the coastal region of western India, extending from Goa to Okha. The stereotypical image of these 'sons and daughters of the sea' was of marginal and disinherited groups. Aggressive, adventurous and sturdy, they were notorious for heavy drinking, gambling and smuggling and were despised by others for their profligacy and for their supposed criminal tendencies.

These 'children of the sea' started offering a portion of their earnings (normally a day's catch each month) at the feet of God. Soon enough they had substantial resources. A productive use for their capital and skills (sailing and fishing) had to be found. Ultimately the suggestion came from Dada that with these funds, belonging to no one but God, they could buy motorized boats and more efficient tools and tackle. Fishing could be their way to express their devotion to the Creator.

Thus the experiment called 'Matsyagandha' (after a legendary fisherwoman) took its shape. The Swadhyayee fisherfolk treat the 'Matsyagandha' boats as floating temples. A crew of six to ten is on board each boat. Fishing goes on all year round except for a three-month pause during the monsoon period which is used for repairs and refitting the boats. The volunteers are many more than the 'Matsyagandha' boats. No individual fisherman gets a chance of more than one trip (of 24 hours) in a year.

The experiment in generating impersonal wealth through fishing on motorized boats and trawlers, and dredging sand from the estuary bed, is similar to divine farming. There is no employer and no employee; there are no owners and no workers;

no one has claim over what they have willingly offered to God. Each fisherman and seaman is a 'pujari' [priest], while he is on his floating temple. The disbursement of wealth created by 'Matsyagandha' is similar to that of divine farming. To date there are about 100 vessels and a few more are added each year. The estimated number of Swadhyayee fishermen and women exceeds 1 million. Every year over 2 million rupees are distributed to needy fishermen who are using the money even for non-fishing entrepreneurial activities such as cyber cafés, trucking and the restaurant business.

'Vrkshmandirs' [tree temples]

For Swadhyaya, trees are a living testament to the omnipresence of God. Acting on this idea, Swadhyayees have started renting or purchasing large pieces of barren land, turning them into 'upavans' [orchards and woodlands] and naming them after an ancient sage. After acquiring an 'upavan' plot, Swadhyayees from 15 to 20 villages around the 'upavan' and from neighbouring towns first rehabilitate its land, dig wells for its irrigation, and then dig the holes for saplings. Most are fruit trees. Finally the day arrives when at a given time thousands of Swadhyayees, from far and wide, stand with a sapling in their hands to lower into the holes. In about five minutes the planting of an orchard of, say, 40 acres is complete.

Once a 'vrkshamandir' is set up, Swadhyayees from neighbouring villages and towns take turns tending the saplings and trees in a spirit of devotion as 'pujaris'. These 'pujaris' number nearly 100,000. As a result, large plots of totally desolate and barren land are now turning into beautiful lush green orchards, where the plants' survival rate is claimed to be nearly 100 per cent. The first 'vrkshmandir' was raised in July 1979. Now there are two dozen, covering an area of over 500 acres. These orchards unite the rich and the poor, high castes and low castes, erstwhile neighbourhood enemies, the learned and the illiterate into the closely knit fabric of the Swadhyaya brotherhood. A work of this magnitude under the government social forestry scheme costs million of rupees, has a high loss rate of plants and attracts numerous complaints against it from those who are supposed to be its beneficiaries.

Water conservation

Through twin projects of water conservation and management, Swadhyaya is changing the face of large tracts of semi-arid parts of western Gujarat where underground water resources have been all but exhausted. Since 1992 Swadhyaya has recharged over 100,000 wells (by replenishing the aquifers) and built or renovated over 500 ponds. Farm productivity has been raised by between 100 and 300 per cent. Moreover the cost incurred by Swadhyaya in recharging a well (about 500 rupees) is nearly one-tenth of the cost incurred by official agencies (5,000 rupees). By spending nearly 5 million working hours of devotional labour on this initiative of water harvesting, by 1996–97 Swadhyaya had freed hundreds of thousands of acres of land from dependence on rain-fed irrigation alone.

Other Initiatives

Using devotional motivation and the experience of local communities, the Swadhyaya family has shown considerable creativity and capacity for constructive activities to reinforce the idea of human dignity. They mainly relate to enriching the diets of marginal groups who are victims of chronic malnutrition; improving the quality of village life through better sanitation and better drainage; enlarging the supply of potable water in the villages; raising farm productivity and rural incomes through eco-friendly techniques, vocational training and occupational diversification; facilitating harmony between farmers and farm labourers and so on. These activities are too numerous to elaborate but examples include: health centres in remote areas run by highly skilled Swadhyayee medical professionals; voluntarily managed stores in large villages and cities that sell Swadhyayee villagers' surplus produce, homemade soaps, matchsticks, milk products, candles and other provisions; and centres for dairy products to ensure that the villagers have the first claim over the milk produced in the village.

All these centres and activities are responses to urgent community needs. When replicated over time and over large areas, they have the potential to become a major programme. Swadhyayees make efforts to conserve what is best in local tradition, though it may not carry a label such as 'sustainable development' or 'greening the earth'. To cite one example, in the month of July many Swadhyayee couples plant saplings around their homes and tend them on a regular basis. Since 1993 more than 8 million saplings have been sown.

Then there is the '*Tattvajnana Vidyapith*', a residential school of philosophy and humanities established in 1956 by Dada on a 13-acre site near Bombay. It currently enrols nearly 200 non-paying graduate and post-graduate students from India and abroad. The institution is run without any support from the government or philanthropic subvention. Professors offer courses on a voluntary basis and the students help to maintain the site in good order. It aims to combine the best of traditional knowledge with the best of the conventional philosophy curriculum pursued in a liberal arts college.

Besides the 'Vidyapith', Swadhyaya has set up several residential higher secondary schools and vocational training centres in Maharashtra and Gujarat at the request of local Swadhyayees. While links with the state educational apparatus are maintained for reasons of certification, there is a continuous effort to inculcate Swadhyaya values through greater emphasis on programmes of non-formal education, the most extensive of which is called '*Vidya Prem Vardhan*' [seeking knowledge for the love of it]. Under this programme some 100,000 candidates world-wide annually sit examinations at seven levels on cultural and philosophical topics, notably Vedic knowledge. Successful candidates are awarded certificates of merit.

There is also a well-developed and popular seven-year non-degree course at Bhav Nirjhar, a Swadhyaya institution in Ahemdabad. It combines traditional and modern course material as well as vocational training for rural students. The intention is that students will take up their family vocations and Swadhyaya work after completing the course.

Conclusion

In this brief overview, an effort has been made to show that Swadhyaya is a new kind of non-sectarian social creative movement. It is difficult to judge the significance of Swadhyaya, either by its spatial spread or its sheer numbers; it is neither a project of identity articulation nor of resource mobilization. It is a project of inner transformation and redefining human relationships. The sacred becomes more personal and serviceable in meeting individual and community needs. These are not material needs. These are needs of love, identity, humility, self-acceptance and self-esteem. Though it is an inwardly focused spirituality, its main concern is human life. Since the idea of the separation of the secular and the ecclesiastical is deeply ingrained in critical minds the world over, religion-oriented visions are avoided in most public discourse. Swadhyaya claims a place in the public sphere because it is both a state of being and a state of action.

The Sarvodaya Shramadana Movement

Kamla Chowdhry with Wendy Tyndale, 2002/04

Early Years

The Shramadana Movement began in Sri Lanka in 1958 when A.T. Ariyaratne, a young science teacher, organized a holiday work camp with the help of his students in a remote and destitute village. 'Shrama' means energy or labour; 'dana' is a basic Buddhist concept that means 'giving'; but it means more than that, as in the process of giving the giver, too, achieves self-respect and self-esteem, and also a sense of peace.

Within a few years this idea of 'shramadana' spread to hundreds of schools and thousands of schoolchildren were participating in weekend village camps to share and donate their labour for development activities that the villagers identified. The students lived with the villagers in their huts, shared their meals and shared their work.

In the early years of his pioneering work, Ariyaratne visited India to learn about Gandhian philosophy and work. He was much influenced by Vinoba Bhave and his Sarvodaya Bhoodan Movement – 'sarvodaya' meaning the 'welfare' or 'uplifting' of all and 'bhoodan' meaning the 'gift of land'. After Ariyaratne's visit to India, the name 'Sarvodaya Shramadana' was given to the Sri Lankan movement but 'Sarvodaya' took on the more Buddhist meaning of 'awakening' of all. This awakening has six major dimensions: spiritual, moral, cultural, social, economic and political.

Joanna Macy, a North American who spent some time living with Sarvodaya in the 1980s, explains:

> Implicit in this goal (of 'awakening') is the belief that a root problem of poverty is a sense of powerlessness. While most modern planners would view the goal of spiritual awakening as idealistic and irrelevant, the Sarvodaya Movement sees any development programme as unrealistic which does not recognize the psychological impotence gripping the rural poor. Sarvodaya believes that by tapping their innermost beliefs and values, one can awaken people to their 'swashakti' [personal power] and 'janashakti' [collective or people's power].[1]

Spirituality and Development in Sarvodaya

At the time when Sarvodaya began, there was a rich fund of traditional cultural and spiritual values such as sharing and mutual help in economic activities in the villages of Sri Lanka, for example in rice farming. It is on this (now fast disappearing) cultural

---

1   Joanna Macy, *Dharma and Development: Religion as a Resource in the Sarvodaya Self-help Movement* (West Hartford, 1983), p. 31.

and spiritual tradition that Sarvodaya has founded its work of material development for rural communities, with special emphasis on the most destitute.

In an interview in 2001, A.T. Ariyaratne spoke of four essential Buddhist values that form part of and emerge from the awakening of a human being: the first is 'metta' [loving-kindness] to humans, animals and plants, which means respect for all forms of life; this leads on to 'real action' based on 'karuna' [compassion] which, in turn, gives rise to 'muditha' [the unselfish joy of living]; and finally, over a period of time, it is possible develop 'upekha' [equanimity or a balanced mind] that brings detachment from loss or gain, achievement or failure.[2] In discussing 'upekha' one Sarvodaya worker said: '"Upekha" is dynamite. It is surprising the energy that is released when you stop being attached to the results of your action. You discover how much can be accomplished when nothing is expected in return.'

Religion for Sarvodaya has always been a way of life rather than rituals. Its motto, 'We build roads and roads build us', points to the inner and outer transformation that happen dialectically through the movement.

The Sarvodaya Movement has used Buddhist concepts and has updated them in terms of village needs and concerns. Over the centuries 'dana', for instance, had become identified with donating alms to the 'sangha' [community of monks] rather than giving one's time and skills and energy for the good of the village. Giving in any form is encouraged in Sarvodaya – rich farmers are encouraged to donate their land for road building or other community purposes, skilled workers are encouraged to donate their skills, and poor people whatever they can spare.

Another core principle of both Buddhism and Sarvodaya is social equality. Sarvodaya has lived out the notion that discrimination is a moral outrage by choosing to build up the movement with people from the most impoverished and outcast villages.

Shramadana Camps

Since it is the villagers who do their own thinking, planning and putting into action, the shramadana camps provide opportunities for real leadership to emerge in rural communities. After six to eight hours of hard physical labour come three or four hours of interaction with others through discussion, dialogue, song and dance. It is through this interaction that an integrated programme of education, health, economic activities and local government emerges.

'Shramadana' has led to the building and repair of houses, digging of wells, construction of latrines, cleaning of irrigation canals, cleaning of temples and sacred sites, planting of trees, growing of food crops, weeding and harvesting of paddies and so on. But for millions of people in Sri Lanka – non-Buddhists as well as Buddhists – it has acquired a profound significance beyond practical action, as a positive force for the liberation of individuals and society. It means removing social and economic

---

2   Interview with Chowdhry and Tyndale in Moratuwa, 10 November 2001.

injustice, and freeing human beings so that they can participate constructively in the activities and development of the community as a whole.

Agnieska Komoch, a visitor from Europe to a shramadana camp, gives this account of her visit to Samagipura, a new village in northern Sri Lanka made up of Singhalese, Tamils and some Muslims whose former villages had been engulfed in landslides:

> The purpose of the three-day shramadana camp was to introduce the villagers to the concept of pooling resources and working together for the common good. Our work consisted of widening the road by at least a meter, digging a water ditch and filling the holes with the surplus dirt. ... It was an amazing experience performing backbreaking work alongside small children and grandmas ... The general feeling was that everybody gave what he or she could and we appreciated each other's work. Our sweat was the same and the work we did was the same.[3]

The work of the shramadana camps often motivates the government of Sri Lanka to come in with its own programmes, such as road improvement and bridge building. However, the people of Sarvodaya criticize the 'top-down' way in which the government works, without the participation of the local communities. This and the fact that the government charges for its services often leads such programmes to collapse.

Village-level Organization

Sarvodaya's five-stage development model for village-level organization gives a good idea of the process that has gone on in thousands of different Sri Lankan villages, even though in practice some stages may not have happened strictly according to plan or may have overlapped with other stages. The first stage is to introduce and encourage functional leadership through shramadana camps. After this, groups and training programmes are carried out according to the needs of each particular village. Mothers, youth, elders, children, farmers, teachers, craftspeople, artists and so on each form their own group.

The different groups then go on to stage three, prioritizing their needs and discussing what projects they want to undertake to address them. It is at this stage that official Sarvodaya Shramadana societies are formed as legal bodies that can take out loans from Sarvodaya's Economic Development Programme and banks. Around 3,000 full-scale Sarvodaya Shramadana societies have now been registered. Savings societies are often started and small enterprises such as community shops or vegetable plots are set up. Several thousand villages have established their own Sarvodaya Village Development Banks. These are staffed largely by local women and the payback rate for their loans is estimated at 98 per cent.

---

3   http://sarvodaya.org/Library/dana/Dana%20Kellog/Workcamp.htm (accessed 6 May 2003).

At stage four, the decentralized, small-scale, labour-intensive and environmentally friendly income-generating activities continue, using appropriate technology such as handpumps for wells, solar energy, ceramic cooking stoves, and organic compost and pesticides. Opportunities for employment and self-financing increase and the social programmes of the groups continue. The fifth stage ideally sees self-financing growing to the extent that the surplus generated can be shared with other communities.

Villagers are guided along the 'middle path' of no affluence and no poverty by keeping in mind Sarvodaya's 'ten basic human needs' when they plan their projects. These are: a clean and beautiful environment, a clean and adequate supply of water, a minimum of clothing requirements, an adequate supply of food, basic health care, a modest house, energy requirements, basic communication, total education and spiritual and cultural needs.

The little village of Dambara in the south of Sri Lanka provides an example of Sarvodaya in practice. The villagers draw up a plan at the beginning of each year and a monk from the temple writes it down. Most of the participants in the Shramadana Society are women, because the men are out working during the day.

Through Sarvodaya the villagers have set up a biodiversity project that includes some forest preservation as well as a flourishing medicinal herb garden, from which they make cures for wounds and snakebites as well as common illnesses. They have also built houses for a number of families, beginning with the most destitute, and installed latrines for many families. All the work is done on a voluntary basis and it is co-ordinated at weekly meetings in the temple that start with a period of meditation and a song. A credit and savings bank functions in a room donated by the temple. The monk has played an important role but has now, according to one woman, made himself redundant: 'At the beginning we needed the monk', she said, 'but now we can manage by ourselves'.[4]

At present the Sarvodaya Shramadana Movement is working in about 15,000 villages. To help the village programmes, over a period of time national-level specialized institutions have been created that include: a society for the relief and welfare of refugees, orphans, the malnourished and disabled; movements for human rights, conflict resolution, legal education, peace education and peace work; and a movement for children's rights and welfare.

More than 5,000 pre-schools throughout the country have been built and maintained by Sarvodaya, providing employment for young women, nutritious food, safe learning activities for children, and often a community centre (see Plate 1). There is also a centre for the prevention of drug addiction and for rehabilitation, a printing and publications department and a school for deaf mute children. The Sarvodaya Economic Enterprises Development Services Bank (SEEDS) provides support for economic development.

---

4   Visit to Dambara by Chowdhry and Tyndale, 10 November 2001.

Role of Buddhist Monks in the Sarvodaya Movement

The 'bhikkhus' [Buddhist monks] play a key role in the success of the Sarvodaya Movement. When a new village is to be introduced to Sarvodaya Shramadana work, more often than not it is the 'bhikkhu' who approaches the villagers and organizes a public meeting, generally held in the temple premises, to discuss their problems. The 'bhikkhus' use religious stories and religious terms familiar to the community to convey the Buddha's ideas of self-reliance and of compassion and fearlessness that are necessary for communities to be able to change their behaviour and relationships.

The 'bhikkhus' in Sri Lanka are particularly respected, and their access to government officials and other important persons makes it easier for the proposed activities to be undertaken by the Sarvodaya Movement in villages. However, A.T. Ariyaratne warns the 'bhikkhus', who have their own Sarvodaya Bhikkhu Association, not to curry favour with the members of parliament, reminding them that the real power is with the people.

The 'sangha' is very much part of Sri Lankan civil society and many monks became caught up in the nationalist movement of the Singhalese that fanned the flames of the war against the Tamils. Through working with and offering training to 'bhikkhus' in the villages, Sarvodaya has made an important contribution towards their return to Buddhist principles of non-violence. The development activities of the 'bhikkhus' have had a profound effect not only on the villagers, but on the 'sangha' itself. The understanding of the 'dharma'[5] has come to include putting spiritual values into practice by involving village communities for village development. The process has benefited the 'sanghas' as much as the village communities.

Meditation and Peace Work

Sarvodaya has been criticized for being too slow in the past to use its influence to counteract nationalism within the Buddhist 'sangha'. It is, however, the only Sri Lankan organization that was able to preserve a centre in Jaffna during the war, and it is now spreading more and more in the north. It has organized mass peace meditations, one of which, in a Hindu temple in Jaffna, drew together 5,000 people from different religious traditions, including many Buddhist monks.

Now the Vishva Niketan, a Peace Centre for Peoples of All Nations, has been set up in Moratuwa, near Sarvodaya's headquarters, 'to pursue the ideal of inner and outer peace'. Training courses in meditation are offered to prisoners, prison officers, senior executives from the private sector, doctors, midwives and lawyers, as well as to thousands of villagers.

Vishva Niketan has been established in the firm belief that enduring peace can only be attained when the participants achieve inner peace – a cessation of conflict within themselves. Training is offered in learning and practising conflict resolution

---

5   The 'dharma' is the teaching and practice of Buddhism but it also means the nature of reality.

and human rights as the basis of peace and justice in every community the world over. The centre aims to promote mutual understanding among people of different cultures and faiths and to encourage engagement in social service and welfare activities with a view to promoting harmonious co-existence.

Sarvodaya pays special attention to young Hindus, Muslims, Christians and Buddhists from villages in the conflict areas of Sri Lanka. Through meditation and conflict resolution courses, they are trained to overcome their fear and to play a leadership role in their communities where they work to build trust and understanding through programmes on health and education for villagers and refugees from other places.

Sarvodaya's Concept of Poverty and Development

Sarvodaya does not see development as a process whereby 'one set of people who are "rich" are trying to do something for others who are "poor"', says A.T. Ariyaratne.

> We at Sarvodaya believe that the 'poor' are rich in some respects and the 'affluent' are poor in some other respects. That is why our development programmes include both. ... In order to deal with poverty it is not only important to empower the poor, but simultaneously to 'de-empower' the affluent. ... It is essential that the affluent be educated to accept the need for a life style which is capable of being sustained.[6]

Some differences between Sarvodaya's view of development and that of professional development agencies became apparent through the relationship of Sarvodaya with several foreign agencies that provided funding for its work. At the beginning, Sarvodaya received no outside funds, and 90 per cent of the professionals working with the movement were volunteers. But as time went on and Sarvodaya became better known, offers of money began to come from abroad, and in 1972, having legally registered as a non-governmental organization (NGO) in Sri Lanka, Sarvodaya received its first outside funding.

For about ten years all went well but disagreements with the donors arose with the result that, in 1993, they began to make radical cuts in their grants. In Sarvodaya's view the donors wanted to change its identity from being a spiritually inspired movement to becoming a centralized development agency, and indeed Sarvodaya had already, at the behest of the donors, turned into a huge and rather bureaucratically run NGO. The suggestion that Sarvodaya should use more modern business management techniques and monitoring systems and produce more professional financial accounts than those that were coming from the villages threw up countless questions about human relationships and the ethos of a movement based on trust.

---

6 A.T. Ariyaratne, speech to the United Nations Development Programme (UNDP), 1997.

The more sceptical donor agencies were unable to appreciate the importance given by Sarvodaya to spiritual empowerment involving activities such as meditation, which fell outside their development remit. They wanted the work on economic development to be separated from the spiritual side of the movement.

For a while Sarvodaya complied with the donors' requests, but such a split between spirituality and economics is alien to the Buddhist viewpoint. Sarvodaya considers a strong spiritual and ethical basis to be essential for the success of any economic or political work. Spiritual empowerment, Sarvodaya believes, leads to people feeling secure enough to give up drinking and gambling and being more open to others whose opinions and beliefs may be different from their own. It also means acting on the basis of genuine love and care for others instead of clinging on to individualistic desires for status and wealth. A.T. Ariyaratne explains:

> If you learn to keep your mind silent and to overcome selfish greed you have the necessary means to take the right decisions. Nothing remains unchanged for a single moment. When you attach yourself to something, thinking it's permanent, suffering will follow. The pre-requisite of lasting happiness is to accept your real Self and let go of the 'I' that is an illusion. By thus putting your heart and soul into what you do, relating to people without expecting anything in return, caring for the environment without wanting to withdraw profits, you can make a positive contribution to 'development'.[7]

The Future

Following the withdrawal of most of the donors' support, Sarvodaya took the decision to turn its entire attention once again to being a Buddhist-inspired movement to bring about social, economic and political change. In 2000 A.T. Ariyaratne's son, Vinya Ariyaratne, who is a medical doctor, took over as Executive Director of the movement. He recognizes that some of the criticisms of the funding agencies were not altogether unfounded. 'The challenge we are facing', he says 'is to build on a movement headed by a charismatic leader in order to meet present needs. We have to look at new ways of doing things but without losing any of our values.'[8]

Sarvodaya will not lose its Buddhist identity, nor will it go back to operating along the lines of a centralized NGO. On the contrary the plan is now that the 3,000 villages with the strongest sense of community and most highly developed spiritual and material resources will help the other villages to link with each other rather than with Sarvodaya's central structure. This model of a network without a centre is closer to the idea of the Buddhist 'sangha' as a self-governed community.

The new emphasis on decentralization is in accordance with A.T. Ariyaratne's vision, shared by many within Sarvodaya, of forming a grassroots movement to challenge not only the government's economic and social policies but the party political system itself. With Sarvodaya's 15,000 villages as the base, the idea

---

7   Interview with Chowdhry and Tyndale, 10 November 2001.
8   Interview with Chowdhry and Tyndale, 10 November 2001.

is to build up a new system of Gandhian inspired participatory democracy in Sri Lanka founded on Buddhist values and consensus politics. Ariyaratne reckons that the Sarvodaya Movement now has enough popular support to be able to bring about profound political changes in the country. In 2001, the Deshodaya [National Awakening] Organization was founded to promote this plan.[9]

Even while becoming a more political movement, however, Sarvodaya is holding on to its development work. An effort is being made to gain more financial independence in the villages through the development of the Sarvodaya Economic Enterprises Development Services, and there is a greater emphasis on linking up with markets, on efficient management and on research to improve the economic effectiveness of the work.

But the vision is still of economic development nourishing the social movement. Sarvodaya has every intention of remaining true to the original idea of bringing Buddhist philosophy to life by providing action that put its principles into practice. Whether this vision will be realized in the future through establishing a new political, economic and social system based on Buddhist principles for the whole country remains to be seen.

---

9   See George D. Bond, *Buddhism at Work* (Bloomfield, 2004), pp. 111–14.

What Kind of 'Development'?

The problem is how, in conditions of continuous and accelerating change, to put people first, and poor people first of all; how to enable sustainable well-being for all.

Robert Chambers[10]

Spirituality

Swadhyaya and Sarvodaya are guided by the belief that a change of consciousness is necessary for individuals to free themselves from the tyranny of egoism and, as taught in Buddhism, of greed, hatred and delusion. It is only through such a process of transformation, they say, that people are able to relate to each other with compassion and respect – a necessary condition for the creation of just and harmonious societies.

With this starting point, Swadhyaya and Sarvodaya are drawing deeply on the spiritual sources of the Hindu and Buddhist traditions, at the heart of both of which is the quest to free our true selves from the clutter of our projected images of who we are so that our action, rather than being merely a reaction to the phenomenal world around us, arises freely and spontaneously from within. This is what A.T. Ariyaratne means when he speaks of 'real' action and what Swadhyaya refers to as 'selfless, righteous action based on devotion'.

To some this may sound suspiciously like 'quietism', like concentration on one's spiritual life at the cost of disregarding the social and material needs of others. But whilst prayer and meditation are of great importance to Swadhyaya and Sarvodaya, they both emphasize the importance of practical action as a means itself to spiritual awareness and self-discovery. 'We build roads and roads build us', says Sarvodaya, and it is through 'devotional activism' that the Swadhyayees aim to arrive at an awareness of the divine presence in every human being. 'Self-study' is a dialectical process, reaching outwards and inwards so that the outer and the inner mutually influence each other. Inner change and social change are parts of the same thing, as inseparable as are body and mind.

Those who are 'awakened' are able to perceive the interrelatedness of all beings and, as Swadhyaya puts it, the 'we-ness' of the human family. Through the interchange of spirituality and practical action, people can overcome their sense of inferiority or superiority in relation to others and are able to take action for the common good without feeling they have to protect their own interests. It is in the light of this philosophy that Swadhyaya states that its focus of attention is not on

---

10 Robert Chambers, *Whose Reality Counts? Putting the First Last* (London, 1997), p. 14.

equity but on 'divine brotherhood'[11] and ego-moderation, and that A.T. Ariyaratne insists that Sarvodaya is a movement of development for all – development needed by both rich and poor alike.

It is impossible to describe exactly the energy, self-confidence and sense of renewal that has been generated among so many millions of adherents to these movements. Some people have likened Swadhyaya to Christian evangelical movements because of the emotional security and sense of belonging as well as the process of transformation that it offers its adherents. It clearly inspires people, too, to 'spread the word'. However, in its openness and welcoming acceptance of people of different religions, it avoids all cultish or confrontational behaviour and it does not exclude non-members. We are told, for instance, that the 'divine communes' are open to villages that are not part of the movement.

Poverty

Neither Sarvodaya nor Swadhyaya condones or overlooks material poverty. Hindu and Buddhist philosophies regard material poverty as a scourge. They see it as a cause of physical, mental and emotional suffering and a real hindrance to human flourishing. The sense of hopelessness so often generated by material deprivation is considered to be among the principle causes of immoral and degrading behaviour such as gambling, drinking and stealing; moreover poverty deprives people of educational opportunities and the possibility of devoting time and energy to gaining deeper spiritual awareness. Both Sarvodaya and Swadhyaya are therefore careful to attend to the needs of the poorest people in their communities. The idea of giving away any surplus gains to those who need it most is always present.

Is not their strategy of personal change, however, too long-term and idealistic to be of any real use in combating poverty? To answer this question we need to return to the dialectical relationship between inner transformation and social change. Since they are so intimately related and each exerts influence on the other, there is no idea of chronology: that first we must transform ourselves and then we can change the world. Right from the start Sarvodaya has always given a high priority to achieving practical improvements in impoverished villages.

Nevertheless, since for these movements the concepts of poverty and wealth embrace more than a lack or abundance of material goods, they do not see the answer to poverty as lying merely in increasing people's income and consumption. Buddhism tells us that one of the main causes of human suffering is the craving that comes from our attachment to material things and the status and power they bring with them. If this is true, suffering can never be overcome by the continual creation of new desires that is the driving force behind the culture of consumerism. Shramadana has given rise to countless initiatives that have raised the material standard of living

---

11 The term 'brotherhood' is used in an inclusive sense. As we shall see later, women are neither disregarded nor segregated in the Swadhyaya movement. They have no less importance in the 'parivar' than men.

of some of the poorest people of Sri Lanka but, as we see from Sarvodaya's 'ten basic human needs', for the Sarvodaya Shramadana societies the opposite of poverty is not wealth but sufficiency.

Indeed, it is not only poverty that is the problem but also disproportionate wealth. One of the driving motivations of Athavale in setting up Swadhyaya was the huge disparity between the living standards of the rich and the poor that he saw around him in India. Because of this the process of self-study must be undertaken by the rich as well as by the poor. The Swadhyayees who set out to dialogue with villagers are very often from the urban middle classes.

Swadhyaya's approach has been less directly aimed at material improvements than Sarvodaya's. The often substantial material benefits that ensue are almost an involuntary outcome of the spiritual and social regeneration that is the life-blood of the movement. But this does not make these benefits any less real or far-reaching; nor does it reduce the value of the contribution of the practical farming, fishing and forestry work as a unifying force within the movement.

Empowerment

The notion of personal and collective empowerment is crucial to understanding what both these movements mean by 'development'. It includes but also goes beyond the sense in which it is generally used in development discourse, that is empowering people to secure their livelihoods, to stand up for their rights or to negotiate political power-sharing within their communities and states. The meaning of empowerment for Swadhyaya and Sarvodaya is essentially to discover and release the power that lies within us to transcend the boundaries of the individual and collective ego and thus to live life skilfully, attaining inner contentment, peace and security. Education has a major role to play in the process whereby this spiritual and moral empowerment gives rise to social, economic and political empowerment.

Swadhyaya's formal educational institutions testify to the importance the movement gives to combining elements of formal contemporary Indian schooling and university curricula with traditional knowledge, thus validating the students' own culture and spirituality. The residential courses are open only to boys, but through its huge non-formal educational programmes Swadhyaya reaches thousands of women too, encouraging people at all levels of scholastic achievement to learn more about their own philosophical tradition and to think for themselves. The provision of vocational training for rural students is also a validation of their way of life. The idea of 'seeking knowledge for the love of it' is refreshing in a world in which education seems to be being narrowed down more and more to a process of training to achieve good examination results.

Sarvodaya shares the view that the purpose of education is to prepare people for life as well as training them for specific types of work. The movement's locally run pre-schools aim to set children off on the right path with a strong grounding in values. Its training courses – ranging from peace education and conflict resolution to teacher training, health education and training in management and legal aid – are designed to give villagers the knowledge and skills they need to engage constructively with society. Its school that helps deaf mute children to play their part in the villages they come from, is a symbol of Sarvodaya's firm belief that everyone has something of value to offer.

Both Swahdyaya and Sarvodaya pay attention to the empowerment of women. The Sarvodaya story tells us how the village Shramadana societies, for instance, are mostly led by women and, commenting on a visit to several Swadhyaya villages, Pawan Gupta, an experienced community development worker, says:

> What came across very forcefully was the confidence of young and old women speaking without inhibitions in front of elders from their own community and strangers from urban areas. ... I think all of us working in the area of women's empowerment and gender sensitization should particularly take note of this and visit Swadhyaya villages.[12]

The academic, T.S. Rukmani, tells of an encounter he had with a Dalit[13] Swadhyayee woman called Pushpa Behn: 'Because of my caste I was not allowed to carry the Gita', she said to him. 'Now not only have I learnt the Gita, I have a head full of its thoughts.'[14]

There are 16,000 women's centres in Swadhyaya whose activities are all co-ordinated by women. Married couples go out on pilgrimages to neighbouring villages and, as we are told in the story, women act equally with men as 'pujaris' or priests. In the midst of a culture which still strongly discriminates against women, these activities, along with the educational opportunities offered, provide the women in Swadhyayee villages with the possibility of fulfilling their potential perhaps as never before.

Organization and Leadership

Both Sarvodaya and Swadhyaya are committed to egalitarian relationships and to the lack of a built-in hierarchy through which villagers might be made to feel that their contribution is inferior to those who have received formal education. For Sarvodaya this means trying to follow the pattern of the earliest Buddhist communities that were organized without social stratification on the grounds that people should see others as human beings rather than as fulfillers of a function, in the way a king might see his subjects.

---

12 Pawan K. Gupta, *Swadhyaya, The Alternative Paradigm* (Mussoorie, 1999), p. 4. www.swaraj.org/shikshantar/resources_gupta2.html (accessed 19 May 2005).

13 Dalits are India's outcasts. They were formerly called 'Untouchables' and then renamed 'Harijan' or 'Children of God' by Mahatma Ghandi, but today they prefer the more militant term Dalit, meaning 'crushed' or 'broken'.

14 T.S. Rukmani, *Turmoil, Hope and the Swadhyaya,* Presentation at CASA conference, Montreal 1999, p. 6. www.infinityfoundation.com/mandala/s_es/s_es_rukma_hope.htm (accessed 19 May 2005).

Of course there are innumerable cases when the practice falls short of the ideal: the monks working with Sarvodaya are warned not to get carried away by their potential influence in society at large, for instance. Furthermore, Sarvodaya's period as a large development NGO meant the introduction of a managerial hierarchy whose role was then questioned.

As with very many organizations based on a spiritual ethos, Sarvodaya has depended heavily on the figure of its founder, A.T. Ariyaratne who, together with his wife Neetha, has provided spiritual inspiration, vision, encouragement and almost parental care to the movement for over 40 years. Although A.T. Ariyaratne's son has now become Executive Director and taken on responsibility for the day to day running of the movement, in some senses such visionary and inspirational leaders are irreplaceable. This inevitably raises questions about the long-term sustainability of the movements they have founded.

Swadhyaya has similarly depended very heavily for guidance on its founder and mentor Pandurang Vaijnath Athavale. Before he died in October 2003, Athavale appointed his daughter, Dhanashree Talwalkar (known as 'Didi'), as his successor. Although some of the senior members of Swadhyaya had wanted a more collective form of leadership for the future, the huge growth of the movement since Didi took over testifies to the strength of motivation of the 'family-feeling' of the Swadhyaya 'parivar'. Its members regard Didi both as their mother and as the embodiment of Athavale's principles, philosophy and values.

The dangers of hereditary leadership at any level are clear but the crucial question is surely about the checks and balances in place to prevent the misuse of power. Fearing that Swadhyaya's rapid growth, both in India and abroad (Swadhyaya is now present in 30 countries) might dilute the philosophy of the movement, Didi has concentrated on bringing in more uniformity. Festivals, for instance, are celebrated on the same date and in the same way all over the world, and programmes are universally the same. Does this denote a move towards a more authoritarian, top-down form of leadership?

Up to now the presence of single strong leaders in both Swadhyaya and Sarvodaya appears to have stimulated rather than stifled the creative participation of people at the grassroots. Sarvodaya and Swadhyaya are above all village movements whose members have been given the necessary confidence and skills to be able to express their views through local leaders who depend on their support. Swadhyayees, for instance, put forward their ideas through their delegates at district, groups of districts and regional levels, and Didi regularly consults with delegates from each Indian state.

The movements' allegiance to their leaders is based on trust – on the belief that they are acting in the best interests of the movement rather than for their own gain. This has worked so far because of these leaders' wholehearted commitment to the spiritual values they share with the movements' members.

Whatever the organization of any movement, people in positions of leadership at all levels are bound to be faced with the temptation to use their influence to push through their own ideas. Some resist it, others succumb to it; but it may well be that the latter have least chance of survival in movements driven by a grassroots membership that is held together by the strength of shared ideals.

Another question that arises concerning organizations that have been so strongly shaped by a single person is how, or even whether, they can be replicated, especially in other cultural contexts. (Swadhyaya's membership outside India is still largely made up of Indians, even though an increasing number of these have been born abroad.) Probably the prime lesson to be learnt is that the life of a movement depends on its being rooted in the culture and beliefs of those that belong to it. But this does not imply fossilization. New challenges are arising all the time: television now lures people away from other activities; an older layer of local and regional leadership has to learn to give way to young people with more energy. To be effective and keep its relevance, every movement or organization of any sort must be open to change.

Political Engagement

Sarvodaya is now at a crossroads. Its view of itself as a social, cultural and political movement based on a spiritual ethos has not changed, but in this new phase of its existence, the intention is to engage to a greater extent with national politics. Since A.T. Ariyaratne's vision has always been of a non-party political system, it will not link itself to any political party; nor will it become a party itself. Its engagement in the political arena will be rather to try to offer a genuine alternative within a completely new framework. The long-term vision is that the villagers' economic programmes will form 'the foundation for a comprehensive social revolution that will bring an alternative economic structure'.[15]

Some people have dismissed this idea as being based on a utopian Buddhist past that never really existed in Sri Lanka, and few would consider Sarvodaya's Gandhian agenda to decentralize political and economic power to the villages to be a feasible plan in the context of the twenty-first century. Moreover, in spite of Sarvodaya's description of itself as a spiritually based rather than a Buddhist movement, Sri Lankans of other faiths have expressed reservations about a state run on Buddhist principles.

Nevertheless, in rejecting the vision out of hand, might one not be running the risk of aligning oneself with those who believe that there is no possible alternative to the present economic and political system? There are experiments of a similar nature in other parts of the world, such as that of the Mayan municipalities in Chiapas, Mexico, that have provided some interesting examples of different forms of power sharing, even if they fall short of offering coherent models for national governance.[16]

Swadhyaya's relationship to politics has been very different from Sarvodaya's. The movement has been criticized for 'disempowering' its members through adopting an explicitly non-political stand. There are two observations to make on

15 Bond, p. 66.
16 Morna Macleod, *Espiritualidad, Movilización Política y Reparación Social: Recursos del Movimiento Maya en Guatemala* (Mexico, 2004).

this: the first is that its reluctance to take sides politically should be understood in the context of communal inter-religious violence in India, the flames of which are more often than not fanned by political parties or groups. The second observation is that, although the movement itself is explicitly non-political, Swadhyaya has given many Swadhyayees the confidence to join other organizations that are taking action in defence of the rights of the poor, such as the National Forum of Fish Workers that seeks to defend the livelihoods of fisherfolk all over India.[17]

Contradictions can arise, however. Pawan K. Gupta tells the story of a Swadhyayee woman called Mangu Behen who told him of the dilemma she felt as a field co-ordinator of SEWA, a highly reputable voluntary organization that mobilizes poor working women. Mangu Behen felt torn between Swadhyaya's belief that people are fully capable of helping themselves and her role with SEWA which put her in the situation of offering them help from a position of power, since she had access to money. In the end she decided to resign from SEWA.[18]

Many development agency workers are frustrated by the fact that the work of these mass movements is not linked into the national development strategies of their respective governments. This has not always been the case with Sarvodaya. Until 1983, the movement co-operated closely with successive governments in the hope on the one hand of influencing them with a Buddhist vision of society, and on the other of being given the opportunity to flourish as a national movement.

At the time, Sarvodaya was accused by some of a naïve underestimation of the inflexibility of the governments' free market economic agenda for Sri Lanka, and by others of a careless disregard for the growing element of Buddhist nationalism that the governments seemed to condone. However, when the ethnic conflict in the north and east began to grow in the early 1980s, Sarvodaya broke off its relationship with the Jayawardene government. After that, in the late 1980s and early 1990s, the movement was viciously attacked by the subsequent Prime Minister, R. Premadasa, who saw Ariyaratne and his movement as a threat to his leadership.

This experience of Sarvodaya is just one example of how extremely difficult it is for a movement based on strong principles, whether religious or not, to keep its integrity and at the same time co-operate with national development schemes based on a very different, if not opposing, set of values.

Funding

Swadhyaya has always followed the principle that financial support must be given in the spirit of devotion to God and sharing with others, just as the members of a family give support to each other. Since all donations are given anonymously, there is no question of rich members exerting influence on account of their wealth. The policy of accepting no funds from individuals or institutions outside the movement has helped to ensure Swadhyaya's independence and to preserve its identity as a spiritual movement.

---

17 See Chapter 5.
18 Gupta, p. 3.

Both Swadhyaya's determined stand against accepting any outside funding and Sarvodaya's experience with European donors provide food for thought about the relationship of outside funding agencies to national or local organizations. The questions that arise are very difficult to solve. Even religiously inspired non-governmental development agencies based in the West are bound to support 'good' development work as the West understands it, both by their governments from whom they receive a sizeable proportion of their money, and by individual contributors who want to help the poor. They cannot risk being laid open to accusations of irresponsibility by transferring money to organizations about whose achievements they are unconvinced.

This can be problematic for organizations in the South[19] that understand 'development' somewhat differently and are reluctant to separate it from their spiritual life. As the case of Sarvodaya shows, it is not merely a matter of the allocation of funds for specific activities but of the entire vision of a movement or organization and the way in which it is run. No doubt the agencies' criticisms were, in their terms, well founded and in their view they were helping Sarvodaya to become more efficient. But the core questions about what constitutes 'efficiency', and especially about what must be sacrificed to achieve it, still remain.

Among the very large majority of Western development NGOs there is a sincere desire to build up authentic 'partnerships' with the organizations for which they provide not only much needed financial support but also useful technical expertise in areas of planning and managing programmes. Over many years, a great deal of time, effort and money has gone into designing more satisfactory patterns of partnership. The results have been varied, with both partners and agencies often experiencing considerable frustration, but there has been progress and interesting proposals are still being made.

These include, for example, suggestions about one of the most controversial issues: ways of measuring results. On the one hand more attention is being focused on planning methods that take into account the conceptual and ideological framework of organizations in the context within which they are working, and involve the participation of a maximum number of the people concerned. On the other hand a broadening out of the measurement of results is being considered in order to include changes in the 'quality of life' – both tangible and intangible – at the personal, organizational and societal level.[20]

There is still a lot of truth in the old saying that 'he who pays the piper calls the tune' but if the funding agencies are willing to 'let go' and open themselves up to other ways of doing things that allow for spontaneity of action, changes can be made and the pattern broken whereby academics and 'experts' (often but not necessarily

---

19 Throughout the book 'South' is used to replace the term 'developing world' and 'North' or 'West' replace the term 'developed', as the concepts embodied in the words 'developing' and 'developed' are inappropriate.

20 See Ann Chaplin, *Metodología para la Medición de Impacto de Trabajos que Buscan el Fortalecimiento de la Sociedad Civil,* Manual for NOVIB [Oxfam Novib] and its Counterparts in Bolivia (La Paz, 2005).

from outside the country concerned) decide what development should consist of in communities whose visions may be very different from their own.

Are Their Agendas and Practice So Different?

In the case of Sarvodaya and Swadhyaya, one of these different visions concerns the very idea of 'progress' that underlies the Western view of development. Since both Hinduism and Buddhism understand life as a cycle or spiral rather than a linear process, the concept of development constituting a change from a more 'backward' to a more 'advanced' way of life does not easily accord with their views. Of course they carefully plan their activities but, in the end, for them development is not so much the result of human planning as the natural outcome of deeper insights into what life is about.

Nevertheless, there are many areas where their agendas coincide with more conventional development programmes. They are, for instance, making a real contribution towards building up at least rudimentary alternative sources of livelihoods for some of the most impoverished people within their countries.

The village-level programmes of both movements are often on a small or even tiny scale, but as the writer of the Swadhyaya story says: 'when replicated over time and over large areas, they have the potential to become a major programme'. Sarvodaya has managed to reach almost half the villages on the island of Sri Lanka, and Swadhyaya is estimated to have drawn in more than 20 million people in 100,000 villages. Its 'divine communes' and 'tree temples' that bring groups of villagers together are already resulting in the beginning of a larger economic experiment, even though economic prosperity is not their aim. The same applies to the programme for fishing communities that has reached over a million people.

However, these movements are more prepared than most development agencies to recognize that lasting change comes about slowly: 'The early Swadhyayees say that they often doubted that anything would happen', says Pramila Jayapal. 'It took eight to ten years, they say, to begin to see any kind of change'.[21]

Furthermore, that the rules of the programmes are different from those of a 'mainstream' economic enterprise is demonstrated through surplus profit being pooled for the good of the community rather than being invested for the benefit of those who make it. However, this practice, even if not always strictly followed, may be seen in the long run as the guarantee of the sustainability of the movements, since an ethos of co-operation and inclusion is likely to enhance the economic functioning of the community as a whole by building up an 'internal market' even for ventures such as the fisherfolk's cybercafés.

The philosophical outlook of Swadhyaya and Sarvodaya guides them almost automatically towards good practice in the realm of protecting and reviving the natural environment. This happens at village level with small fields, medicinal herbs,

---

21 Pramila Jayapal, 'Swadhyaya: Toward a New Order', ICWA *Letters* (India, September 1996), p. 8.

solar technology and woodlands but also, with Swadhyaya, on a grand scale with programmes for water conservation and the planting of millions of trees.

In both stories there are passing comments about government programmes in the same areas in which the movements are working. Their observations that there are complaints by the would-be beneficiaries (Swadhyaya) or that, being run without the participation of the villagers, the chance of success of government programmes is slim (Sarvodaya) give us a glimpse of how local people view the comparative value of the work that they themselves can jointly plan and carry out. Both stories mention, too, that government undertakings cost hugely more than the initiatives taken by the movements. There is no doubt that religious motivation that inspires people to work on a voluntary basis not only strengthens the spiritual and social life of the community but also helps to make any practical programmes carried out extremely cost-effective!

If development is considered to be about building up 'social capital', both these movements must come very high up on the awards list. Social cohesion and community solidarity are, as we have seen, their principal characteristics, both 'bonding' within their own communities and 'bridging' to others outside them.

Both Sarvodaya, in 1969, and Swadhyaya, in 1996, have won the prestigious Ramon Magsasay International Award for Community Leadership, Sarvodaya received the Belgian King Baudouin Award for International Development in 1982, and in 1997, the United Nations named Swadhyaya one of the most significant development models in the world, noting that Swadhyaya communities are 'indeed more wholesome, better developed economically, cleaner and more efficient'.[22] Dhanashree Talwalkar is a member of UNESCO's steering committee on children's education.

Movements for Religious Change

Neither Sarvodaya nor Swadhyaya sees itself explicitly as a reform movement within Hinduism and Buddhism. Nevertheless, both of them are movements for religious change in the sense that they are imbuing traditional concepts and rituals with new meaning.

Sarvodaya's interpretation of 'dana' as giving in the service of others, for example, constitutes a direct challenge to the notion of 'dana' as donating gifts or money to the community of monks in order to store up 'merit' for the giver. This latter idea has become crystallized and widespread in contemporary Buddhist practice and is linked with the accumulation of wealth of many monasteries.

By daring to take seriously the concept of the divinity dwelling within each person, Swadhyaya breaks down the hierarchical and hereditary caste divisions which, despite the Vedic view of the equality of all human beings, have been

22 Quoted by Pramila Jayapal, 'A crisis of imagination – IV, Creating something different', *Michigan Citizen*, 2–8 June 2002, p. 1; www.boggscenter.org/mc6-8-02.htm (accessed 18 April 2005).

embedded in Hinduism for centuries. This and the view of 'bhakti' [devotion] as becoming a social force when practised as devotional action, has given religion a new meaning for millions of people.

Though firmly grounded in the Hindu and Buddhist traditions both Sarvodaya and Swadhyaya are open to including people from other religions or none. Indeed, they do not describe themselves as 'Hindu' or 'Buddhist'. Nevertheless, Sarvodaya has helped to revive Sri Lanka's Buddhist culture as a living philosophy and way of life for the good of everyone. Even the temples have been restored to their former role as centres for community activities as well as for meditation and ritual. They have become inclusive places, too. The Buddhist temple in the village of Dambara houses a statue of a Hindu god so that the local Hindus, who have no temple of their own, can share it.

Swadhyaya is a counter force both to communal hostility as well as the caste system in India. A visitor to a Kajli village, near the Indian town of Veraval, reported that the village had 250 Harijan families, 100 Muslim families and 100 Karari Rajput families, all living together in harmony. 'Before Swadhyaya, the communities were separate', he writes, 'neither eating nor drinking in each other's houses; now they even worship together.'[23] 'Loknath Amritalayam', the building of 'non-sectarian' temples, has been a highly significant innovation that brings Muslims and Christians together with Hindus, but also includes Dalits, even as priests. (Dalits are still forbidden to enter many temples in India today.)

Of course agreement is not always reached. There has been criticism from certain Dalit quarters, for example, of the custom of Swadhyaya's voluntary pilgrims to the villages bringing their own food with them because it could be interpreted as their avoiding having to share food with people of a lower caste. (Pilgrims themselves explain that this custom was introduced because of the way that villagers have often been exploited by social workers and particularly politicians who have expected hospitality.)[24]

Despite all the errors and conflicts that inevitably arise in human organizations, Sarvodaya and Swadhyaya are making an important contribution to establishing harmonious relationships between people of different religions and ethnic origins in Sri Lanka and India – two countries in which the lack of such harmony has often destroyed the hope of development taking place. Both movements also provide a challenge to the more traditional hierarchies of the monasteries and temples by showing how religion can become an empowering force within society, inspiring people to take action for their own benefit and for the common good. In 1997, Pandurang Athavale was awarded the Templeton Prize for Progress towards Research or Discoveries about Spiritual Realities and A.T. Ariyaratne has won many

---

23 Makarand Paranjape, 'Spiritual Sites as Sources of Transformation: Lessons from Svadhyaya' in Paranjape (ed.), *Dharma and Development: The Future of Survival* (New Delhi, 2005), p. 213.

24 Dr Rajesh Parikh, WFDD/VSF workshop, 2004.

peace prizes, including the Gandhi Peace Prize, awarded by the Indian government in 1996.

Chapter 2

Filling State Deficiencies
at the Grass Roots

These three stories tell of small groups that are struggling to improve life in marginalized communities. Two are in urban settings in Brazil and Cameroon; the third is in the mountains of Guatemala. We meet courageous and self-sacrificial women who are empowered by ancient spiritual traditions, in one case mingled with Christianity, and we are challenged by the unshakably principled stance of a Muslim group. There are illustrations of how values are weighted differently in different contexts and of different viewpoints on gender issues. Questions arise about the viability of these small organizations, about how they are run and their style of leadership and also about how funding agencies may 'use' the poor whose support is their raison d'être. In all three cases we see the groups' openness to people of other religious and spiritual traditions making an important contribution to peace in their communities.

Association for Environmental Conservation and
Social Progress: Sarkan Zoumountsi

Ibrahim Salissou, March 2003[1]

General Presentation

Socio-Political Context

Until the 1990s, Cameroon was socially a very stable country: national unity had been achieved and social peace was a reality. Various subsidies and benefits were granted by the state to different sectors of national life such as education, research, health and agriculture. But the arrival of the combined phenomena of democracy

---

1 Translated from the original French by the author.

and economic crisis brought inevitable consequences for social stability. From one day to another everything was radically changed.[2]

Indeed, with a two-fold devaluation of salaries, the reduction of state personnel, systematic savings on all benefits, subsidies and scholarships formerly granted by the state, and the re-emergence of disputes and wars of a tribal nature, Cameroonian citizens in general find themselves in quite the opposite situation from what they might hope for from a well-organized society. The present lack of schooling, the upsurge in the incidence of sickness and death, organized crime and widespread corruption of practices and attitudes all contribute to the lack of well-being of the citizens of Cameroon.

It was in the face of this problem of anti-social behaviour linked to the phenomena of economic crisis and poverty that the movement Sarkan Zoumountsi came into being. To be precise, the Association was born in Yaoundé (the capital) in 1995 – a 'Chain of Solidarity', as its name means in the Haoussa language. It is an apolitical, non-profit association with its head office in Yaoundé, though it has local branches or carries out programmes in Douala and several other places as well. Today it has 400 members.

The Objectives of Sarkan Zoumountsi

The Association was founded with the following principal objectives:

- To fight against poverty and lack of schooling
- To improve the standard of teaching of the underprivileged sectors of the population
- To provide tolerable living conditions by protecting the environment
- To take care of orphans and abandoned children
- And above all to promote the ideals of peace, tolerance and respect for differences.

Sarkan Zoumountsi's mission was to promote development among the socially underprivileged sectors of the population. From this perspective, the first priority lay in the resolution of the crucial problem of unemployment among young people. After that, it was necessary to create and encourage some income-generating activities for housewives and girls who have suffered from early marriages or lack of schooling, because these are the people who constitute the most underprivileged sector of all our target groups.

---

2   The writer is referring to the political upheavals, accompanied by severe repression in 1992, after President Paul Biya had allowed legislative elections but was then fraudulently re-elected. The political unrest was followed, in 1994, by a devaluation of the currency that caused a grave economic crisis for the poor. (Author's note.)

The Association's Target Groups

Our principal targets are thus youth and housewives and girls. However, in another sense we can say that our target group is the whole population in so far as actions to change behaviour in a society are a matter for each and every person. The social environment of the people who benefit from our work is characterized by poverty, violence, unemployment, lack of sanitation and a departure from religious and social rules.

The Founders of the Movement Sarkan Zoumountsi

The idea of setting up a 'Chain of Solidarity' in favour of our brothers and sisters in distress arose among a group of people from different social sectors who shared a vision of the meaning of development and well-being of human beings. A directorate was formed, advised by six 'ulemas' [scholars], imams and other local leaders.

Resources for Sarkan Zoumountsi's Activities

In order to put our ideas into practice on the ground, our movement has collected moral, material and financial resources.

Moral Resources Most important of all are the moral resources that people in our Association can count on, namely the imams and religious counsellors who are well versed in the legal codes and theology of Islam. It is they who enable us to work according Islam's code of life. These resource people act by preaching Islam. It is a question of making the whole population, and in particular our target groups, aware of the value of spiritual development by emphasizing that human beings are present in the world not only in their bodies but also in their spirit. This is crucial, for instance, in highlighting the importance of mutual assistance among the brothers and sisters of a society. In this regard Allah (the Merciful) says in the holy Qur'an (2:177):

> Righteousness does not consist in whether you face the East or the West. The righteous man is he who believes in God, in the Last Day, in the angels and the Book and the prophets; he who, though he loves it dearly, gives away his wealth to kinsfolk, to orphans, to the destitute, to the traveller in need and to beggars, and for the redemption of captives; who attends to his prayers and renders the alms levy; who is true to his promises and steadfast in trial and adversity and in times of war. Such are the true believers! Such are the God-fearing!

Moreover a Hadith[3] of the Prophet Mohammed (Peace and Blessing of Allah be upon him) tells us that: 'In the communion of their mutual affection, believers are like the limbs of the same body. If a single one suffers, it is the whole organism that

---

3 Hadith are narrations about the deeds and sayings of the Prophet Mohammed. (Author's note.)

falls prey to sickness and fever'. So our movement draws its spiritual resources from the well-being of all.

Financial and Material Resources   The financial resources of our chain of solidarity come from: members' contributions; cultural activities (within the Association there is a group that produces theatrical plays and games); a grant from the European Union through the 'Ant' Programme which looks for a participative approach by the people; and a grant from the Islamic Development Bank which has financed the women's micro-projects.

Means of Action

In order to complete our mission and achieve our objectives, we carry out awareness-raising programmes through posters, educational talks, public debates, seminars and sermons; we contribute to the creation or improvement of sanitary, social, cultural and scholastic infrastructures; and we organize socio-cultural events.

Analysis of Sarkan Zoumountsi's Practice

Today, in our so-called 'developing' country the notion of development and of social well-being is always assessed on the basis of the quantity of material wealth that the country has been able to accumulate, independently of the way in which this wealth has been amassed. This implies that development really means concentrating exclusively on the importance of economic growth: the rest can come afterwards. But is this the true sense of human development?

We find ourselves in a capitalist system where the only thing that counts is immediate material profit. In such a context, the aim of our Association is certainly to seek development, the well-being of individuals in society, but not at any price, for in Sarkan Zoumountsi we take action following our great guide, Islam.

In practice, our Association holds monthly meetings with all its leading members. At these meetings we investigate local social problems and bear in mind the ones that the Association judges to be most relevant. We categorize them in order of priority and then hold seminar-workshops with the relevant sectors of the population in order to establish a plan of action with them.

As Sheik Ismaïla, Imam at the Central Mosque of Yaoundé points out, the first verse of the Holy Qur'an, says: 'Allah is Merciful and Compassionate'. 'He is Merciful on the day of the Resurrection and Compassionate here below', says the Sheik. 'He makes no distinction between Muslim and Christian, Pagan and Animist. He enriches whom he will and impoverishes whom he will. Allah has authorized the co-habitation of different communities, lawful trade among them and respect for difference.'

Sheik Ismaïla also tells us that each piece of work that we carry out in favour of other human beings will not be in vain. A reward awaits us in paradise. This is why, as we have already said, guided by our Islamic faith, our action is devoid of any economic interests.

Some of Sarkan Zoumountsi's Achievements

Resolution of a Dispute Among Muslims

In 1996, the city of Yaoundé faced a grave problem of violent scenes in the heart of the large Muslim community. The problem was caused by a divergence of viewpoints on Islam and its practice between the so-called 'traditionalist, conservative' Muslims (commonly known in the Haoussa language as 'Darika') who claim allegiance to the Tidjania brotherhood, and the so-called 'fundamentalist' Muslims (called 'Isala' in Haoussa), who claim to represent the Wahhabite brotherhood. (By 'brotherhood' we understand here an association of laypeople founded on religious principles.)

This divergence of viewpoints between the Darika and the Isala led to fights and the destruction of material possessions among brothers who had lived together for a long time in peace. The result was the generation of deep hatred, with one person mistrusting another, regardless of the ties of family and friendship that had bound them together.

Against the background of this religious violence, we studied all the different aspects of the problem and then created a peace committee. It was made up of members of our Association, administrative authorities, religious leaders, opinion formers and certain members of the Muslim community.

The committee set itself the task of using all possible means to reconcile the brothers who had formerly lived in peace and in solidarity. We got down to it with determination and results followed. At the end of several days of negotiation, sermons and religious debates, peace finally returned among the brothers and we managed to re-establish a climate of safety in the heart of one and the same family.

Peace between Muslims and Christians

In 1998, Sarkan Zoumountsi took on the resolution of another problem in Yaoundé, again in the religious sphere. This time it was a question of a problem among members of the Muslim community and those of the Cameroonian Baptist Church. The problem was tribal in origin. Two tribes from the north of Cameroon made war on each other here in Yaoundé. On the one hand we had the Haoussa tribe of Muslim allegiance and on the other the Mou Fou tribe of Christian persuasion. The Association Sarkan Zoumountsi took concrete action to reconcile the two communities which, after all, are called to live together. To do this we carried out joint working sessions and meetings for debate among members of the two communities. In the end we re-established a climate of peace and safety, and even saw to it that a footbridge was built over a canal to link the two communities (see Plate 2).

Further Achievements

Other development activities of our Association have been: the construction of further footbridges in the city of Yaoundé to open up certain isolated zones and to help bring sectors of the population together; the purchase of a minibus to transport children to school; educational talks to housewives and girls; a programme for the collection of household rubbish, the cleaning out of gutters by the roadside and street sweeping; and a savings and credit co-operative.

How Has Our Faith Influenced the Work of Our Association?

The Case of the Co-operative

In our Association we took the step of setting up a savings and credit co-operative to help each other to develop new initiatives. It should be noted, however, that we started off from the premise that we could not propose anything that goes against Islam. It is very important in this case to make clear that people have their own criteria about what well-being is, and that these criteria vary according to different human groups.

With regard to our co-operative, for example, the most important aspect that we want to highlight is that our practices were in accordance with the Islamic law that forbids anyone to charge interest in the sense of usury. Indeed our aim in the co-operative had never been to charge interest but to share the benefits and risks in equal measure among the partners. To this effect Allah (the Merciful) says in the Holy Qur'an: 'Those who live on usury shall rise up before God like men whom Satan has demented by his touch; for they claim that trading is no different from usury.' (2:275). It is said that Allah has permitted trading but made usury unlawful.

In short, the charging of interest is formally forbidden by Islam; and we believe that it brings no profit to those who charge it. This law was the reason we had to close down our co-operative, because we could not find any funding agencies who would allow us to run it according to the rules of Islam.

The Case of the Struggle against AIDS

We have also made our contribution to the good work being done at an international level to stop the spread of the scourge of AIDS. However, following the guidance of Islam, our contribution has been of a spiritual rather than a material nature.

One of the most effective means to combat AIDS is the use of condoms. But the status of this means of protection in the sight of Islam is truly ambiguous in the sense that while it resolves one problem (protection from catching sexually transmitted diseases and HIV), it creates another equally important one: it encourages the growth of prostitution which is severely cracked down on by Islamic law.

The fact is that our Association refused partnerships with and even finance from certain international bodies that are fighting against AIDS and sexually transmitted diseases because we do not share the same vision of how to tackle the issue, even if we want finally to reach the same objectives. In this context, we focused our actions more on a change in behaviour following the recommendations of Islam: that one should be faithful to a single partner.

Support from Religious Institutions

We receive technical support quite regularly from the Centre of Social and Sanitary Promotion (CASS) of Nkolndongo. Based in Yaoundé, CASS is a Catholic institution that gives us technical support and presents our projects to donors. In most cases this enables us to carry out the projects we have planned. On the other hand we can always count, too, on the religious leaders of the Muslim community (the imams) and certain scholars who kindly give guidance and support to our activities for the benefit of the population.

The Reasons for the Success of Our Activities

The Leaders

The Association Sarkan Zoumountsi is endowed with a group of dynamic and readily available leaders with a strong faith in Islam. Through their activities under the protection of Islam we are able to say today that Sarkan Zoumountsi has made some contribution to bringing about a change in the behaviour of our society.

The Communities

All the communities that form our target groups are genuinely committed to seeking ways to bring about social peace, which is one of the most important pillars of development. Starting from the heart of Islam and its precepts, these communities become aware of their situation and seek to improve it. They model their plans of action on ours. For example over the question of usury in the co-operative, all the communities embraced the Islamic vision concerning the charging of interest.

Difficulties Encountered

Political Hijacking

In their efforts to be successful within a political system characterized as 'multi-party', political leaders who had no plan of action of their own tried to take over and claim responsibility for some of our development activities (the construction of footbridges, for example), despite the fact that these were exclusively the initiatives of Sarkan Zoumountsi. It is important to note here that we declare allegiance to no political party.

Structural Adjustment Programme (SAP)

The state often carries out programmes with no regard for non-governmental organizations. An example of this is the establishment of the social dimension of the SAP which was supposed to be a response to the problem of youth unemployment but failed to take account of crucial social, economic and cultural factors. This programme hindered our strategy of a participative approach that the population was already following.

The Lack of Motivation of Young People

Young people are one of our most important target groups but they often lack interest in our activities. Trapped in their despair, they think that any action to change the situation will be in vain.

Financial Difficulties

We often lack funds to carry out our projects. Left alone and without sufficient finance, we can produce nothing. This happened, for example, in the case of the women's micro-project programme where our system of working based on Islam was fundamentally incompatible with that of the financial institutions.

Conclusion

The Association Sarkan Zoumountsi has fulfilled its objectives in several areas. It has brought the notion of participative development to the community in accordance with the Islamic principle that people should join together to defend and protect their interests. In the spiritual sphere, the Association has encouraged an inter-faith rapprochement among Christians and Muslims. Living together has been made possible thanks to the efforts of all the communities. Another achievement has been the setting up of an organization in an Islamic milieu with an approach similar to that of an NGO.

Assessment and Perspectives

After about ten years of existence, the guiding idea of our movement is still on track. The assessment of our actions up to now is largely positive. We can observe a change of behaviour in the different sectors of the population and this has been beneficial for the self-development of the most deprived people. However, it must be noted that up to now the majority of donors are not ready to finance this form of development. Worse still, today a greater contribution from the very poorest is being called for.

Generosity Comes from the Strength of the Waters: The Socio-Educational Activity of the 'Terreiro' Ilê Axé Omin Funkó

Jussara Rêgo, December 2003[4]

Introduction

The different traditions of Candomblé[5] believe that the universe is made up of two places, two great parts. One is the space of the living, of us human beings, the other is the place belonging to the Enchanted Ones: the 'caboclos', the 'inquices', the 'orixás', the 'voduncis'[6] and the ancestors. Candomblé makes possible the communication human beings need with the world of the Enchanted Ones. It is this continual communication that gives strength to life in society, to the living ones.

In the understanding of Candomblé to live means to try to become better and better; to die is to integrate into a system of communication and support for the survival of all. The people of Candomblé do not live hoping to die and to be sent to another better world. They seek something better in this world of the living, and for this it is essential to act with the strength of the Enchanted Ones.

Thus in almost all the civil associations formed by the Candomblé centres or 'terreiros',[7] people aim to do something for each other, to improve everyone's conditions of life, especially in education and health. It is from the spirituality of people whose faith always has better days for the living in view that the social actions of the 'terreiros' arise.

The 'Terreiros' and the City of Salvador

The 'terreiros' of Candomblé are found most frequently in the peripheral areas of the city. They were driven there for reasons such as persecution and police repression and the search for natural surroundings in which to carry out the cult, as well as by their low level of purchasing power to buy land in the great urban centres. The peripheral areas can be located next to great urban centres but they are characterized by the lowest levels of living conditions and the highest rates of population density in the city.

---

4 Translated from the original Portuguese by the author.

5 An African religion brought to Brazil by slaves between 1549 and 1850.

6 'Caboclos', 'inquices', 'orixás' and 'voduncis' are all deities that receive different names in different Candomblé traditions.

7 Candomblé centres are also known as 'ilê', 'casa', 'axé' or 'manso'.

These areas are almost all inhabited by people of low income who are deprived of their rights as citizens, and who suffer from a lack of basic sanitation and public medical and hospital attention. They are notable for high levels of unemployment and low levels of access to formal education. Within these communities the groups of the cult and the civil associations (legally constituted institutions) which represent them play an important role in the neighbourhood. Their aim to improve the quality of life through offering social services, cultural activities and the defence of community rights is consistently found in most of their statutes. Examples of community services of 'terreiros' are:

- in the Ilê Obá do Cobre: formal and informal education, such as literacy for adults and children, and recreational workshops that seek first and foremost to offer activities to young people and children as an alternative to a life of marginalization on the streets;
- in the Ilê Axé Opô Afonjá: similar activities that have even been supported by UNICEF. This 'terreiro' has a formally established school on its premises with a contract with the municipal education network.

Apart from carrying out these types of activity, many other 'terreiros' try to collect food to supply the least privileged families with basic provisions. The leaders of the 'terreiros' of Candomblé are generally involved in the social and socio-cultural services.

This study was written in the context of the Programme Egbé-Territórios Negros of Koinonia [Ecumenical Presence and Service][8] which gives technical support to the socio-political and environmental initiatives of these religious groups. It is but one example among many.

The Community: the Place and the Population

The Ilê Axé Omin Funkó (from the Yoruba 'Terreiro of the Strength of the Waters') is a Candomblé 'terreiro' of the Ketu nation.[9] Since its foundation in 1985, it has been directed by the 'Iyalorixá'[10] Rosa de Azevedo Souza (known as Mãe [Mother] Rosa).

In 1990, it moved from its original location to the district of Periperi on the edge of the city, in the sub-district of Valéria that is noted for its lack of amenities. Some 55.22 per cent of the housing in the area is categorized as 'deficient living conditions'. This situation is made worse by the community's waste being channelled into a system

---

8　A large ecumenical NGO.

9　The term 'nation' refers to the ethnic origin of the founders of the group of the cult of Candomblé and the ethnic-religious tradition to which this group declares itself to be attached. It is a Brazilian re-creation in which the African ethnic memory is preserved through the liturgy and political groupings.

10　Yoruba name for the title of the highest priestess of a 'terreiro'.

of lakes in the region. Simply passing through the area means coming into contact with the contaminated waters, and so the community is exposed to various diseases caused by parasites and lives are under the constant threat of endemic illnesses.

According to official government figures, 70.66 per cent of Valéria's population belong to households that receive less than the basic wage, and 6.45 per cent have no income at all. As is usual in the periphery of Salvador, almost all the inhabitants are black or of mixed race.

A Self-Assessment of the Terreiro's Mission

The 'terreiro' carries out its ritual activities according to the Afro-Brazilian cult of Candomblé. It would have no other distinctive characteristics were it not for the fact that a priestess is its most important leader. In answer to a question about the activities carried out in the area of the community, the people of the neighbourhood highlighted the great importance of the development of social projects. This is reflected in the statutes of the civil association that was set up to represent the 'terreiro' and enable it to seek collaboration with official bodies: 'Article 3 – The goal of the Charitable Association Omin Funkó is to preserve and promote cultural and Afro-Brazilian activities … embracing education, health and social work, as well as to organize sports coaching and artistic and professional training for children, adolescents and adults.'

The community of Omin Funkó sees this type of action as effective in the struggle against its marginalization. It is also true that the development of social projects helps to reduce the prejudices which still exist against Candomblé.

Activities Carried Out by the 'Terreiro'

Education

When the 'terreiro' moved to its present address, known as 'Loteamento Nossa Senhora de Fátima de Periperi', the building was made of wood, which meant that whoever was inside it could clearly hear the noise coming from the streets. Mãe Rosa, who is also a primary-school teacher in the state education network, was horrified.

> It was absurd what was happening out there: after using drugs, the children, who were all addicted, had sex until midnight: and it was boy with boy, girl with girl … I was distressed by the situation and wanted to see what I could do. I had almost no financial resources but I wanted to change all that.

Recruitment and Offer of Formal Education

In view of this situation, in 1992 the high priestess requested authorization from the board of her school to give some help in the evenings to new pupils resident in her community. She hoped that this could solve the problem of their being on the streets as well as giving the children access to their basic right to education. She tells how, on getting a favourable response, she began to take action:

> Together with the school secretary, I went from door to door to talk to the mothers and children of the whole street, telling them that they could matriculate in the school and that it was only necessary to present a birth certificate and a photograph. It was then that I discovered another problem: none of them was registered. Many mothers were unemployed and addicted to drink and lived the entire day in the streets, wandering about. Others lived from washing clothes and had other chores to do. The fathers, of whom the majority were stone masons, spent the entire day working. None of them knew their rights, nor that they had to register their children. I then told people how to register. I helped them with a little money that I had received so that they could take photographs and afterwards I sent them to matriculate. For the school uniforms we carried out a campaign. We got a dressmaker to make them and all of the children went to school.

Mãe Rosa managed to recruit 50 children who stayed at school until the end of the course – a significant achievement in view of the high levels of school dropout in Brazil and specifically in Bahia, where the rate has historically been 20 per cent. 'The problems at night ended and now many have started off in life. They are parents of families and some are even working', she says.

This story of a simple action of solidarity presents a completely different picture from the normally prejudiced idea that traditional Afro-Brazilian religions carry out practices associated with evil. After this campaign Mãe Rosa, who before had been referred to by the children as the 'high priestess' in a pejorative and fear-filled sense, became recognized by the whole community as 'Rosa our respected teacher, who can solve our problems'. From then on, the 'terreiro' began to be visited by everyone who needed help, even by people from communities further away.

Training for Alternatives of Work and Income

'There is a lack of education here, so people have no employment or income', Mãe Rosa points out. 'Because of this they have no food on their plates. Many families here only get something to eat because they gather up what is left over from the market of CEASA [the Supply Centre of Salvador], and to do this they need to be registered there.'

It was with a view to overcoming this situation that the Professional Cooking Course was planned. The course was offered to the community with the support and active collaboration of Mãe Marlene, the high priestess of another 'terreiro'. Her help was an example of the network of relationships of solidarity among followers of Candomblé. The aim was to train people for work, even if in the informal sector.

Since the course was given without institutional support, there was no finance. To make it feasible, the 25 participants were asked, where possible, to donate a proportion of the ingredients and the 'terreiro' provided the rest. The course was held weekly from May to November 1998. It came to an end because health problems forced the teacher to withdraw, but its success gave rise to hopes for new programmes in the 'terreiro' and the search began for financial support for more courses.

Bahian Cooking Course: Solidarity Training Programme

It was then that the members of the 'terreiro' set up the Charitable Association Omin Funkó so that they could seek finance from outside bodies. Omin Funkó won a competition for a course on 'Dishes of Bahian Cooking', run by the federal government's Programme of Solidarity Training for young people from 16 to 21 years old, from low-income families and with only basic schooling. The Association was awarded 30 scholarships as well as a prize to cover expenses. The course was held for five months until the end of January 2002. There was a very large demand for the course and even after the students had been selected, requests for registration continued to come in. Mãe Rosa explains:

> There were many people in need and I didn't want to leave anyone out. But as I had to select, I matriculated the thirty but left five there unofficially. Funnily enough it was a girl from those five who got an apprenticeship in the 'Tempero da Dadá' (one of the restaurants of typical Bahian food with the best reputation in Brazil), and she is still employed there today.

Mãe Rosa emphasizes that the policies and criteria imposed by the official funding institutions are not always sensitive to the needs of the communities. 'The community leadership is better placed to carry out a more accurate evaluation appropriate to the local situation', she says.

Outbreak of Scabies

Because of the lack of medical assistance, combined with the overcrowding and lack of sanitation in the community of Nossa Senhora de Fátima de Periperi, the population suffers from frequent outbreaks of parasites and infestations of lice.

In the second half of 2002, a scabies epidemic broke out in the neighbourhood of Omin Funkó. With no help, information or resources the community turned to the 'terreiro' for support. The members of the Ilê Axé Omin Funkó battled with the less serious cases using their knowledge of herbal medicine. Mãe Rosa tells the story:

> I started looking after my grandchildren. They were scratching and seemed to have sores all over their bodies. Then it began to attack the intestine, producing headaches and fever. I tried with all the natural remedies I knew. And then people from outside began to appear so that I could treat them too. I did all I could. Some cases had to go to hospital because they had third-degree scabies and had to be treated with serum and antibiotics. I looked after the others at home. Everyone caught it: child, man and woman.

Since the epidemic spread very quickly, many people needed help. Government health services failed to meet the demand. The health centres and hospitals, even in other sub-districts of peripheral areas of the city, were full.

The leadership of Omin Funkó sought support from all kinds of institutions. It recruited health volunteers to attend to the population and transformed the 'terreiro' into a sort of improvised health centre. During the two most serious months of the illness, a doctor, a nurse and three nursing auxiliaries were on weekly duty to attend to patients.

In order to get rid of all sources of contagion, the high priestess and her brothers and sisters of Omin Funkó spent all day washing and boiling the patients' clothes and ironing them with a hot iron. The epidemic was acute for almost two months. During that time the Association of Omin Funkó devoted its energies exclusively to treating it.

Medical Attention and Health Education

Following on from the emergency, the 'terreiro' brought in a medical team that attended to people suffering from parasites and other illnesses, but also helped them to identify the symptoms. However, in spite of the community's need for the doctor's monthly visit, the work was discontinued. According to the high priestess: 'When it was a time of politics (elections) everyone was interested in helping. Afterwards it all finished'. This is an example of the way so many politicians buy votes in Brazil.

Workshop on Women's Health Education

Almost the whole of the community of Nossa Senhora do Paripe is black or of mixed race. Since black women are faced with diverse forms of social exclusion, Omin Funkó drew up a plan of action to improve their sexual, physical, socio-emotional and spiritual well-being. In partnership with the Christian ecumenical agency, Koinonia, and the Afro-Brazilian women's organization, Quilombo Asentewaa, a workshop was planned for which the 'terreiro' mobilized 30 young women of reproductive age.

The workshop focused on the woman's body: sexually transmitted diseases, AIDS and preventative and reproductive health. It raised the awareness of the participants, gave them information, strengthened their self-esteem and motivated them to participate in actions that were already being taken in the community to improve the quality of life of women of African descent. It also gave the community greater capacity collectively to seek co-operation from institutions, councils and government health centres in the neighbourhood and in the city.

The Distribution of Condoms

Aware of the serious situation caused by sexually transmitted diseases and the widespread occurrence of unwanted pregnancies, principally among adolescents, the 'terreiro' sought to provide an alternative by applying for registration with the competent institutions as a distributor of male contraceptives. Through the Gay Group of Bahia it has obtained a quota for monthly distribution and it is seeking to register its civil association with the Health Secretariat of Bahia to enable it to reach a larger number of people.

Community Wishes and Frustrated Initiatives

Nursery School

At present, the Omin Funkó Association is operating a nursery school in its rooms. The appropriate state registration for this has already been completed. Theoretically, this qualifies the Association to receive institutional support, but in practice no state funding has been made available.

Courses on Information Technology, Pre-College Entrance Examinations and the African Language Yoruba

These courses were proposed by official teaching bodies in collaboration with Omin Funkó. Students were selected and the courses planned so as to offer a real opportunity to the community. However, at the final stages, the process came to a premature halt because the public employees appointed to teach the courses refused to do so. 'The place does not offer personal security', they said and they alleged that people appointed to work in this area could be subjected to all kinds of physical violence.

Final Considerations

If it were not for the 'terreiro' of Omin Funkó, the community of Nossa Senhora do Paripe would find itself not only deprived of its social rights but also subjected to a chaotic situation of violence and fatal epidemics. It is through the 'terreiro' that people of great generosity and deep spirituality can express their social commitment by giving fraternal help to the least favoured.

At present the 'terreiro' is struggling because it does not have even the minimal resources to make this possible. This is because public programmes for such activities are scarce and demands for a share of them are treated unequally in this city of countless inequalities.

An Experience of Development with a Christian and Mayan Focus: The Case of Awakatán

Antonio Otzoy, September 2003[11]

The women elders smile tenderly as they say: 'This is a testimony of the life that God has given us, here in the mountains of Awakatán, of Guatemala, a country in Central America.'

Awakatán is a municipality in which three Mayan cultures – K'iche', Chalchiteko, Awateko – and *mestizos* (mixed indigenous and Spanish) live together. It is situated 339 km from the capital city.

Through their social and cultural work in their locality and their plans for the future, these people keep two elements of their lives closely linked together: spirituality and work. Spirituality involves their thinking, feeling, being and their presence in their community or church. Work relates them to the economy, health, education and many other things. In their world view there is no separation between the two.

The Context

In 1985, the armed conflict between guerrilla groups and the government in Guatemala had already been going on for some 25 years. It had led to the displacement of countless families. Many of them fled to Mexico but some sought refuge inside Guatemala. Thousands of families had disappeared or were divided. Widows with large numbers of children were left to play the double role of father and mother. In addition to these problems, strict military controls prevented people from carrying out their daily activities. Agricultural work suffered incalculable losses, above all in the smallest communities, because people were forced to spend up to 65 per cent of their time patrolling their community. The conflict lasted more than 35 years. Even today many families are still suffering from its consequences.

The Story Begins

The story starts in 1983–84, when the Bethlehem Church of the Central American Mission in Awakatán divided into two groups. One group, led by Awatekos, considered that faith cannot be separated from daily life: the Church should attend to material as well as spiritual needs. The other group believed the Church should play an exclusively spiritual role even with regard to its own members. To help the 'unconverted' or 'pagan' – terms commonly used to describe Catholics as well

---

11 Translated from the original Spanish by the author.

as followers of the ancient Mayan spiritual tradition – was out of the question. The Awatekos who expressed their disagreement with this doctrine were excluded from the Church. Later they joined the Presbyterian Church whose theology was in accordance with their own beliefs.

Awateko Evangelical Confraternity of Integral Development

In 1987 this group of Awatekos, led by two brothers, Pedro and Juan Castro, founded the Awateko Evangelical Confraternity of Integral Development (CEADI). CEADI's assembly is made up of 45 people representing 20 communities. The members are not all Protestants; some are Catholics and others have kept the practice of their Mayan spirituality. This integration of Christianity and Mayan spirituality is a very unusual and courageous step in Guatemala, and it has greatly enriched the practice of CEADI.

CEADI's members began by identifying the needs of the people living in the area. Awateko families were struggling to survive through their own efforts, and were faced with the challenges of family disintegration and a precarious economic situation. These were exacerbated by the unequal social relationships arising from the racist and discriminatory nature of Guatemalan society.

Education

Education was a prime need. Schools were few and far between and the lack of roads and transport meant that children normally had to walk for one or two hours to get to school. Refusing to be intimidated by the continued hostility of the leaders of the Bethlehem Church or by the difficulties they faced in negotiating the official registration of a school, CEADI's members began an educational project with 185 children. An NGO offered them four classrooms free of charge and they got some second-hand blackboards from local schools. The teachers began by working for six months voluntarily and then for six months on a partial salary.

Today there are more than 400 boys and girls at CEADI's school in Awakatán. In spite of having signed a contract with the Ministry of Education, no state funding has yet arrived so they depend on voluntary contributions from individuals, families and churches, institutional contributions and monthly quotas from any students who are moderately well off. The teachers work for about half the salary they would earn in a state school. At the moment 35 girls and five boys in situations of extreme poverty receive scholarships. For the most part support is given to girls because there are insufficient resources to be able to attend to all the boys and girls who need help. 'We want the children to leave with confidence that they can do things for themselves', says Juan Castro.

Women and Agriculture

When, in 1986, the armed conflict abated and rural activities became possible once more, families began to dedicate themselves full time to agriculture, but they soon came up against serious problems. On the one hand there were the unscrupulous intermediaries who in many cases paid up to 60 per cent less than the market price for their products; on the other hand sometimes no sales at all were possible since the few existing roads were impassable when it rained.

The only hope for Awateko families was to migrate to the coastal coffee plantations for up to six months a year. However, the appalling living conditions on the plantations often led to whole families coming back ill and having to spend the little money they had earned on medical treatment – if indeed they could find any, since health services were almost non-existent in rural areas.

Another dream of the families who formed CEADI had thus been to buy some land for communitarian agricultural production and they did not wait around with their arms folded! They went out to look for resources and managed to get some land in association with the Conference of Evangelical Churches of Guatemala (CIEDEG).

The families already counted on long experience in the cultivation of garlic, onions and basic grains and they put the relatively small piece of land to immediate use through obtaining low-interest credit from a national association of NGOs working on development and service. However, the market for garlic and onions collapsed at the end of the 1990s. This put an end to their aim of a wider co-ordination with other peasant farmers, but all was not lost.

In 1998, 14 women began to play a prominent role in CEADI when they took part in a training programme for health and animal husbandry promoters, co-ordinated by the Australian government's co-operation programme. Two of the women managed to become fully qualified promoters. They started a chicken vaccination project and in the first two years they vaccinated 3,700 chickens belonging to a total of 115 families.

Encouraged by this experience, in 1999 the women organized themselves into the Association of Community Women of Awakatán (ADEMCA) with the aim of promoting sustainable agriculture. In 2002 they went on a tour of the department of Chimaltenango, 350 km away from their community, to get to know the 'peasant to peasant' method of learning, whereby peasant farmers teach each other. Now they talk of their work as 'peasant woman to peasant woman'. The women's leader is Señora Rosalinda de Castro, wife of the pastor, Pedro Castro.

In the community of Agua Blanca, ten women have got organized to grow strawberries, flowers and citrus and other fruit trees on a piece of land measuring 1,500 sq m. They chose strawberries because they are not grown in the region and so they offer a better sales opportunity on the internal market. In fact the demand for both strawberries and flowers has been so great that they are unable to meet it with their present production, but they predict that in the medium term they will be able to supply enough to cover the market (see Plate 3).

This is just one example of agricultural work in which more than 60 families from the surrounding communities are involved. They are making an effort to improve their agricultural production, their technology and the variety of their products, concentrating above all on products which are not common in the region. Up to now they have made surprising gains through having no competition.

These 60 families have now joined up with 40 more and they are planning to spread their ideas and activities wider by linking related activities. Since the land requires constant and adequate fertilization, they are proposing to take up chicken rearing. Through this they will boost their agricultural production with the hens' manure as well as producing chickens and eggs for eating. Their long-term investment costs will fall because they will spend less on fertilizers, but they consider that the greatest benefit will be to health because the products will be cultivated ecologically without polluting the soil.

All the while, the women lay emphasis on their social relationships to families beyond their own group and they are self-critical about their attitude to others. 'We have devalued the work of the rest', they say. 'Sometimes we go in for criticizing but we believe that we should abandon this attitude and dedicate all our efforts to doing our best and sharing with families from the neighbourhood and those of other communities.'

Women and Health

CEADI has focused on improving health by making the most of local resources, including herbal medicines. Women play a very important role in this area. At the moment there is a group of 40 women who meet every two months for training in integral health care. All are midwives. Sixty per cent of them became midwives on account of the 'gift' or 'vocation' that God has given them, as is the tradition. Others were urged to do so because of the community's needs. They explain how they are motivated by a profound sense of service.

> We are very keen to work. We don't mind walking for five or even six hours, whether to learn or to serve our neighbour. We do it happily. Being together or sharing with other families are moments of happiness, listening to other ideas, exchanging experiences. We laugh at things we do and that give us strength. We carry out all our activities according to the advice of the elders (men and women) who say that we should take care of and respect each other and have confidence in the family. We hope to continue to share our experiences, including the failures, as long as God allows us to and gives us life.

The women invest the small amount of income that they get from their work in long-term benefits for their children. 'We have great hope that our work will help our children to study and get a better training than we did', they say.

Their meetings give the women great support and encouragement. They say they see them as a spiritual space that provides opportunities to discuss their needs and their plans:

We are paying attention to ourselves, because being women we have been forgotten and, of course, ill-treated. We are aware of the reality around us and we have ideas to remedy our situation. We are very interested in carrying out our work for the benefit of the community. We want to take advantage of what we already know and to integrate young and old women into the groups in order to share with them.

There is a strong awareness of the importance of a sense of community and the therapeutic role that the community plays in the life of the people who participate in it. This is in spite of the fact that the women face multiple problems ranging from marginalization to cynical trickery. They seldom have the opportunity to make or even contribute to community decisions which affect them and their families. Even if there are still some features of a communal way of life within the family, outside it women suffer extreme exclusion. The most common reasons for their being marginalized are jealousy, mistrust and the fact that their work is undervalued. They are often cheated. Even though they walk for hours to reach outlying houses, many families do not even offer them food and then, on top of everything, they fail to pay them. This is the experience of 85 per cent of the 40 midwives. In spite of all this, the women say:

We shall not stop serving. The difficult situations show us the way we should go. The way is not at all smooth and easy, on the contrary, it is tortuous. But thanks to God, we receive many blessings, more than we deserve. We do not fall ill; we have always had something to eat. Even at moments of scarcity, someone arrives and shares their food with us.

The Spiritual Part of These Experiences

In all this, there is always space for dialogue with the Creator, a moment which makes all the difference to every other activity. Both men and women agree when they say: 'It is not possible to stop talking to God. He is with us from the time the sun rises. He looks after us, he gives us wisdom to carry out our daily tasks. Everything is in the hand of God.' They talk of God as present in another way as well: 'We breathe, we move, we reap the harvest of our work; the earth, the heat and the water make the seed germinate and grow and produce its fruits.'

The Christians see their religious services as a thanksgiving for everything they have received. They are a remembrance of God's goodness and at the same time a renewal of vows to be in communion with him. This can be seen in the words of their prayers.

Those who practise Mayan spirituality understand their rites in a similar way. They are about gratitude for the past, present and future. They remember that nothing is hidden, nor do things happen on their own through inertia.

For Christians and for Mayas, the religious element is fundamental to their existence and to the development of all their activities. Spirituality is given space and importance. Training, for example, must be continual because it is part of life and life has constantly to be nourished: that means that receiving training implies a spiritual re-creation of life.

They firmly believe that no knowledge belongs to one individual alone. It has to be shared as it can bring advantages for the whole community. It is important to pass the ideas of one generation on to the next, to equip oneself and to be clear that there is an alternative to everything. This avoids confusion and dispels any fear of confronting the realities of everyday life.

Their life in communion with God gives them credibility as leaders in the eyes of other women. This, they say, is translated into benefits for themselves, for the community and for the generations to follow:

> We must be ready to know how to deal with what is coming in the future and for this we must not forget what we have now and what the elders left us. We want constantly to build a bridge between the future and the past, between what others know and what we know, without forgetting the Creator, in the sight of whom everything has developed. Knowledge is a path and it is also an opportunity.

These Awakateco women are deeply concerned to:

> emphasize what makes us human beings, through respect for life and human dignity, to make known the experiences we have had so that others know about them and can be helped in their work and service and to adapt ourselves to the people's vision of the world, their ways of worshipping God and of being aware of his presence. We are poor. We live in remote, rocky, forgotten places but with a lot of love for life.

The Mayas invite us to notice everything and to know that there are possibilities. They are very aware of the meaning and the strength which religious practice brings. In other words they show us that faith and spirituality are permanent forces, present in the life of the communities.

Viable Work?

> When the mind joins the heart, everything is possible.
> *Grandmother Margarita, Mayan elder, Mexico*[12]

These three stories are about the struggles of small grass-roots organizations to improve the lives of very poor people in a situation of general abandonment by the state. The leaders face misunderstanding and rejection from those who could help from outside, and even in some cases from others within their own communities. And yet, for all the disappointments they suffer, their struggles are not bitter; nor are they hopeless. While they fully recognize the difficulties that have to be confronted, the stories are paradoxically imbued with a spirit of self-confidence, pride and joy.

Spirituality as a Source of Strength and Guidance

In common with probably all religious and spiritual traditions in different places and different historical contexts, Mayan spirituality and Candomblé provide the means by which people who have been suffering for hundreds of years from untold repression and marginalization have held onto their feeling of self-worth as individuals belonging to a community. Their spirituality has enabled them to keep a hold on a sense of themselves as Mayan and Afro-Brazilian rather than as pagan peoples of a worthless culture and no wisdom as their societies would have it.

To outsiders, characteristics of these spiritual traditions – such as the trances of the Candomblé priestesses and priests, during which they take on the identity of the 'orixá' and utter prophecies, the sacrificing of cockerels and pigeons in Mayan rituals, and the 'reading' of the Candomblé conch shells or the Mayan fire – may seem more like magic than religion. But it is not at all impossible that the Christian tradition of Holy Communion might make a similar impression on someone from outside. Is it not ultimately the motivation and attitude of the people involved that are all important: whether power is sought with the desire to dominate and manipulate or in an attitude of self-surrender, resulting in compassion arising from a love-filled spiritual energy?

The actors in all three stories tell us that they depend on a source of spiritual power for the strength to carry out activities of every kind in their lives because there is no separation of the spiritual from the secular: 'Human beings are not only present in the world in their bodies but also in their spirit', says Sarkan Zoumountsi. The Mayas see no difference between spirituality and work, and the 'terreiros' of Candomblé are equally spiritual places and centres of social services.

Faith and spirituality are 'permanent forces in the community' as the Awakatán story puts it, and they give life its meaning. Mayan spirituality may express most

---

12 Ima Sanchís, *La Vanguardia*, Sección 'La Contra' (Mexico, 28 April 2005).

clearly the spirit of the divine in everything when the women say: 'We breathe, we move, we reap the harvest of our work; the earth, the heat and the water make the seed germinate and grow and produce its fruits'; but this belief clearly influences the way all these communities understand and carry out development. Spirituality or religious teaching is integrated into the work. It goes without saying, for instance, that Omin Funkó should include 'spiritual well-being' in the plan for women's health, and Sarkan Zoumountsi cannot countenance ways of working in its credit co-operative or AIDS programme that do not integrate the teaching of Islam.

Their source of spiritual power is also a source of guidance for all their activities: 'We take action following our great guide Islam' says Sarkan Zoumountsi, and the Mayan women say that God gives them wisdom for all their tasks. For this, constant communication with the divine presence is necessary – communication which is at the heart of all religious practice. We are told that 'Candomblé makes possible the communication human beings need with the world of the Enchanted Ones', and among the many descriptions of the righteous man in Islam is 'he who attends to his prayers'. The Mayan women say 'it is not possible to stop talking to God' as he is with them from the time the sun rises.

Different Values, Different Priorities for Development

As with Sarvodaya, the fact that there is no concept of a separate 'secular' side of life in any of these communities has contributed, in some cases, to a reluctance on the part of the state or development agencies to recognize what they are doing as 'effective development'. The attempts made by all three organizations to obtain state recognition or outside funding testifies to an acknowledgement of the overlapping areas in their agendas, such as their common aims to improve health and education (especially for girls), to provide training in skills that will help people to get jobs and to promote productive activities. But their religious motivation often leads to their holding different views about the way in which these common aims should be achieved.

In the case of Sarkan Zoumountsi, it was their insistence on refusing to distribute condoms or charge interest on loans that led to potential donors refusing grants for their AIDS programme and credit co-operative. Sarkan Zoumountsi sees clearly what the conflict with the agencies was about when it states quite openly that 'one of the most effective means to combat AIDS is the use of condoms'. But there are forces at work in Sarkan Zoumountsi that are more important than immediate practical effectiveness.

Does this mean that its leaders are content to stand by while people die of AIDS? Clearly not. The fact that Sarkan Zoumountsi has the programme at all is an indication of its commitment to get rid of the scourge of AIDS. They 'want finally to reach the same objectives' as all the other organizations doing good work on an international level. The difference lies in their 'vision of how to tackle the issue'.

Underlying this vision is an over-arching, long-term view of how society should be ordered. Any shorter-term project must be in harmony with this framework. With the issue of HIV and AIDS the focus is on fidelity within marriage and strict rules about sexual relationships. Sarkan Zoumountsi shares the predominant view within Islam that condoms are a gateway to promiscuity, the breakdown of the family and the 'anything goes' attitude to sexual morality that they consider to be the source of chaotic and unhappy societies no longer living according to the laws of God. When they speak of the 'spiritual nature' of their contribution, they are referring to the advice they give on how to prevent AIDS through behaviour that accords with the ethics of Islam. This includes respectful behaviour towards women.

Such a position (not adopted so strictly by all Muslim organizations in Africa) leads to frustration and indignation among the staff of development agencies, as well as people beyond them, who consider the refusal by many religious groups to distribute condoms to be, to say the very least, highly irresponsible – just as irresponsible as the distribution of condoms seems to Sarkan Zoumountsi. Up to now the two views have been irreconcilable. Nevertheless, there is common ground to be found in the recognition that a key element in the battle against the spread of HIV and AIDS must be a change in cultural attitudes concerning the position of women in society.

The grounds for the conflict over charging interest on loans are not dissimilar. Within the framework of Muslim ethics, the leaders of Sarkan Zoumountsi consider interest to be a form of exploitation that leads to an increase in the inequalities between the rich and the poor, and thus a lack of just and harmonious relationships within society. Muslim economics forbids the charging of interest and requires any losses as well as gains resulting from a loan to be shared between lender and borrower. The development agencies concerned, however, seem to have believed that to lend money without charging interest is unsound economic practice. Again it is a question of a different view of, or maybe a greater focus on, the kind of society that 'development' is supposed to bring about in the longer term.

With regard to the issue of condoms, there is a marked difference between Sarkan Zoumountsi and the 'terreiro' of Omin Funkó, which has actually gone to some lengths to find a way of distributing condoms and intends to obtain state registration in order to reach more people. Since its main focus is on gathering strength from the Enchanted Ones to improve people's lives here and now, such immediate measures to reduce the incidence of STDs does not contradict Candomblé's overall vision of what development is about.

This does not, however, mean that the 'terreiro' is necessarily at one with the view of development held by state of Bahia. When it came to the allocation of scholarships for the course in Bahian cooking, for example, Mãe Rosa complained that 'the policies and criteria imposed by the official funding institutions are not always sensitive to the needs of the communities'. Whereas the state gave priority to maximum efficacy by restricting the course to 30 students, Mãe Rosa's prime concern was to include as many people as possible. Better a course with rather fewer facilities to reach more people than the most effective course possible for a limited number? In the end Mãe Rosa's resources only allowed for the number to be increased by five, but the results vindicated this expansion at least as far as it went!

The activities of the Awateko midwives provide an example not so much of a different vision of what development is about as of how to go about achieving it. The women's devoted service and their gratitude for the opportunities offered to them, as well as their determination to continue their work in spite of their exploitation by those they serve, fly in the face of the notions of gender equity as well as the 'rights-based' view of development promoted by many agencies. It is the right of mothers giving birth to receive the attention of a midwife, but equally the right of the midwives to be paid fairly for their work. Some might even see the midwives' attitude as 'anti-developmental' in the sense that by acquiescing to their exploitation as women they are helping to prolong rather than to change an unjust situation.

Here again it is a question of a different order in a hierarchy of values. In Christianity as well as in Mayan spirituality, generous service freely given is a very highly valued virtue, even a sacred obligation. Moreover in the Mayan world view, harmony within the community is of such importance that people will put up with a great deal in order to avoid a conflict.

Gender Issues

The midwives' lack of militancy about their rights does not reflect a lack of interest on the part of the Evangelical Confraternity of Integral Development (CEADI) in improving gender relations within the Awateko communities. Priority is given to girls in the school scholarship programme. Moreover, even though the perennial problem of increasing women's workloads is not addressed, the training provided for women in areas such as the vaccination of poultry and strawberry cultivation indicates an awareness of the need to provide the opportunity for them to play roles within the community beyond their traditional role in the home.

Seen from this point of view, it is a mistake to regard the midwives merely as victims. When they say 'Being together or sharing with other families are moments of happiness, listening to other ideas, exchanging experiences', they are appreciating the opportunity they have to broaden their horizons and make new friends. The integral health training programmes they attend may not have resulted yet in an end to their exploitation but they provide a space for learning, leadership and increased autonomy in a context in which many Mayan women are struggling to survive in a society that discriminates against them for being indigenous, poor and women.

Under the leadership of Mãe Rosa, Omin Funkó seems naturally to make women – the most disadvantaged of all – the focus of its attention. It is the girls who are given an opportunity to join the labour market through attending the cooking course, and the health workshop is specifically designed for the most marginalized women in the community.

Conversations with Sarkan Zoumountsi in November 2002 revealed that its work to raise awareness about the need for education for girls and women, and particularly about the undesirability of early marriages for girls, had met with some resistance within the community and also among some of the imams.[13]. But this has not led to a change in the Association's priorities. Moreover the women's micro-project programme financed by the Islamic Development Bank is a sign of space and encouragement being given to women to set their own agenda. Sarkan Zoumountsi is one of the many Muslim groups, movements or organizations in different parts of the world that are working from within Islam to change the culture of oppression of women which is often associated with Islam, even though many Muslim scholars stress that such oppression is certainly not in accordance with the spirit of the Qur'an.

Leadership

The women in Awakatán lead by example. Far from using the knowledge they gain from their training opportunities as a tool to create powerful positions for themselves, they consider that an important part of their leadership consists in sharing it. The re-creative experience of the training courses, understood to be part of their spirituality, is to be made available to all.

The story tells us that 'their life in communion with God' gives the women leaders credibility. As with Swadhyaya and Sarvodaya, the trust of the rest of the community on which their leadership depends is enhanced by the spiritual foundation to their work.

Mãe Rosa's experience as a spiritual leader has been a different one. Her role as a priestess had evidently led to those in the community who are not adherents of Candomblé regarding her with fear rather than trust. Only when she went from house to house informing people how to register their children for school did she come to be regarded in the neighbourhood as 'our respected teacher who can solve our problems'.

It was through her actions in serving the community that Mãe Rosa managed to draw people to the 'terreiro' so that it has become an accepted reference point for social assistance. The story points out, too, that the social work of the 'terreiro' has helped to change people's habitually negative views about Candomblé as a spiritual tradition. This negativity did not lead Mãe Rosa to question the power of Candomblé, nor has she ever for a moment felt it necessary to underplay her role as a priestess. On the contrary, she called upon the priestess of a neighbouring 'terreiro' to help out with the first cooking course, thus strengthening the spiritual connection of the social work. Like the women of Awakatán, Mãe Rosa leads by example. She personally got the children off the streets and into school; and during the scabies epidemic she was in the thick of it, washing and ironing the clothes.

Sarkan Zoumountsi says with some pride that it has managed to set itself up in an Islamic milieu with an approach similar to that of an NGO. It has the managerial

---

13 Visit to Sarkan Zoumountsi by Tyndale, 2 November 2002.

structure of many an NGO, with a directorate consisting of a general co-ordinator, general secretary, treasurer and so on, but the advisory group of the religious scholars and imams who enable Sarkan Zoumountsi 'to work according Islam's code of life' has the last word when it comes to the overriding principles of the organization's aims and ways of working. In this way Sarkan Zoumountsi has managed to maintain its position as an integral part of the Muslim community in Yaoundé.

The cohesive force of the community's commitment to Islam was shown when the people willingly supported the leadership in their difficult and sacrificial decision to forgo the grants for the AIDS programme and the credit co-operative. To some people their intransigence in taking these decisions may seem rigid, but within Islam great store is set by consensual decision-making and thus we can presume that a decision to accept the grants would have caused deep malaise both within Sarkan Zoumountsi itself and in the wider circle of the people they work with. From the story of how the leaders managed to reconcile warring factions within the community, it is clear that they have won the trust not only of the religious leaders but also of the local people.

It is this vital ingredient of trust that makes the way leadership works in these organizations different from the mode of leadership found in development agencies and most NGOs. This is not to say, of course, that NGO managers are mistrusted by their staff – this would lead sooner or later to disaster – but the relationship of the leaders in these stories to the members of their organizations is a personal rather than a professional or managerial one. They are natural leaders who come from the communities themselves. Their leadership is entirely dependent on the continued support of the people alongside whom they live as well as work, and to whom they are directly and personally accountable. Mahatma Gandhi's adage 'My life is my message' is tried and tested at close quarters.

Such leadership may not lead to maximum 'efficiency' – a lot of time can be spent on reaching consensual agreement as well as on building up relationships of trust. It may not even result in maximum transparency. At a meeting of East African faith-based organizations with the World Bank, one Muslim explained why his community never used receipts. 'We send the imam shopping', he said. 'We trust him.'[14] To ask for receipts would have been a sign that this trust had been lost.

It is clear that funds provided by the World Bank or any other governmental or non-governmental agency cannot be dealt with in this way. The ability to call people to account not merely by popular consent but on the basis of duly recorded evidence is integral to most people's notions of good development practice. Moreover the idea of leaders spending a lot of time chatting to people would not necessarily be considered compatible with good time management. These differences have something to do with how very small organizations can be run compared with larger ones but, as a comparison with Sarvodaya and Swadhyaya confirms, they also reveal very different cultural attitudes and ways of doing things that are particularly

14 World Bank meeting 'Improving Access of Faith-based Organisations to Funding from National HIV/AIDS Programmes', Addis Ababa, 13–16 May 2003.

characteristic of many religious communities. The receipt of outside funding brings inevitable changes to some of these characteristics, but whether they are necessarily changes for the better is a moot point.

Exploitation of the Poor

Both Sarkan Zoumountsi and Omin Funkó strongly object to the manipulation of marginalized people in the interest of other organizations. Both have experienced opportunistic interference by political parties: in one case falsely claiming that they were responsible for successful work and in the other withdrawing collaboration as soon as the elections were over. Their rejection of this behaviour is not at all surprising, but the issue brings us close to the delicate question of the extent to which many funding organizations use the materially poor communities in whose favour they are working, and indeed sometimes seem almost forced to do so, in order to keep their own institutions (and thus their ability to continue their support) going.

Sometimes this 'use' may amount to fraud – siphoning off disproportionate amounts of money for the institution and its staff or giving false accounts or reports in order to deceive potential donors – but it is the more subtle cases that are the most difficult to deal with. 'Personal stories' of how poor people have been able to use grants to 'lift themselves out of poverty' can be told, very often unwittingly, in patronizing or sentimental tones that belie the strength and talents of those involved. Photographs can give images of degradation and almost inhuman hopelessness. Supporting organizations can claim more than is their due for successes achieved. And the philosophy or spirituality of the people on the ground can be overlooked or distorted when their stories are told merely in terms of material achievements.

When institutions resort to this kind of 'advertising', they may be opting for what they see as the necessary 'professional' approach to keep their work and the projects they support going, particularly if they depend for a large proportion of their funds on voluntary giving. People quite naturally like to know that their money will go to 'deserving' people who desperately need it and will use it well. It is probably also the case that many grassroots communities accept that this is part of the deal. But there is something about this sort of commercialization that seems to betray the kind of solidarity we see at the heart of the development work of Awakatán, Omin Funkó or Sarkan Zoumountsi.

Religious Identity and Relationships: a Contribution to Peace

Through their openness to people of other religious traditions, it is probably safe to say that these three organizations are making a particular contribution to peace in their societies that no secular groups could make.

In refusing to go along with closed attitudes of the Bethlehem Church, the members of the Awateko group were protesting against what they felt was an unacceptable narrowing down of the Christian imperative to serve others (based on the example of Jesus himself as well as his teaching). But they were also protesting against the exclusion and even condemnation of people of other religious groups. The rejection of Catholicism by Pentecostal churches was strengthened in Guatemala as the result of a deliberate government policy to set other churches against the Catholics during the civil conflict. This was because the military perceived Catholics to be actively participating on the side of the poorest communities, and particularly of the indigenous population whom they accused of supporting the guerrilla front. As a consequence of this, many Mayan people joined the Pentecostal churches as the safer option.

The open inclusion of Mayan spirituality on an equal footing with Christianity is also a remarkable step forward after 500 years of ostracism of this ancient world view by the large majority of churches in Guatemala. The story shows that the women from these different traditions are united by their common commitment to improving life for their children and to serving the community. However, they are also united by their common Mayan culture, which is inextricably interwoven with Mayan spirituality. This has led to the Christians among them consciously or unconsciously incorporating elements of Mayan spiritual tradition into their Christian faith. Nevertheless, their courage in so openly stating the 'interfaith' basis of their work should be seen as a brave example for the hundreds of Mayan communities that have been split down the middle by intransigent religious groups.

With Omin Funkó we see a similarly remarkable alliance between people of a traditionally despised and feared ancient African cult and others in the neighbourhood whose prejudices against Candomblé were clearly very strong. The support of Koinonia, the large Christian ecumenical Brazilian NGO mentioned in the first section of the story, is an important validation of the work of the 'terreiros', as well as a statement of solidarity with the people of Candomblé who, like the followers of Mayan spirituality, have been ostracized through the centuries by the churches.

Sarkan Zoumountsi is making a significant contribution to peace in inner-city Yaoundé through mediating among opposing factions in the community. Since the conflicts have been among people from different religious as well as tribal groups, Sarkan Zoumountsi's own clear religious affiliation gives it a certain authority to intervene; but this is only possible because of its attitude of openness and respect. The building of a footbridge over the canal to the Baptist community is a powerful symbol of a Muslim organization reaching out to people of other faiths.

An Insignificant Contribution?

Are small religiously inspired organizations like the ones in these stories too insignificant to make a difference in the development arena and too far removed from modern development thinking and practice to be able to scale up their work? Are they struggling against all odds in an environment that is likely to grow more and more hostile to their vision and their ways of working so that they are in danger of ending up as failed idealists out of touch with the reality of the twenty-first century?

One of the main criticisms often levelled at faith-based development work is that it is too local to count in the context of the enormity of the problem of poverty in the world today. As President of the World Bank, James D. Wolfensohn repeatedly urged faith-based organizations to 'scale up' their work by joining together or creating bigger umbrella institutions that enable small projects to be replicated if not enlarged. As we saw in Chapter 1, it is not impossible for them to do this while maintaining their roots in very local communities; but the question lingers as to whether programmes should be expanded – as seems often to happen – principally for the convenience of the funding institutions.

It is true that it would be beneficial if CEADI, Omin Funkó and Sarkan Zoumountsi could provide schooling for more children, more widespread midwifery and other health services, micro-credit schemes to benefit thousands rather than scores of women, and training courses enabling many more young people to find employment. (This could equally be said, of course, about thousands of small secular NGOs.) However, the experience of these organizations points to various factors to be borne in mind when considering what scaling up would mean.

If it were initiated from outside such a change might even be in danger of destroying them, since their very identity has been formed by a vision of development based on the spirituality of their local communities and leaders and by the culture and geography of the areas in which they have grown up. The crucial point is that the motivation of the three organizations we have been looking at in this chapter only partially coincides with those of institutions more focused on technical aspects of development. Scaling up might improve the results of their work on one level. But if it did not happen organically, from within, the new managerial structures that would inevitably be part of the endeavour might well mean that these small organizations would be hard pressed to maintain their culture of solidarity and relationships of trust within the community, which can be more important to them than a higher level of achievement.

If there is doubt about the possibility of such programmes being scaled up, the question must then be: to what extent are they replicable? No clear answer can be given here either. Replicability belongs to the realm of science. If I do a scientific experiment I would expect the outcome to be exactly the same if you do it. But this is not so with spiritual motivation, which is experienced differently by different people. Moreover the specific nature of the context of the initiatives in each of these stories might well mean that in a different place an attempt to carry out the same sort of work would bring very different results.

Nevertheless, if these caveats are borne in mind, neither of these possibilities should be rejected out of hand. The organizations themselves are all trying to extend their work to reach more people, but they want to do it on their own terms.

Another criticism that is often aimed at spiritually inspired movements is that they have a romantic view about keeping everyone in the countryside when it is clear that the prevailing trends in the modern globalized world are leading to very rapid urbanization. Two things should be noted here: first that the fact that the current economic model leads to massive migration from rural to urban areas does not mean that faith-based organizations should agree with it. Many do not. On the contrary, they see the rapid growth of urban areas as the source of untold human problems, some of which are graphically highlighted in the stories of Omin Funkó and Sarkan Zoumountsi. The second observation is that both Omin Funkó and Sarkan Zoumountsi have actually arisen in urban communities. Thus, whatever their own views on urbanization are, they are not hesitating to try to find solutions to the challenges it presents.

There seems no reason to suppose that the usefulness of the 'development' work of small faith-based organizations is coming to an end. The prognosis that in the modern age religion will cease to be an important factor in the life of humankind seems in its turn to have been a 'romantic' one. The fact is that these groups continue to give material, spiritual and moral support to people whom the state does not regard as a priority population for its services and who, without these organizations, would be in danger of losing all hope for the future.

Chapter 3

Tribal People Take Development into Their Own Hands

This chapter looks at two large programmes of integrated development with tribal mountain peoples. The people who started them – a Hindu doctor in India and a Christian missionary in Cameroon – were both profoundly influenced by the people they went to help. Once again, religion 'brought down to earth' is experienced as a source of hope and of faith in oneself and other people. Taking a critical look at the role and motivation of development workers, the stories emphasize the importance of people carrying out their own development according to their own cultural traditions, though these are by no means seen as immutable. We see the interplay of modernity with traditional cultures and consider whether tribal values, such as a strong sense of community, can survive the values brought by globalization.

Vivekananda Girijana Kalyana Kendra

K.R. Usha, April 2003

Set off the main road, which ascends into the thickly forested Biligiri Rangana (B.R.) Hills in the southern Indian state of Karnataka, are the stone and clay-tiled buildings of the Vivekananda Girijana Kalyana Kendra [Tribal Welfare Centre] (VGKK). The VGKK is a voluntary organization working among the Soliga tribes who are said to have lived in these hills for thousands of years. What began as a precarious venture in a hut 30 years back now has a radius of over 60 km, taking in its ambit a tribal population of 20,000.

VGKK: The Beginnings

In 1979, H. Sudarshan, a 29-year-old doctor from Bangalore, first arrived in the B.R. Hills wanting to serve the Soliga people. 'If you want to find God, serve man!' his preceptor Swami Vivekananda had urged. The one hitch to Dr Sudarshan's plans, however, was the reluctance of the Soligas to be served. But he persisted, living in the forest, hoping to win their trust. 'For three years he lived amongst us,' says Shivane Gowda, President of the VGKK Council, adding with a touch of pride, 'but he did not get our measure. It was only after three years that he understood our problems.'

A dramatic cure for snakebite helped to establish Dr Sudarshan's credentials, but it was not until October 1981 that the VGKK was formally founded, with Dr Sudarshan as secretary, one of the volunteers working with him as treasurer and eight representatives from the Soliga community on the executive committee.

The Soligas

The Soligas or 'Children of the Bamboo' are traditionally a semi-nomadic people, practising shifting cultivation and living off the minor produce and small game of the forest. They live in 'podus' or settlements of 10–50 thatched huts. The barter system has been their basis of economic transaction. Even today, despite the Indian Penal Code, disputes are settled by the 'Nyaya Sabhe' or the people's congregation. Though women have still not been elected to head their 'podus' or as 'nyaya' judges, they speak openly at the congregational meetings and take on all work, from cultivating crops to hunting. The caste system of mainstream Hindu society, which might well have begun as a system of division of labour but has now developed into a privileged ordering, is absent among the Soligas.

The religion of the Soligas could broadly be described as nature worship. Deep in the B.R. Hills stands the Doddasampige, the gigantic Champak tree, believed to be over 2,000 years old, and revered by the Soligas as a manifestation of their god Madeshwara. The Soligas speak directly to their deities and celebrate them in the most lyrical of songs and poetry. The nature worship of the Soligas captures the spirit of Rig Vedic culture where forces of nature were deified.

Whenever the Soligas cut down a tree, they perform a small ritual in penance. To plough the land, the Soligas use a spade and not heavy animal-drawn implements, so that the earth is not hurt.

After the year's harvest, the whole 'podu' meets in a festival of thanksgiving to God, the ultimate protector from whom everything comes. Pancakes are offered first to Lord Jadeswami, in acknowledgement that all human endeavour is an offering to God (echoing the Bhagavad Gita) and then shared among the whole community. No one goes hungry as long as there is food in the 'podu', which takes care of all its inhabitants. The community is thus the backbone of Soliga existence and the forest their natural habitat.

The End of 'Splendid Isolation'

In 1971, after rapid deforestation owing to the British policies of commercializing the forest and the post-independence growth mode of industrialization, the B.R. Hills were declared a 'protected' area. The Soligas were evicted from their interior 'podus' and their traditional way of life was ended. And so began the vicious cycle of land alienation, exploitation by landlords and indebtedness often resulting in bonded labour.

The government rehabilitation schemes, though well-meaning, were neither culture-specific nor needs-based, and they often went awry because the Soligas remained ignorant of them. The Soligas, unused to heavy tilling, were not able to cultivate the land given to them in compensation. Monetary compensation was whittled away in no time at all. Branded as 'lazy and land-hungry', the community sank further into poverty and disease, and also into their shell, refusing to trust any figure of 'authority'.

The Formulation of VGKK Objectives

The Spirit behind the Objectives

Common to the Hindu view of life – from the philosophical flights of the Upanishads to the nature worship of tribes like the Soligas – is a belief in the divine nature of every living being and the inseparable unity of the material and the spiritual world. All the Hindu sects that subscribe to Vedantic/Upanishadic philosophy see the human quest as one of 'self-realization', of union with the 'eternal soul' or Brahman, or simply, freedom. One of the ways to attain this union is the path of Karma Yoga, the concrete and practical path of work.

When Swami Vivekananda founded the Ramakrishna Mission in 1897, it was Karma Yoga as a system of ethics which advocated unselfishness and good works as the path to spiritual development that he brought to the fore. As a young man, Dr Sudarshan worked with the Ramakrishna Mission, and he has always regarded Swami Vivekananda as his guide and mentor.

According to Swami Vivekananda, a social worker should meet three requirements: truly to feel the pain of his brothers as his own; to find a remedy for their ills and act on it; and constantly to question his true motives. A combination of 'immense idealism with immense practicality' was required. Vivekananda exhorted his monks, 'You must be prepared to explain the intricacies of the 'shastras' [sacred texts] now, and the next moment go and sell the produce of the fields in the market.'

According to the Bhagavad Gita, only unselfish, detached work carried out as worship is truly regenerating. By working in freedom through love, without a slavish attachment to the results, the worker will not be disappointed if the receiver is not grateful to him, or if his schemes miscarry. What is really achieved by doing good unto others is improving oneself. By questioning his motives constantly, the worker can make sure that duty does not degenerate into self-aggrandisement or selfish attachment.

The Objectives of VGKK

The VGKK evolved the following objectives for its integrated tribal work:

- To realize the vision of a self-reliant, united and progressive Soliga community.
- To identify the potential of the Soligas and help them build their confidence through motivation, education and training. Development efforts would have to encourage them to retain and build on their intrinsic values, traditions and culture; efforts at modernization must combine synergistically with the positive dynamism of their life: ('Keep the gold and remove the dross of the old ideas' as Swami Vivekananda had urged).
- To build up people's organizations in order to educate the people about their rights and to work for social justice and fundamental rights.

Support for the VGKK

In the initial years, before the days of government grants and international interest, the VGKK survived on the generosity of its well-wishers. (All services of the Kendra were, and still are, free.) European non-governmental development agencies followed with financial help. The Kendra now gets regular grants from programmes run by the Indian government's Ministries of Health, Education and Rural Development and it works with several specialist organizations in different areas.

Education

The VGKK school, which started with six students in 1981, today has a total of 566 students in its school, junior college and on vocational courses. Of the 451 students in the school section, 180 are girls. The success rate of students taking the state-level exam has improved from 17 per cent in 1989 to an average of 55–60 per cent today, with a dropout rate of only 2 per cent.

The VGKK system of education reinforces the Soliga way of life while incorporating the benefits of mainstream education, particularly of modern science. Optional courses in forestry and animal tracking and vocational courses have been introduced in the high school for those students who do not want to pursue conventional academic subjects. The classrooms overlook the hillocks and the residential hostel was designed with the Soliga 'podu' in mind.

The morning prayer at the VGKK school is a tribal song in praise of the sun, the giver of life. This is followed by the 'Suryanamaskar', the salute to the sun, a yoga 'asana' and in the classroom the scientific process of photosynthesis is explained, thus completing the knowledge loop.

The school builds on the sense of fellow feeling that exists in the Soliga community. When one boy injures another he is not punished but made responsible for taking the other to the dispensary and for washing his clothes. Children undergo leadership training programmes and are actively involved in educating the community on matters of health and hygiene, nutrition and individual and community rights. Recently the junior college shifted to the plains in Yelandur so the Soliga students now mix with non-tribal students. According to M. Revanna, the college principal, this has given them the semblance of a spirit of competition and, through travelling by bus, a sense of time.

The VGKK kitchen, run largely on solar power and gobar gas (fuel from cattle dung), provides students, staff and visitors with simple, nutritious meals. While this is of practical convenience, the act of the entire VGKK community breaking bread together is an indirect way of negating the caste rules of Indian society and of reinforcing the equality of all human beings as one of the founding principles of the VGKK.

'One of the most important things the school did for me,' says Jadeya Gowda – one of the first six students of the school, who today is working towards a PhD in agriculture and is a member of the VGKK Governing Council – 'was to instil a sense of pride in myself and my community, to give me a sense of worth. It is this sense of pride which will form a counter weight against all the blandishments of the modern world.'

The Soliga Concept of Development

The concept of progress or development in the Soliga mind, adult and child alike, is linked with the community as a whole and with education. The old days of isolation are over, they agree, and it is education for both boys and girls that they see as their passport to the modern world.

For the VGKK's high-school students, development entails not just education but political awareness and the ability to think for themselves. To Sankala, who aspires to study law, this means reassessing certain tribal customs, such as the belief in being 'possessed'. While their scientific training makes them think of it as illogical, their customs reinforce it. 'We must decide for ourselves what we want to think,' he sums up. Jayeda adds that students also need moral guidance to reassess customs such as eloping in one's teens, the sanctioned system of marriage among the Soligas.

Remarkably, the Soligas do not seem to fear that modern education will alienate their children from their culture. For the younger Soligas, this is largely because the VGKK school has brought the advantages of the city to the hills while simultaneously strengthening the Soligas' cultural roots.

Health

Rising from its 'solitary hut' beginnings, the 18-bed VGKK Tribal Hospital is now the base hospital for the region. In the year 2001–02 it treated over 500 in-patients and almost 11,000 out-patients. Its laboratory has a range of facilities, from haemograms to ultrasound scanning. The special programmes include drives to eradicate leprosy, control tuberculosis and to support HIV/STD awareness and detection. While curative medical care was the VGKK entry point into the Soliga community, the emphasis has shifted to a preventive community health programme that includes the immunization of children against polio and other diseases.

The VGKK hospital works on a three-tier system. To entrust grassroots health care to the villagers themselves, the Village Health Workers (VHW) and traditional healers who form the first level are selected by the villagers and trained to handle first aid, community health and health education. The Multipurpose Worker and Auxiliary Nurse Midwife form the second tier. Three medical officers, including a surgeon and a paediatrician, form the third tier.

A special effort is made to encourage the use of traditional herbal medicine, especially at the VHW level, including homeopathy and Ayurveda. Dr Sudarshan estimates that '25 per cent of the health problems can be managed through traditional systems' (see Plate 4).

The government has now evolved the Karnataka model of primary health care management, largely based on the VGKK hospital. Dr Sudarshan's appointment to head the state's Task Force on Health is seen as a vindication of the VGKK's methods.

Vocational Training and Cottage Industries

The Vocational Training and Cottage Industries section trains the community, particularly the youth, in weaving, carpentry, knitting, tailoring and printing, as well as other trades, in collaboration with government training centres. The raw materials for the industries come from the forests and its surrounding areas. The 15 centres in this section, including honey and food processing, hand-made paper, leaf-cup making and screen printing, generated sales worth over 1.5 million rupees in the year 2001–02.

The Kendra has assisted in the training of the Large Scale Adivasi Multipurpose Co-operative Society (LAMPS) to enable the Soligas to manage their cottage industries and market their goods by themselves. The Industrial Training Institutes train students in tailoring, motor mechanics, home appliances and welding. A credit union which gives loans at nominal rates of interest is also run by the Soligas.

Environmental Preservation

The VGKK has launched a series of environmental projects in collaboration with organizations such as the Tata Energy Research Institute and the University of Massachusetts in Boston. They focus on the conservation of local health traditions, medicinal plants, nursery and seed storage techniques and also assess extraction levels of forest products, harness and regulate the collection of non-timber forest products and herbal medicines, and develop forest management programmes.

Community Organization

The VGKK's philosophy of people development puts into practice Swami Vivekananda's quest for a religion/philosophy 'which will give us faith in ourselves … self-respect, the power to feed and educate, the power to relieve the misery around [us] …'. Through personal involvement in the Soliga struggle against the intransigence of government authorities and the strong-arm tactics of influential landlords, the VGKK realized that it was imperative to develop a grassroots power base and organize the solidarity that already existed in the community. VGKK workers would act as catalysts or change agents in the process.

Out of a leadership training workshop conducted in 1985 was born the Soliga Abhivruddhi Sangha [Development Council] – (SAS) – made up of 'taluka sanghas' or groupings of individual 'podu sanghas'. Young Soligas are very active in them, as are also the traditional leaders. All Soliga men and women are members of the 'sanghas' and efforts are made to include at least one woman in the organizing committee. Local problems are discussed and solutions worked out, and often contact meetings are organized with officials to work out contentious issues. With the Forest Department, for instance, the SAS negotiated the right to harvest the produce of certain trees, as well as irrigation, housing and drinking water schemes. But by far the most important contribution of the 'sanghas' has been the management of minor forest produce by the people themselves. Further, the Soliga systems such as their 'nyaya' have been rejuvenated by the unity that the SAS has created.

'Now, thanks to the "Sangha",' says Shivane Gowda, 'the government knows we come 20,000 strong. With such numbers, the government is our mother's house, a source of strength. It takes our demands seriously.' The state cabinet meeting held at the B.R. Hills in January 2002, where the Chief Minister addressed the problems of the local people, was seen as a sign of recognition of the legitimacy of the tribal people's claims.

Philosophy of the VGKK's Work – What's In It for Me?

The VGKK's success in empowering the Soligas has been largely due to the commitment of its workers and their ability to work as a team. Its workers at all levels are challenged to go beyond a professional analysis of the problems and possible solutions to continuous self-questioning regarding their motives: What's in it for me? – the 'working with awareness' that completes the VGKK's approach.

VGKK's total of 120–150 workers fall into three categories: honorary workers who are not remunerated by the organization but whose basic requirements are met by the Soliga community, those who are paid a small honorarium and those who depend on their VGKK jobs for a livelihood and are paid a regular salary. For some VGKK workers, their inspiration has been the teachings of Swami Vivekananda. But for others, it is simply the satisfaction of doing their work to the best of their ability and the joy in discovering their own growth through empowering others.

In order to reinforce its work culture, strengthen team spirit and update skills, the VGKK holds staff meetings from time to time with open discussion forums. The decision-making machinery is transparent, and in a conscious effort to decentralize authority, work units are planned and executed through committees. Since the organization ultimately aims at withdrawing from the community once it is self-reliant, efforts are made to draw on the tribal community for VGKK staff.

As in all organizational endeavour and human dynamics, the VGKK has had its share of conflicts. Conflict resolution, whether with the government or within the organization, is understood as a dialectical process involving the willingness to listen to others, transparency and a focus on their common goal. 'With long interaction and understanding, differences disappear', says Venkat, who is involved in youth training, 'but investment in the community and acceptance of the people are a pre-condition'.

Learning from the Soligas

The VGKK workers realize that many of the Soliga strengths have gone unconsciously into building the organization. Team spirit, which is the backbone of the VGKK's success, owes much to and is perhaps a reflection of the communitarian spirit of the Soligas. While the 'unworldliness' of the Soligas can still exasperate VGKK workers, it has made many workers reflect on their own attitudes, and their lives and needs have been simplified as a result.

Many have seen in the way the Soligas live their lives, their modes of worship, their songs and dance, a simultaneous reverence for life and a celebration of it, an affirmation of the many and mysterious ways in which nature or the divine regenerate the human spirit. Dr Sudarshan admits that many things he had earlier dismissed as superstitions, such as the Soliga practice of hugging trees, he now knows are positive stimuli. He can understand why the Soligas dance when it first rains. 'Here,' he says, 'I have learnt to appreciate beauty and understand the regenerative power of love.'

Tokombéré: A Project for Human Development Founded on Faith

Etienne Zikra, March 2003[1]

Introduction

Every community needs to organize in order to deal better with the daily issues it has to face. Our underdeveloped, or rather developing countries experience various problems and have become an experimental field for development experts. But development theory as it is understood and applied by many experts has brought dissatisfaction because the principle component of any true development project – human beings – has been pushed to one side.

No development project can give signs of hope if it does not regard people as the agents of their own development. All aspects of human beings must be considered, with all their capacities and deficiencies. This poses the problem of faith: faith in humankind (because, since they are created in the image of God, human beings have capacities that must not be overlooked) and faith in God (the principle source of all positive inspiration).

The word 'faith' is understood here not only as belief in God. It is also that which allows one to remain hopeful and expectant. The faith of the men and women of Tokombéré upholds all their activities for the development of the region. And results have come, even if the way is long and sometimes full of disappointments and difficulties of all sorts (including jealousy, lack of understanding and many others).

Background

In 1959, one of the first Catholic Cameroonian missionaries, Simon Mpeke, set off to explore northern Cameroon, where there were three dominant religious practices: the religion of the mountains, Islam and Christianity. The followers of the religion of the mountains were given the name 'Kirdi' or 'unbelievers' by the Muslims, but to everyone's surprise this priest who had come to evangelize admitted that he did not know what to teach the Kirdi because they knew God already. 'I have found people who lead a natural life to unite them to God,'[2] he said. 'If it weren't for the fact of Jesus Christ which seemed to me something new, which completes creation, I would have gone back home'[3]

---

1 Translated from the original French by the author.
2 Televised interview, 1972.
3 Interview with the writer J.B. Baskouda, 1975; see also Baskouda, *Baba Simon, le Père des Kirdis* (Paris, 1988).

Father Mpeke was adopted by the mountain people, who gave him the name of 'Baba' (which means Papa) because they saw that he wanted people to live fraternally, crossing all religious or ethnic boundaries. Baba Simon (as he was called from then on) did not envisage any activity without the participation of the Kirdi; everything had to be done with them, often by them, and for them. And everything had to be done with faith and devotion to the gospel message based on love of one's neighbour. Every single person was important to him: the sick, the despised, men, women, the misunderstood. Seeing life as a commitment to the struggle for each person to grow, he set up a primary school to give the Kirdi enough education to enable them to open themselves up to the whole world.

Since the time of Baba Simon, a team of catechists from different backgrounds has been meeting regularly to meditate and pray and to discuss how the gospel can be practised in our villages through tackling questions such as how to prevent our young people from falling victim to the misfortune of AIDS. Everyone in the Tokombéré Project, even if they are not all Christians, draws upon the same gospel truth to bring together all the members of the community, paying special attention to the young, the poorest and the most vulnerable. The emphasis on a spirit of service and sharing assumes a real commitment on the part of the workers to respect everyone, exercise tolerance and acknowledge differences.

The Health Structure

In 1975, Christian Aurenche, a medical doctor and priest, arrived to take over the small bush hospital that was serving the Kirdi (today around 90,000 people). Influenced by the philosophy of Baba Simon, Dr Aurenche converted the hospital into a Health Promotion Centre with a primary health care orientation. This was the first step towards the formalization of Baba Simon's concern to take people just as they are, in their life context, and to involve them in different actions with a view to their development.

The new concept of health took all aspects into consideration: prevention, cure, accompaniment[4] and social integration. According to Jean Marc Ela, who worked with Christian Aurenche: 'The struggle for health should be seen from now on in the context of the struggle for another society, another human being, another system of production, another way of living among people, as much at the heart of the family as in the global society.'[5]

The villagers, whose average annual income is 100,000 CFA (150 euros), set up health committees and the nurse, from then on known as the 'Itinerant Agent'(IA) became the link between the hospital and the villages. The Village Health Leaders, as they are called, watch over the grassroots work in the different areas of the health project, such as nutrition and the rehabilitation of disabled people. The

---

4   This term, commonly used in Latin America and by the Catholic Church in general, means working alongside people rather than for them.

5   Jean Marc Ela, *Ma Foi d'Africain* (Paris, 1985), p. 115.

hospital provides training and accompaniment (follow-up work) with Village Health Leaders.

At the beginning the leaders were almost all illiterate. But they were capable of reflection and analysis and of showing initiative and solidarity – indispensable qualities to play a leading role in the changes. Their appointment and their acceptance by the community were the result of long discussions.

The IA's meeting with a health committee is an occasion for listening and interaction about themes such as new health habits or the problem of infant mortality, as well as how to get drinking water or how to deal with witchcraft. The IA can share their difficulties and any solutions they have found in 'forums' that help co-ordination and allow the management team to assess the problems at the grassroots and to reflect on possible solutions.

It is striking how ready the villagers were (and are) to commit themselves to health activities in partnership with the hospital. 'If the nurse hadn't made the sacrifice to spend time with us, and if we hadn't been willing to join together to work for health, where would we be today?' comments one villager.

All the administrative authorities who have followed one another in Tokombéré appreciate the project: 'It is an invaluable opportunity for the people to have a development project like this one, which begins with health in order to end up with general well-being. Without this project no one would ever talk about Tokombéré', says one.

It was not long before the Village Health Leaders began to bring up other challenges in the villages, such as how to work with young people or how to ensure food security. After a great deal of thought, the decision was taken to set up further structures in the Project for Human Promotion.

The Youth Project

The question of who would supervise the children from Baba Simon's school who wanted to continue their studies was a thorny one. At that time the nearest secondary schools were 30–60 km away. Eventually, together with the catechists and the parents, the decision was taken to set up secondary 'sarés' [centres] in the towns where the young people would live and take charge of themselves: their studies, health, prayers, cleanliness, cooking and so on. The parents are organized into voluntary teams of attendants of the 'sarés'. In the case of a dispute, the different students in charge meet to find a solution and only call upon the adults if they are unable to do so.

Another initiative was the reopening, in 1984, of a youth centre that had been founded by Jean Marc Ela but then closed by the administrative authorities who claimed that its innovative programmes were subversive. About 1,500 youths are involved in the activities of the Youth Centre of Tokombéré. A management team called the Youth Project Council makes sure that things do not get out of control and that no one is excluded.

At the request of the young people themselves, this experience was later brought to the villages with the creation of (now over 20) mini youth centres. These are places of entertainment, reflection and training also managed by the young people themselves with the support of the Youth Project's Itinerary Agents who are the link between the village youth and the whole of the Human Promotion Project.

It is impressive how the young people themselves are already talking about development and feel concerned about the issue. Mangavé, present Youth President, explains what motivates her:

> Faith in God. Faith in the New Person. The Bible calls upon us to help each other. I am convinced that people have worked very hard in order that we should be where we are today. Now we, too, are finding support in our faith to leave our mark on the development of our village.

Education

In 1990, the Baba Simon College was set up to respond to the dual need of training and education. In the morning the students learn classical subjects (history, maths, French and so on) and in the afternoon practical disciplines called 'footbridges' (bridges between the school and the village) such as agriculture, building, carpentry, small livestock farming, mechanics, health and family education. They also study their traditions so that, firmly rooted in their own culture, they are well prepared to deal with modernity.

This college has solved the problem of the lack of secondary schools in Tokombéré. Once more, it is faith which prevails over everything. Each morning starts with prayers and an hour a week is devoted to catechism; but this does not consist only of learning to pray or to know the Bible and it is certainly not a course in doctrine. It is much more about drawing the pupils' attention to a spirit of solidarity, of service and commitment. Discussions and debates are organized around themes of daily life.

The teachers are also Itinerant Agents. They meet the parents, listen to their problems and exchange views about their children's education. An annual Parents' General Assembly tackles all aspects and demands of school life and education.

Here again, we see the method of dialogue and consultation. And here too the fruit begins to 'ripen'. Are not the pupils of the college who do not have the chance to continue their studies frustrated or hurt to see school friends coming back from the town better dressed than they are, often with big motorbikes? Sewya, a former pupil of the college, who keeps animals and works in the fields, says that he is not:

> I'm proud of having been through the college. Today I'm practising what I learnt and I'm not disappointed. On the contrary! I think each person is important in the place where he is. I can give some help towards development in the village and I can see that life is changing around me. The housing is improving, the level of reflection is rising, tribal quarrels have disappeared and now everyone is working for the same cause: to improve village life.

The Agricultural Project

In 1987, after numerous meetings, it was decided to set up the Peasant's House – an agricultural project to meet the challenge of natural disasters and the reduction of yields because of poor soil. The peasant farmers are organized into about 150 'Peasant Groups' in all the geographical sectors of the area. They cultivate community fields together and put aside a reserve ('the child's part') in a granary called the 'Child's Granary' to be used only in times of scarcity.

At the Peasant's House information and training are provided, experiments carried out and new techniques for agriculture and animal husbandry disseminated. The focus is on the management of the common good (see Plate 5). The first concern of the agricultural project was to improve the local crops and, thanks to the support of qualified people, yields increased. The grassroots committees then came to an agreement: the young had to learn the techniques of the 'white man'. After two years' training at the Peasant's House they would receive a loan and a plough and seeds in exchange for disseminating what they had learnt in the villages. Those who were trained did not receive a diploma, as is usual elsewhere, in order to avoid falling into a relationship of graduate to villager, a relationship similar to that of master and slave.

Very soon the groups diversified their crops and since food security was almost assured, the surplus had to be sold. So in 1994, the 'North–South Granary' was set up. Through this the farmers pooled their products to sell them in the south of Cameroon and bought other products to re-sell in the north. This worked well, as it enabled them to avoid exploitation by middlemen. With the profits they were able to provide for the other needs of their families.

All these activities earned the official recognition of the administrative authorities, who were particularly impressed by the organization of an agro-pastoral market in Tokombéré which showed the peasant farmers' achievements.

The experience of the North–South Granary served its time but had to be brought to a close because the partners in the south did not understand the vision of the project. Their focus only on the economic aspect risked leading the North–South Granary into a mercenary mentality which could have distorted the original objectives. Besides this, they lacked the necessary facilities in Yaoundé to receive the products from Tokombéré. Today the farmers' groups function as a network. They hold annual meetings to debate their problems, propose new initiatives and evaluate their past activities.

Challenged by issues of financial security, after much thought the Peasant's House agreed to an outside institution carrying out a feasibility study for a Decentralized Rural Credit Project. The project went ahead, setting up savings and credit banks in the villages. The aim of the banks was to help villagers solve their financial difficulties and to train them to manage their resources, but today the project is causing great hardship. Many families have been forced to sell their land or their harvest in order to escape imprisonment because they have been unable to pay back their loans on time.

In our opinion, the problems have arisen because the project began at the suggestion of an outside organization rather than of the villagers themselves, and there was no real process of reflection with the people to make them aware of the risks involved.

And the Women?

In our traditional societies, the woman carries heavy responsibility: doing domestic work, bringing up the children, managing the family and working in the fields. Unfortunately these responsibilities are ignored by the man, who is the absolute master of the house. In the light of proposals made by the women themselves, the management team decided to create the 'Women's Promotion' embodied today in the 'Woman's House'.

At first the programmes were aimed at young women who had stopped studying. With enthusiasm and creativity they formed groups in each district, and they now have responsible roles in village organizations. Today the aim is to show the woman that she is the kernel of her family and is thus capable of changing her living conditions.

Apart from practical activities that include agriculture, sewing, childcare and handwork, the women organize regular sessions for reflection on themes such as: 'How can a woman spread peace in her home?' or 'How can a woman contribute to the development of her region?'.

Madame Kokof (former President of the Women's Promotion) recognizes that the Woman's House still has some way to go: 'We still have to attract many women into the group who don't realize yet how important such a structure is for them', she says. However the following account by a member of the Woman's House shows what has been achieved:

> At the beginning we had a lot of difficulties with our husbands because they saw our programmes as useless recreation but many husbands understand now that we learn important things there for the life of the couple and for the development of our region. I've learnt lots of things but I've chosen to make doughnuts to sell. I manage to meet some of the family's needs. In the discussions among women it's easy to pick out those who have been at the Women's Promotion by the quality of their reflection.

There are several more structures that belong to the Project for Human Promotion such as the Adult Literacy Programme, the Association of Pupils' Parents, the Popular University of Tokombéré, the handcraft industry ARTOK and the young Chamber of Economics. All of them have Itinerant Agents – the key links between the people and the management team.

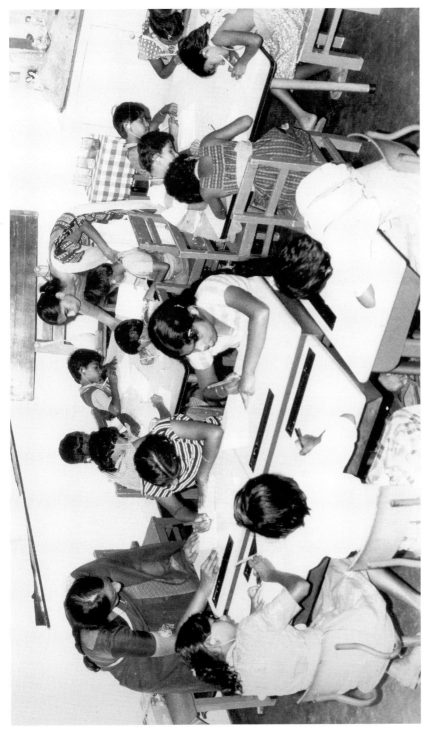

1. Sarvodaya: pre-school

2. Sarkan Zoumountsi: footbridge linking two communities

3. Awakatán: strawberry picking

4. VGKK: Dr Sudarshan examines a Soliga woman

5. Tokombéré: Peasant's House meeting

6. Sebastián Acevedo Movement against Torture: 'Secret Police Continue Torturing'

Small Enterprises to Change the Face of the Village, of the Region

As the standard of living changes, so new needs are created. Nowadays Tokombéré has become the sector with the highest level of schooling in the region and it has an abundance of high fliers. People are changing from walking to riding a bicycle or even a motorbike, and even little by little to driving a car. Eating habits are changing too.

Small enterprises have been set up by the young people of Tokombéré to provide the conditions for this kind of progress. A general store in the heart of the town is managed by a young man whose products range from food to ironmongery. Another man has opened a garage to fix and repair engines and to sell spare parts and fuel, and a traditional bakery along with a restaurant-bar-hotel is managed by a group of young people. Other young people have gone into agricultural farming or into 'modern' livestock rearing.

With these enterprises one has the impression of having suddenly made a leap forward because today we have things on the spot that ten years ago we used to travel 50 km to fetch. All these young people benefited at the beginning from financial support from the Tokombéré Project, but today they are autonomous and are even creating employment for others.

Finances

The Tokombéré Project serves a very poor population and is poor itself. It tries to find resources on the spot by charging for services, but as cheaply as possible because of the surrounding poverty. Since it has no help from public authorities, it needs to mobilize Christian and international solidarity. Each of the 'structures' receives regular support from non-governmental organizations in France, usually to cover 40 or 50 per cent of its costs.

It is this solidarity that has provided the Project for Human Promotion with the sure and stable financial support that allows it to function. All must be staked on the stability and sustainability of the actors of a project. They must have a certain guarantee which allows them really to commit themselves. They must thus be provided with a reasonable and permanent income so that they can be freed from any inclination to go and look for something better elsewhere.

These two aspects (sustainability and stability) enable progress and prevent people repeatedly having to begin all over again. They have been achieved in Tokombéré thanks to the long-term commitment from people outside who share the project's vision.

Conclusion

According to Dr Souleymanou Mohamadou, a Muslim doctor in Tokombéré: 'Human promotion in Tokombéré is inspired by the word of God and rooted in the local culture, with a vision for the future of integrated and sustainable human development. The human being is at the heart of this project, as the absolute priority.'

It is our conviction that for a development project to succeed it is absolutely necessary to work in the field and live on a daily basis with the future beneficiaries. This is in order to understand them better, know their stories, their origins, their aspirations and their difficulties and to include them in the thinking that can give rise to a programme or an idea. The management structure must not be the source of ideas; it should be the sounding board which seeks to give material form to the ideas coming from the grassroots.

As Father Grégoire Cador, parish priest of Tokombéré says: 'No development without faith', which means not a step forward without knowing where we are coming from and what we want to walk towards. All this is not for the short or medium term. People must be allowed to become firmly rooted in the spirit of the project, to ponder on it and then to try it out, adapting it from day to day while keeping to the original aim.

If we were to make a diagram of the Human Promotion Project of Tokombéré, we could compare it to a tree whose roots are the local tradition and the people of the region. The gospel is the sap of this tree, the health project is the trunk and the different branches are the structures which have been created over time at the instigation of the population.

'It is the way one human being sees another which allows people to flourish, to develop' maintains Sababa Michel, a student in Yaoundé. 'They draw their ideas from the gospel but this is the new perception of evangelization, because hungry people cannot follow the gospel. The ground for good living conditions must be prepared, which means recognition, freedom and the capacity to take initiatives in all areas'. For Nicole Payelle, former Director of the Baba Simon College: 'The Tokombéré Project is to walk to the rhythm of the people and to accompany them in their responsibilities, allowing them to be the agents of their future and encouraging them to commit themselves to their life and that of those around them.'

Faith in Ourselves

Keep the gold and remove the dross of the old ideas.
Swami Vivekananda

Religion as the Opium of the People?

Similarly to the previous ones, these two stories tell us about the regenerative power religion can have when it is brought down to earth and made real, so that people's beliefs are intertwined with practical matters. Faith does not only mean belief in God but 'faith in humankind' and 'in that which allows us to remain hopeful and expectant' says the Tokombéré story. Prayer, meditation and the study of sacred texts are an important part of everyday life as sources of inspiration, power and insight, but they are not the only ingredients of a living religion.

Is this not exactly the type of religion or philosophy that Swami Vivekananda was searching for: one 'which will give us faith in ourselves ... self-respect, the power to feed and educate, the power to relieve the misery around [us] ...'? These people are very far away from sin-obsessed, dogmatic and rigid versions of Christianity, focused only on the salvation of the individual's soul and from caste-based, exclusive and intolerant versions of Hinduism!

In both stories we see how the nature worship of the tribal people is not considered by the programmes' founders as 'pagan' or necessarily alien to their own Christian or Hindu beliefs. As a Christian missionary, Simon Mpeke believed that Jesus Christ adds 'something new' that 'completes creation', but he was quite open to the reality that there are many ways of knowing and uniting with God.

Today the people from different ethnic groups living in the region of Tokombéré are divided more or less equally between Christianity, Islam and their traditional animist spirituality.[6] The Tokombéré Project has a strong Christian ethos but its leaders continue to share Father Mpeke's openness as well as his beliefs. 'Thus, according to the website: 'Christians of Tokombéré affirm that they are engaged in the promotion of the human being together with the believers of the traditional religion, Muslims, all the ethnic groups'.[7]

In the light of this, the recognition that 'everyone in the Tokombéré Project, even if they are not all Christians, draws upon the same gospel truth to bring together all the members of the community ...' should not be understood as a resort to the patronizing attitude sometimes found among well-meaning Christians that others are Christians really even though they don't realize it. On the contrary, it is a respectful

---

6   http://www.tokombere.info/ (accessed 22 March 2005).

7   http://www.tokombere-partenaires.org/B/B0206%20-%20projet%20pastoral.htm (accessed 22 March 2005). Author's translation.

recognition that gospel truths such as the importance of love and service can be shared by people of whatever faith or spiritual tradition. It is not doctrine that is centre stage but values and practice. While the sap of the tree of the Tokombéré Project is the gospel, its roots are the Kirdi people and their traditions. They are both equally essential to the life of the project.

Whereas in the story of Tokombéré we are told that Christianity complements rather than contradicts the Kirdi's 'religion of the mountains', the VGKK story explicitly includes the Soligas' nature worship in a 'Hindu view of life', capturing the spirit of Rig Vedic culture. Hinduism, unlike Christianity, has traditionally been open to accepting other religions as equally valid ways to reach the ultimate truth. But Dr Sudarshan has been humble enough to realize that the Soligas' spirituality contains a depth of truth and joy that are not only valid but that greatly enrich his own with its quality of a 'regenerative power of love'. In both Tokombéré and the B.R. Hills, this 'power of love' becomes visible through the vigour, resourcefulness and cheerful commitment of the tribal people.

Agents of Their Own Development

'No development project can give signs of hope if it does not regard people as the agents of their own development.' This central message of the Tokombéré Project arises directly from its grounding in the Christian belief that human beings are created in the image of God, and that one of the essential meanings of Christ's incarnation is that the Holy Spirit dwells in every person (Romans 8. 9). If this is the case, then each human being not only 'has capacities that must not be overlooked' but is potentially a wellspring of extraordinary power and creativity.

It is not only out of respect or because he wanted to win them over that Simon Mpeke insisted that the Kirdi be included in all activities. He realized that he needed their contribution if the project was to be successful. Their insights, experience and knowledge were complementary to his own. Thus when the new health programme was founded there was no question of waiting for higher levels of literacy among the Kirdi as a prerequisite to their taking on leadership roles (although literacy is now one of the programmes in Tokombéré). They already possessed the necessary skills in reflection and analysis and the qualities of showing initiative and solidarity.

Every single part of the Tokombéré Project has been set up at the instigation of the Kirdi themselves. The project is based on their inspiration and practical analysis of what is needed. Outsiders with specific expertise and technical experience have helped them to plan and implement the programmes but they have not needed anyone to tell them what development should be about! On the contrary, when this happened – with the village credit and savings banks – it ended in disaster for many of the people involved.

The experience of the VGKK has been strikingly similar. With Swami Vivekananda's precept 'If you want to find God, serve man' ringing in his ears, Dr Sudarshan very soon realized that to serve other people means to learn from them and to meet their needs in the way, and above all at the moment, they want you to. 'It is not a question of romanticizing them but of understanding their strengths', he explains.[8] This is what 'development' with the Soligas has been all about: focusing on the people's own experience and ideas.

How different from the British administrators' or the state's development programmes of exploiting the forests for lumber or declaring the B.R. Hills a protected area, ignoring the right of tribal people to their ancestral home! It was their own lack of regard for the Soligas' culture and their needs that led the authorities to think that the Soligas were lazy. It also led to increasing poverty and mistrust among the Soligas themselves.

The Ethics of Development Workers

Development is about change. This is normally seen in terms of societal change from a disadvantaged economic and social situation to a better one. It is seldom that development literature focuses on the need for the development workers who wish to play a role in bringing about changes in society to change themselves as well.

However, in these, as in the other stories in this book, the motivation and attitudes of the development worker are very much in focus. 'Whatever is in microcosm is also in macrocosm and since the individual, society and nature all exist in dynamic equilibrium, if you don't change yourself, it is not possible to change the world', says Dr Sudarshan[9]. 'Social workers' inner conflicts can be projected onto the community', he goes on, 'so unless they have inner harmony, they can do more harm than good.'

Then, elaborating on Swami Vivekananda's requirement of social workers that they should constantly question their true motives, he observes: 'Mindfulness, awareness of our own intentions is essential. Is what I am doing merely to promote the institution? Am I imposing my own beliefs? Am I really giving others the autonomy necessary for their self-determination? If you lead an authentic life, social transformation takes place.'

It is this emphasis on motivation that one finds again and again among faith-based groups. No doubt we almost always have mixed motives for anything we do, but motivation matters. In both the Catholic and Hindu traditions we are urged not to be attached to the results of our actions as slaves of our own success or failure. 'According to the Bhagavad Gita', says the VGKK story, 'only unselfish, detached work carried out as worship is truly regenerating.' Ignatius Loyola, the Spanish founder of the Society of Jesus (Jesuits), recommended 'holy indifference', made possible by acting as if all depended on us, while knowing that all depends on God.

Genuine motivation to serve others will result in a certain attitude towards them and way of treating them. As Sababa Michel in the Tokombéré story says: 'It is the way one human being sees another which allows people to flourish, to

---

8   WFDD/VSF workshop, Delhi, 9–11 February 2004.
9   Ibid.

develop'. Technical knowledge, analytical skills and the ability to plan strategically are all needed in development work; but equally essential is openness on the part of development workers to learn from and be changed by the people they are supposed to be helping. It is only through such openness that the workers can, in the words of Dr Sudarshan, 'unfold their own divinity'. This openness results in a heightened awareness of cultural differences and in carefulness not to impose the workers' own cultural norms. Nicole Payelle, former Director of the Baba Simon College, is referring to this when she says: 'The Tokombéré Project is to walk to the rhythm of the people'.

The pressure to achieve results within a certain length of time, and thereby unduly to hasten or even to ignore the social processes that are necessary for these results to be sustainable, does not fit in with an attitude of awareness and respect. Yet it is under this sort of pressure that development workers from government agencies and NGOs are very often working. Long-term processes come to be considered unviable if continued funds, as well as the workers' own jobs or promotion, depend on producing visible achievements within a two- to three- or even, in some cases, a one-year funding cycle.

Relations with the State

The Tokombéré story tells us that the state authorities admire the work of the project. In the past, however, relationships have not always been so happy. The first Youth Centre that was set up by Jean Marc Ela in the 1970s was closed down by the state authorities, who considered it to be 'subversive'. (Did this have something to do with the Kirdi taking control over their own lives?) Today's good relations with the state are characterized by tolerance rather than co-operation. The Project for Human Promotion receives no financial support from the state but relies entirely on international solidarity (mainly small solidarity groups in France), supplemented by local contributions.

The VGKK, on the other hand, receives regular government funding for its health, education and rural development programmes. Moreover not only has the state of Karnataka modelled its own health programme on the VGKK hospital but it has appointed Dr Sudarshan as the head of its Task Force on Health – a job that includes tackling the problem of corruption in the health service. What are the implications of this for the independence of the project?

Dr Sudarshan is very clear. 'Faith-based groups should not be part of the government nor co-opted into it', he says. 'They should act as outside advisers focusing on the value system underlying government programmes and policies.'[10] The VGKK has been willing to co-operate with the state and for its hospital to become the main hospital for the region; but at the same time it has encouraged the Soligas to strengthen their own organizations so that they can put pressure on

---

10 Ibid.

the state to claim their rights. Moreover, when it became evident that the Soligas were losing their land, the VGKK did not hesitate to take sides against the powerful landowners and the state that protected them. Dr Sudarshan even went to jail because of his identification with the Soligas' struggle. The VGKK has remained true to its role as an 'outside adviser' and a highly critical one at that!

Community

A central notion in both of these stories is that development is for the whole community. Individuals are encouraged to develop themselves through education and training and through deepening their own sense of cultural identity as well as their spiritual life; and no doubt the Kirdi, like the Soligas, become more personally competitive when they go to schools and colleges outside the community. But with the return home of at least a good number of those who have gained education outside, there is plenty of evidence that individuals accrue knowledge and skills with the development of their community in mind.

'Community' as described in these stories contains the notion that all its members and all their different contributions to the common good are of equal worth, for they have, as Paul says, 'all been made to drink of the one spirit' (1 Corinthians 12.13). The Peasant's House in Tokombéré refuses even to grant diplomas for fear of creating the relationship of 'master and slave' that they have experienced between graduates and peasant farmers in other circumstances. We also have the moving testimony of the young man who feels no resentment that others have been able to further their education and buy motorbikes which, for reasons unknown to us, he was unable to do. His contentment lies in his sense of his own value and in the knowledge that he is making a worthwhile contribution to the development of his village and the region.

The strong sense to be found in so many indigenous cultures that the individual gains his or her identity and self-worth first and foremost as the member of a community is emphasized in the VGKK story too. The sense of community has been allowed to seep through not only into the education programme but into the way the VGKK works as a whole. There is no hesitation in acknowledging that the 'team spirit, which is the backbone of VGKK's success, owes much to and is perhaps a reflection of the communitarian spirit of the Soligas'.

Adherence to any religion necessarily involves belonging to a community, usually based on a temple, church, synagogue, gurdwara, mosque and so on. The image of us all being united as one body is to be found in several religions, and it is known that the early Christians pooled their worldly goods and lived in communities. The notion of the 'common good' that underlies all the social teaching of the Catholic Church reinforces this focus on the importance of life in community. From the ironical fact that the sense of community is being eroded most quickly in many countries with a strong Christian tradition we can only conclude that much of this original communal spirit of Christianity has been lost in those societies.

Within Hinduism there is also a tradition of community life, though the discrimination through the caste system that is still so entrenched in Indian society militates against it. In the VGKK story, particular mention is made of communal meal times being 'a way of negating the caste rules of Indian society.'

Dr Sudarshan points out that the core values of Hinduism are found in the Brahmasutras, Upanishads and Bhagavad Gita as opposed to the Smriti [codes of conduct] –and particularly the Manusmriti – that have been a source of discrimination against women and through the caste system. '… We can only gain freedom through a realization that Reality is just one, even if called by different names, through a belief in the oneness of everyone. Unity in diversity, is not enough. We have to experience it and feel it', he says.[11]

Maybe it is this feeling of 'oneness' that is essential as a safeguard against communities – and not least religious or tribal ones – becoming hierarchical, oppressive and closed or even hostile to outsiders. Strong communities are not necessarily havens of bliss, as many people, especially women, who suffer from oppressive communities will tell us! If they are based on the imposition of the kind of consensus that allows no one to ruffle the waters, close-knit communities can stifle growth and new ideas.

Both Tokombéré and the VGKK recognize that conflict is a necessary part of healthy communities. In the Youth Project of Tokombéré there is provision for the young people to call upon their parents if they cannot solve a conflict themselves and the VGKK notes the importance of training in conflict resolution.

All this has, of course, considerable consequences for how 'development' is understood. Individualism, competition leading to the superior status and wealth of some over others, the lack of a sense of responsibility for the welfare of the most vulnerable members of society as well as of future generations, individual greed, and the unwillingness to share are all incompatible with a world view that emphasizes the need to live in harmony with and take care of others.

But are Tokombéré and VGKK merely trying to prolong a way of life that is already doomed to extinction in our age of increasingly industrialized and fragmented societies? Questions about what 'community' can mean in the context of the twenty-first century are no rarity, nor indeed are assertions that it is not even a relevant concept for our time.

The increasingly dysfunctional societies of the industrialized world leave little room, however, for a complacent belief that society can flourish merely as an agglomeration of individuals, as Margaret Thatcher, a former prime minister of Britain, would have had it. The financier George Soros is among very many people from all sectors of society who are worried about the issue: 'Market fundamentalists believe that the common interest is best served by the untrammelled pursuit of self-interests. This belief is false, yet it has become very influential', he writes.[12]

---

11 Ibid.
12 George Soros, *Open Society* (London, 2000), p. 117.

The value of strong communities is recognized by development agencies when they speak of the need to build up 'social capital' but because of its economic connotation, the very term seems to indicate that the aim is to strengthen relationships between people first and foremost as a way of helping to increase economic prosperity. This leads once more to the question as to whether there is sufficient awareness of the danger of subordinating all other dimensions of life to the economic – a danger that exists equally at the level of the 'international community' as at the level of national, regional and local development programmes.

Culture and Development

Denis Goulet tells us that traditional values are useful if they can 'supply meaning to people's lives, guide their actions in their present environment and circumstances and provide them with criteria for accepting or rejecting outside influences bearing upon them.'[13] The people in these stories would not accept that the values promoted by modern consumer societies do this to the same degree as the values they are trying to uphold, if indeed they do it at all. As Benjamin Barber says in his book *Jihad vs. McWorld*:

> The complaint against McWorld represents impatience and not just with its consumption-driven markets and its technocratic imperatives but with its hollowness as a foundation for a meaningful moral existence. These absences translate into profound civic alienation that disconnects individuals from their communities and isolates them from nonmaterial sources of their being.[14]

Both the VGKK and the Tokombéré Project hold the view that the only way that the Soligas or the Kirdi will be free to make their own decisions about what they want to accept or reject from Western ideas and attitudes and the culture of global capitalism is by being rooted in their own traditions. They need to have a strong sense of their own identity and of the values they hold dear. 'If a person has two legs, it is in order to be able to walk with one foot in modernity and the other in tradition', says Christian Aurenche.[15]

Culture is the means by which people give meaning and order to their world. As we have seen with the exploitation of the forests of the B.R. Hills, development programmes that disregard or go counter to local cultures leave people in disarray. The Soligas' loss of their forest home did not only mean the loss of their livelihood but also of the place in which their spirituality is grounded.

But cultures are neither static nor impervious to outside influences; nor is any culture wholly positive. In the case of the VGKK and Tokombéré, the Soligas and

---

13 Denis Goulet, *Development Ethics* (London, 1995), p. 138.

14 Benjamin Barber, *Jihad vs. McWorld* (New York, 1996), p. 275.

15 http://www.tokombere-partenaires.org/ (accessed 15 September 2005). Author's translation.

the Kirdi are deciding for themselves which of their cultural beliefs and practices no longer serve the interests of the community and what elements of other cultures would be beneficial to them. Jayeda at the VGKK is ready to reassess the practice of teenage elopement that interrupts Soliga girls' schooling for example, and new dietary habits are being adopted in Tokombéré.

Both the Kirdi and the Soligas recognize that modern technology can bring benefits to their communities: the VGKK school lays stress on the importance of learning science, and the Peasant's House in Tokombéré decided that the young people should learn and teach others the agricultural techniques of the 'white man'. But traditional ways of doing things are also valued and built upon: 25 per cent of the health problems at the VGKK are managed through traditional systems and the VGKK's economic activities include traditional crafts such as weaving as well as motor mechanics and a micro-credit bank that is enabling the Soligas to enter the monetary economy successfully.

The section on small enterprises in the Tokombéré story gives a picture of young people who have come back from the towns with new ideas which will open up their region (through motorized transport) and also encourage a more urban type of economy (buying bread from a shop). Nevertheless, their lives are still based on the traditional occupations of agriculture and the rearing of livestock, albeit enhanced by modern methods.

It is to be welcomed that development agencies are paying increasing attention to culture but as has been said elsewhere:

> The desire to understand the culture of a community is not always disinterested. There have been cases when the knowledge or partial knowledge of cultural issues has been used to integrate communities into programmes designed in another context by people of another culture, or even to deceive communities into believing that non-existent benefits will come their way.[16]

The use of traditional practices and cultural mores in the service of activities whose aims may be at variance with the values of that culture will either end in the failure of the programme concerned or in uprooting the people involved. Both the VGKK and Tokombéré show that such destruction is not necessary to bring about change. They point instead to the existence of a dynamic within traditional cultures that allows for change while preserving the integrity and identity of the people concerned.

Will it be possible for the Soligas and the Kirdi to keep their culture (and their language) in the long run? Jadeya Gowda says that the sense of self-worth and of pride in the community instilled in the Soligas through the school will 'form a counter weight against all the blandishments of the modern world'. Only time will tell if their faith in themselves will enable them to withstand the inevitable onslaught of the

---

16 Thierry Verhelst with Wendy Tyndale, 'Cultures, Spirituality and Development', in Deborah Eade (ed.), *Development and Culture* (Oxford, 2002), p. 6.

materialistic culture of consumerism and the individualistic values that globalized capitalism brings with it.

Chapter 4

Working with Women

In this chapter we get to know three women's organizations: two of them, in Ethiopia and Indonesia, are Muslim and one is run by people from the Bahá'í faith. Salient issues arising from the stories include the close link that the women see between rights and responsibilities and the role of men alongside the women in their struggle. In their view 'development' means getting rid not only of poverty but of injustice in all areas of society, the family included. We see the astuteness of the women but also their integrity as they wrestle to bring about the necessary cultural, institutional and political changes to achieve the justice they are looking for. With their focus on their faith not merely as a set of rules and their insights about the meaning of their scriptures, the Muslim women are helping to set in motion some deep and long-lasting changes for the future.

Addis Ababa Muslim Women's Council

Bedria Mohammed, October 2003

Background

The modern multi-ethnic state of Ethiopia was formed in the second half of the nineteenth century when the expansion of Abyssinia was launched from Shewa, its southernmost principality. Introduced by emissaries of the Prophet Mohammed himself and strengthened by the arrival of the first Muslim refugees, Islam had been a minority faith in Abyssinia for over a thousand years. There was, however, such a close relationship between the Abyssinian rulers and the Orthodox Christian Church at the time of the wars of expansion that the Abyssinian kingdom was virtually synonymous with the Church. Today the conquered lands to the south, east and west make up all but two of the nine regions of the Federal Democratic Republic of Ethiopia, and are home to over three-fifths of its total population.

The people of the conquered lands resisted the Abyssinian invasion and suffered greatly as a result. They were slaughtered and taken into slavery. Their possessions were looted and their lands were measured and divided so that two-thirds were expropriated by the state and one-third was given to the Orthodox Church, whose supremacy was continued by the claim that Ethiopia was a purely Christian state.

In a speech before the United States Congress in 1954, Haile Selassie described the country as an 'island of Christianity in a sea of Islam'.

Even though the successive governments of the multi-ethnic state of Ethiopia attempted to improve the image of Ethiopia's modernity in the eyes of the European powers, the people of the conquered lands were politically excluded and economically exploited. Furthermore, they suffered religious repression at the hands of the Abyssinians. In this contradictory situation, Islam made significant advances among groups that had been superficially integrated into Abyssinian culture and society in the north and it became the dominant religion among the people of the lands that had been annexed. However, aware of the governments' deep suspicion of Islam, Muslims refrained from establishing formal associations and generally avoided involvement in civic affairs.

Ethnicity and religion remained social factors of major significance in Ethiopia until 1974. The complexity of the situation created by the forceful incorporation of a large number of diverse ethnic groups on the one hand and the fact that Orthodox Christianity remained the state religion on the other was compounded by the drought-induced famine that ravaged the northeast during the years 1972–74. Strikes and popular demonstrations throughout the country eventually ended in the overthrow of Haile Selassie's government.

The military junta known as the Dergue [Committee] that seized power from 1974 to 1991 denounced the Abyssinian cultural chauvinism of the previous regime. The status of Islam was raised through the recognition of Muslim holidays, while the Orthodox Church lost its official status. But before a year was out, having purged the top leadership of the Ethiopian Orthodox Church, the Dergue opted to bring it under its control, overseeing appointments to key posts in the administration of the Church and secretly allocating the budget. At the same time, the Dergue discouraged religious teaching as being contrary to its so-called socialist rhetoric.

Several armed groups were formed in opposition to the military dictatorship. Most of them demanded a democratically elected government as well as recognition of their cultures, religions, languages and identities, and a say in local and national affairs. When finally the Ethiopian People's Revolutionary Democratic Front (EPRDF) overthrew the military dictatorship in 1991, it issued a call to all ethnic organizations to send representatives to the conference that established the Transitional Government which then issued the Transitional Period Charter. This Charter served as the basis for the Constitution of the Federal Democratic Republic of Ethiopia that came into effect in August 1995.

The Present Situation

The Constitution of 1995 rectified historically unjust relationships between women and men. With the consent of the parties in dispute, it also recognizes (Article 34(5)) the adjudication of personal and family disputes in accordance with religious laws. Furthermore, it allows for the recognition of religious courts. Accordingly, the Sharia courts have been recognized by the country's justice system and they continue to function in line with the Constitution.

In the name of standing up for women's rights in general and the rights of Muslim women in particular, various individuals and local NGOs started to denounce Article 34(5) of the Constitution. These interest groups stated in one of their advocacy papers: 'Article 34(5) of the Constitution is simply out of place and its removal must be seriously considered.' They repeatedly portrayed Islam as an oppressor of women and painted it in dark and dismal colours.

The favourable political environment created by the Constitution encouraged us Muslim women to challenge the present state of affairs and fully to participate in all social, economic and political endeavours of our country. The rights and protection guaranteed to women by the Holy Qur'an regarding their involvement in the political, social and economic activities of their country also inspired us to be active.

It is a well-known fact from experience that the performance of the Sharia courts in Ethiopia has not been satisfactory concerning women's rights. In addition, traditional customs and practices are inhibiting both Muslim women and men from practising their rights and fulfilling their responsibilities when entering into marriage, during marriage and at the time of divorce. To question and oppose entrenched practices that are based on customs requires awareness on the part of Muslim women. This is necessary to achieve liberation. We thus decided to make some kind of intervention in order to challenge the interest groups that portray Islam as an oppressor of women and to overcome the customs and practices that do in fact oppress Muslim women.

The Beginnings

Our task was not easy as few of the Muslim women who were aware of the rights and protection guaranteed to women by the Holy Qur'an and the Constitution were convinced that it was necessary to be organized in order to realize those rights. Islam has also given people the right to freedom of association and to form organizations. Addressing Muslims, the Holy Qur'an declares: 'You are the best community which has been brought forth for mankind. You command what is proper and forbid what is improper and you believe in Allah' (3:110). If the Muslim community as a whole does not perform this duty then 'Let there be a community among you who will invite [people] to [do] good, command what is proper and forbid what is improper: those will be prosperous' (3:104).

The women who believed that the Muslim community had collectively neglected its obligations decided to form a group prepared to meet those obligations. We were lucky enough to find a chairperson from the Islamic Affairs Supreme Council of Addis Ababa (IASCAA) who was also seriously concerned about the issue. On 4 October 1997, we thus managed to found the Addis Ababa Muslim Women's Council (AAMWC) under the auspices of the IASCAA.

The Formulation of AAMWC Objectives

Having made a critical assessment of the problems surrounding the realization of women's rights, the AAMWC determined to raise the awareness of Muslim women and men to liberate them from the customs and practices that prevented them from practising their respective rights. Consequently, they agreed that the AAMWC's overall goal should be to strengthen the capacity of the Muslim community in general and women in particular to participate in, and benefit from, the social, economic and political development of their country.

In order to achieve this goal, the Council has been conducting awareness-raising workshops in Addis Ababa targeted at the Muslim community in general, and Muslim women in particular. In addition, it is engaged in advocacy, education, economic empowerment and the promotion of reproductive health rights.

Activities of the AAMWC

Raising Awareness

The AAMWC believes that one of the major processes in nation-building is ensuring the political participation of citizens in general. As Ethiopian citizens, Muslims have a responsibility to participate in the economic, social and political activities of their country. The AAMWC and IASCAA together outlined a strategy of explaining how the concept of social responsibility is derived from the Holy Qur'an and the Constitution. Based on this strategy the AAMWC conducted several awareness-raising workshops on the rights and protection of women provided by the Constitution and Sharia law.

The topic covered a wide range of issues. With regard to women's rights in Islam, the presenters cited several verses from the Qur'an and Hadith[1] to show that social responsibility, rights and obligations are derived from the Holy Qur'an. What this opportunity meant for the participating women and men is best expressed in their own words:

> For me it was very important to know that women and men have to work together to fulfil their obligations to society. I was able to understand that traditional customs and practices prevented Muslim women from fulfilling their obligations. Above all, I was delighted to hear what several Qur'anic verses and Hadith state about women's rights. I think that I will go on from here with a better sense of who I am, and with the will to fight for my rights and also to stand up for the rights of others. (Fatuma Abdi)

> Now we know our rights. However there is injustice in the Sharia courts. Some judges of the Sharia courts do not interpret the law correctly. They discriminate against women. Our next task should be to fight against those judges. (Amina Kamal)

---

1   Hadith are narrations about the deeds and sayings of the Prophet Mohammed. (Author's note.)

We men believe that we know everything. However, what I have been able to learn today has helped me to realize my responsibility with regard to the promotion of women's rights. It was an opportunity to understand that Muslim women's and men's equality, responsibility and accountability is a well-developed theme in the Qur'an. (Mohammed Sufi An)

Reproductive Health

The presenters pointed out that sexuality is considered part of our identity as human beings. To this end, they quoted several Qur'anic verses and Hadith relevant to reproductive health rights in general and female genital mutilation in particular. The presenters explained that the practice of clitoridectomy preceded the introduction of Islam in Arabia and in different parts of Africa. Moreover, it was pointed out that the practice is totally un-Islamic because it is a direct violation of both the Qur'an and Hadith, which clearly stress the importance of sexual satisfaction for both the husband and wife.

With regard to the female genital mutilation issue, both women and men said to us: 'We took for granted that female genital mutilation was mandatory in Islam. We thought it was a religious obligation.'

Education

The Holy Qur'an expresses deep concern for the welfare of children, whether they have parents or are orphans. The Qur'an mandates that children should be properly nurtured and raised on the basis of mutual consultation by the parents. Children who have become orphaned are the responsibility of the community and the Holy Qur'an stresses the importance of treating orphans with kindness and of protecting their property as well as their identity.

To discharge this responsibility, the Muslim community needs to have appropriate institutions through which it can take care of orphans and provide every possible means to advance their overall education. Being aware of this, and also encouraged by the importance placed by the Qur'an on the sharing of one's resources with those in need, the AAMWC initiated a programme for orphans and needy children. To implement the programme, it approached individuals in the country and also communicated with the Muslim community in the diaspora. As a result, through the sponsorship it received from the Muslim community inside and outside the country, the AAMWC has managed to enrol 376 orphans in elementary schools.

Tackling Poverty

There is deep-rooted poverty in Addis Ababa. Poverty is a complex and multidimensional issue. A thorough understanding of poverty as well as the common effort of the community is essential in order to take measures to alleviate it.

Consequently, the AAMWC carried out a participatory needs assessment to identify the existing socio-economic conditions of its target community as well as to know their priority needs to improve their lives. Then it organized a one-day meeting to present the main findings of the needs assessment. Muslim religious leaders, private enterprise owners and civil servants were invited to participate in the meeting. Having listened to the presentation, most of the participants were touched by the situation and decided to sponsor vocational training for young boys and girls. As a result, the AAMWC managed to establish a training centre for young women. So, it trained 50 needy girls in sewing and embroidery. Some young boys and girls have also been enrolled in a private vocational training school.

The Addis Ababa Muslim Women's Council used the notion of social responsibility within Islam to mobilize the Muslim community to support their fellow members. According to the AAMWC, social responsibility in Islam is derived from the Qur'anic verse which states: 'And [as for] the believers both men and women – they are friends and protectors of one another' (9:71). By calling Muslims' attention to the above Qur'anic verse, the AAMWC encourages believers to do good to others and to spend their wealth in the service of the needy.

Philosophy of the AAMWC's Work

The Qur'an, Sunnah[2] and Islamic history provide ample evidence of women undertaking various types of active roles in society and thus practising their rights as stated in the Holy Qur'an. However, traditional customs and practices are used as a justification to exclude women from active involvement in the economic, social and development activities of their country. There are even some individuals who, in order to justify women's exclusion, argue that men are superior to women.

To overcome this attitude the AAMWC believes that its strategy should be based on the divine sources of Sharia, that is the Qur'an and the authentic teachings of the Prophet Mohammed. The AAMWC explicitly recognizes that individuals cannot abandon deeply rooted cultural practices against women if there is no collective will to change, so it uses a collective approach. Moreover, the strategy adopted is grounded in the local context and evokes some of the strongest values and practices of local culture, parental love and Qur'anic piety to challenge other practices.

The AAMWC has involved religious leaders and imams who can remind people that Islam recognizes women's rights. The strategy has been to empower women. This means that, while rooting awareness-raising activities in personal testimony and the transmission of the true information contained in the Qur'an, it leaves resolution and action up to the initiative of each community and its members. It inserts the problem of women's rights, the education of orphan children, and the issue of female genital mutilation into the larger framework of Muslims' responsibilities and obligations

---

2   The Arabic word 'sunnah' has come to denote the way the Prophet Mohammed lived his life. (Author's note.)

– topics of importance to men too. The result has been that people have not only voluntarily supported the initiative but have also been ready to spread the word.

What Have We Learned?

We have learned that women can be empowered only if they believe in their own strength. In order to believe in their own strength, there must be a consciousness-raising process that allows them to see and to comprehend the power mechanisms that create inequality and gender discrimination. We have gained understanding of the importance of the participation of men in the programme. Through their participation, men can become aware of their own responsibility in the fight for women's rights in general and reproductive rights in particular. Finally we have gained the knowledge that people will fight to end their own oppression when they recognize it and when there is a clear solution. Generally, we have learned that social responsibility in Islam is derived from the Holy Qur'an. Thus in order to be a Muslim, one should not only be practising the pillars of Islam but should also take care of the needs of those who are in poverty.

Women's Empowerment through Islamic Organizations: The Role of Nahdlatul Ulama in Transforming the Government's Birth Control Programme into a Family Welfare Programme

Christopher Candland and Siti Nurjanah, February 2004

Throughout Asia, religious associations and religiously motivated individuals operate thousands of associations involved in community development. Muslims make significant financial and professional contributions to social welfare activities through Islamic associations. These contributions go well beyond a Muslim's individual obligation to aid the poor through 'zakat' [obligatory contribution for distribution to the poor in proportion to wealth owned]. Some of these associations are important agents for social change. This study focuses on the work of the world's largest Muslim association, Nahdlatul Ulama (NU), and its two women's associations, Muslimat NU and Fatayat NU.

Religion and the State in Indonesia

At independence in 1945, Indonesian leaders struggled with the question of whether the state ought to endorse Islam, as some Muslim leaders demanded. Muslims are a majority in Indonesia, but a substantial number of Indonesians are Christians (Catholic and Protestant), Confucians, Hindus and Buddhists. A variety of other spiritual practices are recognized not as religions, but as 'kepercayaan' [faiths]. One of these faiths, Kejawen [literally, 'Javaneseness'] is widely practised. Kejawen refers to the principles for the conduct of life in harmony with society and nature and is rooted in the pre-Islamic culture of Java.

The 'Pancasila' [Five Principles] has been Indonesia's state ideology since independence in 1945. It has strong Kejawen overtones – emphasizing faith, humanity, unity, consensus and obedience, democracy and social justice. Governments, especially the New Order government under General Suharto (1966–98), have used the 'Pancasila' to promote loyal and obedient citizens. The first principle of the 'Pancasila' promotes belief in God but does not endorse any particular religion. The accommodation with other religious communities left some Muslim leaders feeling that the government had unfairly sidelined Islam.

Nahdlatul Ulama

Religious leaders established Nahdlatul Ulama [Revival of Religious Scholars] in 1926, in part as a counterweight to other Muslims leaders who wanted to make Indonesian Islam a stronger political force. Today, Nahdlatul Ulama may have as many as 40 million members. Nahdlatul Ulama members are highly tolerant of diverse religious views and practices, including those that derive from Kejawen. After a long debate, Nahdlatul Ulama adopted the 'Pancasila' as its 'single principle'.[3]

The membership of Nahdlatul Ulama draws largely from humble backgrounds – mostly farmers – from rural areas and smaller towns. The life-blood of Nahdlatul Ulama is Indonesia's network of 'kyai' [Nahdlatul Ulama term for religious scholars] and 'pesantren' [Islamic boarding schools]. There are around 10,000 'kyai' and 8,000 'pesantren' in Indonesia which have educated millions of students of Islam.[4] These students study 'fiqh' [jurisprudence], theology and 'kebatinan' [spirituality].[5] In many parts of Indonesia people respect greatly and consult regularly with 'kyai' on religious and spiritual matters, as well as on career, family, community and health concerns.

The Philosophy of Nahdlatul Ulama

To explain their outlook and philosophy, Nahdlatul Ulama members often refer to the blessing bestowed by Allah on the entire universe. According to Nahdlatul Ulama scholars, all of the organization's activities are based on the recognition that Allah's blessings belong to everyone, without regard to their religion. The former leader of Nahdlatul Ulama, Abdurrahman Wahid, used to say that 'the inter-religious movement is more important than everything else.'[6]

The other basic principles of Nahdlatul Ulama are the five principles or basic human rights, derived by the scholar, Imam Al Ghazali, from the Qur'an and the Hadith. These are 'hifdz al deen' [the right to one's religion]; 'hifdz al aql' [the right to think for and to express oneself]; 'hifdz al nafs' [the right to life]; 'hifdz al mal' [the right to livelihood and property]; and 'hifdz al nasl' [the right to have a family].[7] Like other Muslims in Indonesia, those associated with Nahdlatul Ulama follow the Syafe'i School of Islamic jurisprudence which is known for considering the social context of the Hadith and for reasoning by analogy.

Nahdlatul Ulama and Formal Politics

Nahdlatul Ulama has had considerable influence on but also a complicated relation to formal politics. It operated as a political party from 1952, when it broke from

---

3   Andrée Feillard, *NU vis-à-vis Negara* (Yogyakarta, 1999), pp. 233–61.

4   Masdar F. Mas'udi, Presentation to the International Workshop on The Role of Islamic Women's Organizations in Advocacy and the Elimination of Discrimination: A Comparison of Southeast Asia and the Middle East, Yogyakarta, 28 July 1999.

5   Aminoto Sadoellah, Kyai Pesantren Al Alawi, interview with authors, Tuban, Indonesia, 16 January 2004.

6   Abdurrahman Wahid, then Ketua Umum [General Chief] of Nahdlatul Ulama, interview with Candland, Ciganjur, Indonesia, 22 August 1998.

7   Ibid.

a coalition of Muslim political associations. In 1984, Abdurrahman Wahid, then leader of Nahdlatul Ulama, persuaded the leadership and members to withdraw from formal politics and return to their roots. However, with the downfall of President Suharto in 1998, Nahdlatul Ulama returned to formal politics and established a new political party, the 'Partai Kebangkitan Bangsa' [National Awakening Party – PKB]. The PKB came fourth in the national elections in June 1999.

Some scholars have written about Nahdlatul Ulama, demonstrating the political wisdom of Islamic associations in exploiting openings in an otherwise authoritarian system. Others have found that the Association's foray into formal politics undermined its social power. Few scholars focus on the community development work of Nahdlatul Ulama or on the work of its women's organizations.

Muslimat NU

The most effective Nahdlatul Ulama bodies involved in community development are its women's organizations. The impetus for Muslimat NU was the desire of Nahdlatul Ulama women to 'improve the well-being and status of Muslim women.'[8] Although many of Nahdlatul Ulama's boarding schools are for girls, its leadership is composed exclusively of male religious scholars. Therefore, it is a male-oriented association. Many wives of religious scholars felt that they needed a separate association within Nahdlatul Ulama to promote the welfare of Nahdlatul Ulama women. Thus, they established Muslimat NU (originally in 1940, though under another name).

Muslimat NU represents Nahdlatul Ulama women above the age of 40. It is structured at national, provincial, district, sub-district and local levels. It has local leaders in more than 14,000 villages. Muslimat NU leaders often regard their connection to thousands of villages and millions of women through the concentric structure of Nahdlatul Ulama as one of their greatest strengths.

Fatayat NU

The younger women of Nahdlatul Ulama are organized within Fatayat NU, which focuses on leadership training, Islamic principles of organizational management, and the principles of Nahdlatul Ulama.[9] It was established in 1950 for Nahdlatul Ulama women between the ages of 20 and 40. Many of the women in Muslimat NU and Fatayat NU are graduates from Nahdlatul Ulama boarding schools.

Fatayat NU is structured in the same way as Muslimat NU, with five levels, beginning in thousands of villages and, through sub-district, district and provincial leadership, reaching a national leadership based in Jakarta. Each of the five levels of Fatayat NU maintains nine departments: organization and management; leadership

---

8   Safrina Tristiawati and Munir Rozi, *The Nahdlatul Ulama*, mimeograph, 1995.

9   Masdar Mulia, former *Ketua* [Chairperson], Nahdlatul Ulama Fatayat, interview with authors, Jakarta, Indonesia, 13 January 2004.

and education; economic and co-operative activities; health and sports; 'dakwah' [propagation and information]; advocacy and legal affairs; social, artistic and cultural activities; research and development; and foreign connections. Each of these programmes is led by a group of several women.

Development and Population Control in New Order Indonesia

Soon after the resignation of President Sukarno, General Suharto's government launched an aggressive national development programme. Development assumed the status of an official ideology. New Order Indonesia stood for the sacrifice of political liberties for the sake of national economic growth. Suharto referred to himself as the 'Father of Development'. For more than three decades, development ('pembangunan' – literally 'to stand erect') was offered as the rationale for foreign investment and ownership and restrictions on political and civil rights.

A key component of the New Order's development programme was birth control. Like most Muslim associations, in the 1950s and 1960s Nahdlatul Ulama had been opposed to birth control. The deposed President Sukarno had favoured rapid population growth as a way to strengthen the Indonesian nation, and opposed birth control. President Suharto, in contrast, energetically supported family planning and accepted major funding from the United States. A national family planning co-ordinating body, the Badan Koordinasi Keluarga Berencana Nasional (BKKBN), was established in 1970 with United States assistance.

Some Muslim associations perceived these family planning programmes and the BKKBN, funded and operated by foreigners, as a Western imposition. There was a widespread feeling among Muslims that family planning was a foreign concept introduced in Indonesia to minimize the number of Muslims and thereby limit Muslim power.

In the first two decades of the New Order, from 1966 until the early 1980s, the government assumed an instrumental and coercive approach to family planning. Its purpose was to promote national development by limiting population growth. The police and military often accompanied government officials when they visited women in their homes to introduce contraception. Allegations of coercion were widespread.

The programme was target driven: visit as many homes as possible and introduce as many contraceptives as possible. Incentives were given to officials who surpassed their targets. The favoured contraceptive devices were intrauterine devices (IUDs) which prevent pregnancy for five years, Depo-Provera injections, which prevent pregnancy for three months and, later on, Norplant subdermal implants, which also prevent pregnancy for five years.

Conditions, lifestyles and attitudes in Indonesia, as in most countries of the world, do make it difficult for women and men to use some other contraceptives, such as diaphragms and the Pill. But the government's heavy reliance on implants and injections suggests that government officials were less interested in educating or enabling women to use contraceptives themselves than in meeting contraception 'acceptance' targets.

The use of implants requires knowledge about how they work in women's bodies. Women were not equipped with that information. Many women became ill and permanently infertile. As a result, many Indonesian women are now highly suspicious of contraception and have a strong fear of government family planning programmes. The government's approach to family planning – as an instrument for national development – lowered fertility by abusing women's rights.

Nahdlatul Ulama on Reproductive Health

Initially, many 'kyai' of Nahdlatul Ulama campaigned against contraception, as they believed it to be an attempt to oppose God's will. However, realizing that without the support of the 'kyai' the family planning programme would have limited success, the government attempted to involve them in their birth-control programmes. Eventually, Nahdlatul Ulama did get involved, but in the process it helped to prevent the coercive approach used by the government and transformed the very purpose of the programme.

Many religious scholars had long argued that the strength of the Muslim community is directly dependent on the number of believers and thus requires the birth of as many Muslim children as possible. Supporters of the view that children are instruments of power often quoted the following passages from the Qur'an:

> And make ready against them all you can of power, including steeds of war, to threaten the enemy of Allah and your enemy. (Surah Al-Anfal: 8: 60)

> Allah has made for you mates of your own kind, and has made for you, from your wives, sons and grandsons, and has bestowed on you good provisions. (Surah An-Nahl: 16:72)

Opponents of family planning also referred to passages from the Qur'an and Hadith that supposedly advocate that Muslims procreate and multiply.[10] The relationship between these passages and family planning seems indirect at best, but opponents of family planning remained strong.

A major shift in Nahdlatul Ulama's thinking about family planning was signalled in September 1969, when it released a 'fatwa' [religious instruction] that encouraged family planning for the creation of family welfare. There were eight parts to the fatwa: that family planning should be practised to space births not to prevent pregnancy; that family planning should emphasize the health and welfare of the mother and children rather than the fear of poverty; that abortion should be prohibited; that permanent severance of any part of the body of husband or wife should not be permitted; that family planning must be voluntary; that family planning is to be practised only with

---

10 Abd Al-Rahim Umran, *Islam and KB* [Islam and Family Planning] (Jakarta, 1992), pp. 98–102.

the consent of both husband and wife; that implementation of family planning should be practised in accordance with Islamic laws and values; and that family planning should not aid acts of immorality.[11]

'Kyai' found justification for this fatwa from the Qur'an and Hadith. The Qur'an stresses that marriage is an institution designed for the satisfaction of both wife and husband, not merely for the purpose of procreation. The Qur'an does not make specific mention of contraception, but the Prophet Mohammed did. He was aware that many of his companions and some of his family members practised 'azal' [withdrawal] as a form of birth control. He did not disapprove of their practice. Indeed, he advised those who did not want to have children to practise 'azal' but warned that the method would not prevent pregnancy if conception were God's will. 'Kyai' were able to elaborate on the Prophet Mohammed's teaching to argue that family planning is supported by Islamic teaching for the promotion of a better life for the Muslim community.

Muslimat NU and Fatayat NU deliberations played an important role in encouraging the 'kyai' to study the teachings of the Qur'an and Hadith related to family planning. Nahdlatul Ulama men and women found in the Qur'an and Hadith encouragement and injunctions to promote the health and welfare of the family. Thus in the Nahdlatul Ulama family planning is referred to as 'keluarga maslahah' [family welfare] rather than family planning. The Indonesian word 'maslahah' is derived from the Arabic word 'shalih' [virtuous and prosperous].

Once the 1969 fatwa was issued, Muslimat NU and Fatayat NU became extensively involved in the promotion of 'keluarga maslahah'. The Muslimat's Welfare Foundation set up a 'Lembaga Kemaslahatan Keluarga' (LKK) [Family Welfare Institute] as a body within Nahdlatul Ulama to promote family welfare through reproductive health and family planning. LKK supports more than two dozen hospitals and health clinics.

LKK conducts training programmes for health care workers, works with domestic and international governmental and non-governmental agencies, and produces and distributes pamphlets and books on reproductive health. Muslimat NU and Fatayat NU women run most of Nahdlatul Ulama maternity hospitals, birthing centres and clinics. In 1979, a group of senior 'kyai' reviewed the 1969 fatwa and concluded that all contraception that does not produce permanent infertility is permitted by Islam.[12]

The Nahdlatul Ulama women who run LKK maternity hospitals, birthing centres and clinics and conduct reproductive health education programmes are motivated by the sentiment that humans are a community whose blessings can be enhanced through

---

11 Saifuddin Zuhri et al., *Fatwa: Keluarga Berencana Ditinjau dari Segi Syari'at* Islam, [Religious Opinion: Reflections on Family Planning from the Perspective of Muslim Law] (Jombang, Indonesia, 1979), p. 68.

12 Zuhri. Also Abdullah Aziz Masyhuri, former Director, Bureau of Information and Motivation, Nahdlatul Ulama Institute for Family Planning, interview with authors, Jombang, Indonesia, 16 January 2000.

training, education and the promotion of both practical knowledge and awareness of fundamental rights. According to Musdah Mulia, a Deputy Chairperson of Muslimat NU and former Chairperson of Fatayat NU, the greatest resource of Muslimat NU is not material or financial, or even organizational, but spiritual. It is the commitment of Nahdlatul Ulama women to 'to work to satisfy the inner self', she says.[13]

Musdah Mulia describes one of the sources of 'satisfaction of the inner self' as the discussions and deliberations in which Muslimat NU and Fatayat NU women regularly engage. Every three months, 'kyai' engage in round-table discussions or 'problem solving' using the Qur'an and Hadith to develop solutions to issues of contemporary social concern. Muslimat NU and Fatayat NU hold parallel discussions and make the results of these deliberations the focus of their educational work for three-month intervals.

Total fertility rates in Indonesia decreased rapidly from 5.6 births per woman in 1971 to 2.8 births per women in 1997.[14] The rate of reduction decreased most rapidly only after religious associations, such as Nahdlatul Ulama, became involved in family planning and the government focused on the welfare of parents and children rather than on limiting population growth.

Findings

In the story of Nahdlatul Ulama's involvement in the national family planning programme, religion can be seen as the basis of social solidarity and a powerful force for promoting human development. The women of Fatayat NU and Muslimat NU are motivated not by money or by power, but by the desire to be good Muslims. According to a Hadith authenticated by Imam Bukhori and quoted by Nahdlatul Ulama women, 'those who do not care about the problems of others are as if they are not Muslim.'

The story shows, too, how Islam can be a powerful resource for women's empowerment. Muslimat NU and Fatayat NU were able to promote reproductive health, in an area of the world where reproduction is the single greatest threat to (women's) health,[15] by reference to the Qur'an and Hadith. Islamic associations helped Indonesians to achieve one of the highest mother and infant survival rates among lower-income developing countries.

The achievements of Indonesia's family planning programme depended upon the transformation of priorities from controlling and reducing national population rates to promoting family welfare and empowering women to make reproductive choices.

---

13 Interview with authors, Jakarta, 13 January 2004.

14 S.A. Wilopo, H. Sigit, T. Hatmaji and K. Mohammad, *Country Population Assessment* (Jakarta, 1999).

15 Nafis Sadik, Executive Director of the United Nations Population Fund, quoted in 'UN Warning, As Population Nears 6 Billion', *New York Times* (23 September 1999), A5.

Fatayat NU and Muslimat NU helped to effect that transformation from a coercive and instrumental approach to a voluntary and principled approach.

Women's empowerment is highly dependent upon men's attitudes and, therefore, requires that men are a focus of educational activities. The involvement of and positive reception by 'kyai' was necessary for Fatayat NU and Muslimat NU's progress in promoting women's health and women's empowerment. Thus, the education of men about women's rights is the key to the promotion of women's reproductive health.

At the core of socially just and sustainable development is the empowerment of individual women, especially with respect to their health and that of their families. An increase in the wealth of the 'nation' is not an adequate definition of development. Sustainable development depends on individuals who have the education and capacity to behave in socially just ways.

Empowering Women to Improve Rural Lives: The Story of the Barli Development Institute for Rural Women

The Bahá'í International Community, July 2003

In the Beginning

The story of the Barli Development Institute for Rural Women is the story of more than a thousand young women whose lives have been transformed by their experience at the Institute. Although Bahai'í experience in the field of development stretches back to the beginnings of the faith in Iran more than 150 years ago, widespread involvement in social and economic development is a relatively new thrust for the Bahai'í world community. In 1983, the National Spiritual Assembly of the Bahá'ís in India decided to take part in this worldwide effort to create projects that would transform society through the systematic application of spiritual principles.

Guided in their consultation by the admonition of Bahá'u'lláh (the founder of the Bahá'í faith): 'Be ye anxiously concerned with the needs of the age ye live in and centre your deliberations on its exigencies and requirements',[16] the Bahá'ís in India decided to address India's historic oppression of women. They based their decision on the Bahá'í principle that men and women must participate in the process of social and economic development as equal partners:

> Until woman and man recognize and realize equality, social and political progress here or anywhere will not be possible.[17]

> The world of humanity possesses two wings: man and woman. If one wing remains incapable and defective, it will restrict the power of the other, and full flight will be impossible.[18]

The remedy prescribed for this inequality is education and equal rights for women: 'If woman be fully educated and granted her rights, she will attain the capacity for wonderful accomplishments and prove herself the equal of man.'[19] So it was that the Bahai'í Vocational Institute for Rural Women was created.

---

16 Bahá'u'lláh, *Gleanings from the Writings of Bahá'u'lláh* (Wilmette, IL, 1976), p. 128.

17 `Abdu'l-Bahá, *Promulgation of Universal Peace* (Wilmette, IL, 1982), p. 76.

18 Ibid., p. 318.

19 Ibid., p. 136.

Locating the Institute

Madhya Pradesh is one of India's largest, most populous and poorest states. The tribal people who comprise one-third of the state's 66.18 million people are the poorest of all, and the least valued among the tribal people are the women and girls. In 2001, female life expectancy in Madhya Pradesh was 57, the lowest in the country.[20] In 1994, only 92 out of every 1,000 tribal girls were literate; only three in every 1,000 made it as far as middle school; and just one in every 1,000 actually completed her secondary schooling.[21]

Women are the primary cultivators of the land, yet they own very little of it, so they have almost no say in any decision regarding their environment or their own lives. Jobs are scarce. The economy is for the most part based on family farming, often limited by lack of water. The Bhilala tribesmen in the district still carry bows and iron-tipped arrows – a reflection of the degree to which most of them remain outside the mainstream of Indian society.

First Steps

In order to serve this population, the Bahá'í Vocational Institute for Rural Women was established in the city of Indore, Madhya Pradesh. The Institute began simply, with short courses to train rural women in income-generating skills such as candle making and jute mat weaving. The training was accompanied by lessons on spiritual subjects such as the acquisition of virtues as the key to happiness, progress and prosperity.

Funding in the early days was provided exclusively by the Bahá'ís, and courses were taught by volunteers and part-time staff. However, the demand for the courses increased and in 1985, with a grant from the Indian government's Department of Science and Technology, Miss Janak Dulari Palta (now Janak Palta McGilligan) was appointed as the Institute's director. Although she arrived to find no buildings, no equipment or materials, no infrastructure and no trainees, within three weeks Janak had started a residential programme.

In contrast to the rote memorization typical in many Indian schools, classroom instruction at the Institute adopted an experiential approach to learning which helped the women develop confidence in their capacity to learn, to express their views and to take initiatives. Within a year, a total of 180 tribal women from three districts had received ten days' training and returned to their villages.

---

20 Indian Human Development Report, 2000.
21 National Commission for Women, 1994.

Early Challenges

One of the major challenges in the early days was recruiting trainees. It was not easy to convince parents to send their daughters to a place 200 kilometres away. Trust was gradually developed as Janak learned their language, staying with them in their homes and eating with them, sometimes for days and weeks.

Another major challenge arose in 1988, when Janak married a Northern Irish Bahá'í, Jimmy McGilligan, a land reclamation and drainage contractor who had come to India to help with development work. Rumours ran wild in the villages that the girls would be sent overseas. Fears were quelled and trust re-established when the parents were invited to meetings at the Institute for three days at a time.

As the Institute's courses lengthened from ten days to three months, the changes in the young women became more pronounced. Although they returned home happy and eager to apply what they had learned, their families were not always pleased with the transformations they saw in their daughters and wives. The young trainees were now able to read and write and earn a living, and they had also become accustomed to making decisions about their lives. Their newfound confidence and assertiveness was sometimes perceived as a challenge to the authority of male family members.

To address this problem, the Institute established residential courses that allowed husbands and wives to explore together such principles as the equality of women and men and unity in diversity. Kami Chauhan says, 'When I first got married my husband drank and beat me. We then took family-life training at the Institute and I saw many changes in my husband. Now our family is a happy family. Without spirituality this is impossible.'

Spiritual Principles of the Institute

'Although literacy, vocational and health training are essential, we believe that one of the most important things we do at the Institute is to help these young women recognize their full potential as human beings,' says Janak. 'This is where the element of moral education comes into play.'

Bahá'ís view development as a global enterprise whose purpose is to bring prosperity to all peoples, an enterprise which is best understood in the context of the emergence of a world civilization. Humanity is in transition from its collective childhood to its collective maturity. The revolutionary changes that are occurring with bewildering swiftness in every department of life are the throes of our collective adolescence. The hallmark of the age of maturity will be the unification of the human race, which, in turn, requires the establishment of the principles of justice. To create a just society, in which all the earth's inhabitants are able to enjoy the fruits of a materially and spiritually prosperous global society, it is essential that people everywhere be empowered to participate in the constructive processes that will give rise to it.

Some of the main spiritual principles on which Bahá'í development is based are: unity in diversity (the principle of the oneness of humanity 'does not ignore, nor does it attempt to suppress, the diversity of ethnical origins, of climate, of history, of language and tradition, of thought and habit, that differentiate the peoples and nations of the world'[22]); equity and justice; equality of the sexes; trustworthiness and moral leadership; independent investigation of the truth ('... all the nations of the world have to investigate after truth independently and turn their eyes from the moribund blind imitations of the past ages entirely'[23]) and the harmony of science and religion – ('When a religion is opposed to science it becomes mere superstition: that which is contrary to knowledge is ignorance.[24])

The Institute Today

In September 2001, the Institute became independent with its own board of directors. It was then that it took on the name 'The Barli Development Institute for Rural Women'. Built on what was once a neglected 6-acre piece of urban land, today it is an oasis of fruit trees and bushes kept green by sprinklers using recycled water. It accepts 75 trainees every six months: 60 are totally illiterate learners and 15 are school dropouts, who are simultaneously trained to teach the 60 learners with the help of master trainers. These trainers are former graduates from the Institute, many of whom have gone on to higher education and have returned to serve on the courses.

The training programmes, which now typically last either six months or one year, continue to seek to overcome obstacles that have traditionally hindered the development of women, and thus the development of all. In a special kind of educational experience – founded on respect and infused with spirit, joy and possibility – courses include literacy, tailoring, agriculture, artisan crafts, human rights, environmental awareness, self-esteem and personality development, social commitment, nutrition and health, and income-generating skills. Art, music and dance are also incorporated into the curriculum. Graduates receive a certificate through the National Open Schools programme.

The aim is for the women to return to their home villages and become 'pillars' of their families and communities – agents for changing the social and physical environments. 'Barli' is the local word for the central pillar of the house.

Since its foundation in 1985, the Institute has trained more than 1,300 young women and girls. Ninety-nine per cent of graduates leave fully literate in Hindi, and 96 per cent seek employment or set up their own small enterprises using the income-generating skills they have learned. Empowered by their training, graduates have not only improved their own lives, they have become agents for social change in their villages. Through instruction and through example they have shared what

---

22 Shoghi Effendi, *The World Order of Bahá'u'lláh Selected Letters* (Wilmette, IL, 1974), pp. 41–2.

23 'Abdu'l-Bahá, *Japan Will Turn Ablaze: Tablets of 'Abdu'l-Bahá, Letters of Shoghi Effendi and Historical Notes About Japan* (Osaka, 1974), p. 35.

24 'Abdu'l-Bahá, *Paris Talks* (London, 1972), p. 141.

they have learned about health and hygiene, education of children and consultation for problem solving.

Many villagers now proudly show how they have learned to clean their family water pots daily and keep them covered. Corn, millet and peppers are stored in neat piles within the homes, and there is a new emphasis on cleanliness. By boiling the water they drink, villagers have been able to reduce the incidence of a number of diseases. In addition, women in five villages have planted approximately 2,500 trees.

Studies have shown that the women have helped to create a new atmosphere of mutual respect and unity in their villages, helping to displace prejudices in tribal communities once notorious for their high crime rate and alcohol abuse.

Developing Personality and Instilling Values

One unique aspect of the Institute's programme is personality development and leadership training. Its purpose is to help women take initiatives, and to show the importance of women's role in developing society and in respecting and reinforcing the value of their culture. A scientific temperament and a spirit of inquiry are also cultivated. Through classroom training and daily interaction with Institute staff, volunteers and peers, ethical and human values such as love, respect and unity, as well as work as a form of worship and service as a form of prayer, are taught and practised. The students become sensitive to social development problems and learn to mobilize and develop local resources to solve them. Among the key values practised at the Institute are consultation, responsibility, trustworthiness, self-reliance and service.

Consultation is both a principle and a technique for non-adversarial decision making. It seeks to include a wide diversity of ideas and information in order to discover what is best for the group as a whole. The women plan their day in groups of four. They learn how to express themselves in group discussions, how to listen, how to address an audience and how to give reports.

Responsibility and trustworthiness are necessary for success in every undertaking. The kitchen store, training materials and garden store are controlled and managed by the trainees. Gulab Alawa, who completed the three-month course in 1995, tells us of an experience she had at the market:

> When I asked the shopkeeper for what I wanted, he was busy stacking the shelves. He told me to take what I wanted, put my money in the cash drawer, and take whatever change I needed. 'You have taken training at the Institute and they give education on truth and honesty, so I can trust you', he said.

Self-reliance and service are combined in the work to maintain the Institute. Trainees take care of the institute as if it were their own home, in a spirit of service and self-help.

Literacy

The empowerment of women is not possible without literacy. Literacy is incorporated into every aspect of the curriculum, supported by two hours of formal literacy classes a day. The Institute provides each trainee with basic literacy in Hindi to enable her to understand herself and her world. She learns to read and write and also to carry out simple arithmetical calculations and to measure length, weight and time. Trainees learn through practical experience to write a receipt, calculate stock, estimate costs, count cash and give change. They also learn to approach a bank or a local government official to apply for loans. Some trainees rise to the level of being able to sit for a National Open School theoretical exam at the end of the six-month course.

J.S. Mathur, the District Collector of Jhabua – home district for many of the Institute's trainees – marvels at the level of literacy accomplished by these young women in just three months. 'Most government organizations have not been able to accomplish this, even in programmes lasting a year', he says.

Environment

Environmental awareness is one of the main emphases of the Institute. Trainees learn conservation strategies through practice. Students are taught about planting and maintaining trees, finding local sources for seeds, and using environmental and energy conservation techniques such as composting, vermiculture, the use of biodegradable products, and proper waste management. At the Institute itself, rainwater is harvested and, in an innovative arrangement, used to recharge the underground aquifer. Gardens, tended by the trainees, provide most of the Institute's food.

Bahá'ís see no conflict between science and religion. There is no fear of technology, but there is a real concern that technology be appropriate and sustainable. For the last 17 years, the Institute has been a leader in researching, experimenting with and using solar cooking technologies. Now, for approximately 250 days in a year, 100 per cent of the Institute's cooking is powered by solar energy. Trainees who show an interest in the technical side can become the experts who adjust and maintain the solar cookers.

All trainees are encouraged to propagate the use of energy-saving devices in their villages. Sakaram Dawar, who works at the Institute and helps his wife with the cooking, says: 'If we cook on a fire we need wood for fuel and if we cut the trees for the sake of getting fuel it will affect the rains and our future will be darkened. ... We should use the sunlight properly in order to cook meals.'

'Kokila' Newsletter

The newly literate trainees are encouraged to write postcards to the Institute to keep them from falling back into illiteracy. All the graduates' news, views and stories, plus some educational messages, are published in a monthly newsletter, 'Kokila', which is sent to all Institute graduates. 'Kokila' is also left in the centres of the traditional weekly markets, where women can pick it up and share it with their friends. Environmental concerns, health suggestions, social issues, legal dilemmas and success stories of Institute graduates are accompanied by song lyrics and black and white photographs. The 124 issues of 'Kokila' published so far have reached the hands and hearts of thousands, as it circulates through homes and villages, spreading the voices of women.

Funding

The initial funding provided by the Bahá'í community of India and the Indian Ministry of Rural Development was increased in 1990, and an additional sum was given by the Canadian government to enable the Institute to construct a dormitory with space for 20 trainees, an office and workshop building and on-site housing for the Institute's director. The Institute now obtains funding from a range of sources, including the Bahá'í community of India, the Swedish International Development Agency and a private development fund.

Collaboration with Government and NGOs

The Institute is sought out for collaboration because of its innovations in social work, education, science and technology. It collaborates actively with government officials and non-government organizations, exchanging information, methodologies and research information. Institutions such as Stanford University in the United States and Cooperative Cold Store send volunteers, and professionals such as doctors, teachers, artists and designers come to give assistance, also in a voluntary capacity. The Institute's work has been honoured by government officials, university professors and leaders of political parties as well as by many international institutions, including UNICEF and faith-based groups. In 1992, it was made a member of the United Nations Environmental Programme's Global 500 Roll of Honour for outstanding environmental achievement for its role in eliminating guinea worm from 302 villages in the area surrounding the Institute.

Bahá'í Approach to Development

As a result of the development experience accrued by the worldwide Bahá'í community during the last 20 years, of which the Institute is a part, we see a distinctively Bahá'í approach to development emerging. The principle of service underlies all the work. This means that development projects are not conducted for the purpose of public relations or as a means of converting people. Other principles include that funds should be accepted from governments and donor agencies only for projects of a humanitarian nature (never for internal community affairs), and that development programmes should be locally controlled.

But at the heart of the Bahá'í approach to development is the application of spiritual principles to all collective action. Spiritual principles not only point the way to practical solutions, but they also induce the attitudes, the will and the dynamics that facilitate the implementation of those solutions. At the same time ways of applying these principles to social transformation have to be learned.

Science and religion work together as two complementary knowledge systems. Learning to apply spiritual principles to solve development problems implies experimentation, application and the creation of systems and processes whose results can be validated through observation and the use of reason. Moreover, the advancement of civilization requires the multiplication of material means like the solar cooker and improved methods of capturing water and increasing crop yields. These are generated and perfected through scientific endeavour.

Ultimately, development is a learning process that can best be described as action, reflection, consultation and more action – all carried out in the light of religious teachings and drawing on scientific knowledge.

Rights and the Bargaining Power to Claim Them

'The main thing for the powerless is to have a dream', [Aunt Habiba] often told me while I was watching the stairs, so that she could embroider a fabulous one-winged green bird on the clandestine *mrema* she kept hidden in the darkest corner of her room. 'True, a dream alone, without the bargaining power to go with it, does not transform the world or make the walls vanish, but it does help you keep a hold of dignity.'

Fatima Mernissi[25]

Women's Rights and Responsibilities

The women in these three stories have been motivated to take action because they have seen the suffering of women around them and consider that the oppression and disempowerment of women is contrary to the principles of the religious traditions to which they belong.

In the Bahá'í faith there is no controversy about the teachings of Bahá'u'lláh, the founder of the faith, on the equality of women with men (even if within the Bahá'í community, as in all human communities, practice may fall short of the principle). However, the Barli Development Institute works in the midst of various cultures in which women find themselves ignored, denigrated and in general 'without a say'. Thus one of the 'needs of our age' about which Bahá'ís are exhorted to be 'anxiously concerned' is the need to open up opportunities for women to 'be fully educated and granted their rights' so that they can play their essential role alongside men to bring about social and political progress. The rights of women are intertwined with their responsibilities.

The AAMWC story tells us that it is the responsibility of Muslims to participate in the economic, social and political activities of their country. Muslims in general were given the chance to do this by the new constitution in Ethiopia. But it was their understanding of the 'rights and protection guaranteed to women by the Holy Qur'an' that gave the AAMWC's founders the confidence to begin to prepare the ground for Muslim women to take full advantage of this opportunity.

Here too, rights and responsibilities are understood to be two sides of the same coin. The AAMWC's awareness-raising workshops emphasize the duty of men and women to work together to fulfil their obligations in society. The basis for such action is the Qur'anic theme of 'Muslim women's and men's equality, responsibility and accountability'. Responsibility and accountability are obligations but, along with equality between men and women, they also involve rights in the sense that it is only if their rights are recognized that women are able to fulfil their responsibilities in the societies they live in.

---

25 Fatima Mernissi, *Dreams of Trespass: Tales of a Harem Girlhood* (New York, 1995), p. 214.

The story of the Nahdlatul Ulama women is also about rights and responsibilities – the right and responsibility of women to space pregnancies for the sake of their own and their families' welfare.

Western development agencies have been emphasizing the need to respect women's rights, both in the public and private sphere, for several decades. However, despite the statement in the UN Declaration of the Right to Development that: 'All human beings have a responsibility for development, individually and collectively',[26] it is unlikely that their gender awareness training courses would place the same degree of emphasis on the relationship between rights and social responsibilities as these women's organizations do. Is this because they see women in the past as having had to take the responsibility for their families while men have enjoyed the rights? Or does their focus merely reflect the more individualistic viewpoint of the West regarding the relationship of rights to social, political and economic obligations? Whatever the case, the three faith-based organizations in this chapter would consider that social harmony can only be realized if these two concepts are held together.

Rights-based gender and development courses are problematic for Muslim women for other reasons too. On the one hand, the emphasis that is usually placed on the equality of men and women can be seen to fail to take into account the Muslim view of the complementarity of men and women, according to which they are not necessarily expected to play the same roles.[27] On the other hand, some of the notions embodied in the UN charters on women's rights not only highlight individual rights more than social responsibilities and community rights but, in their opposition to any form of discrimination, they are also incompatible with some of the Islamic inheritance laws and family values and practices. According to Islamic law as it is generally interpreted, for instance, men are duty bound to provide for women's material needs and, in the light of this obligation, inheritance laws are weighted in favour of men.[28]

Women Only?

The women of all three of the stories in this chapter have taken the vital step of recognizing that the subordination of women is not 'natural'.[29] There is no doubt in their minds that the discrimination they suffer is caused by an uneven power relationship between women and men. Experience has led the AAMWC to conclude

---

26 UN Declaration on the Right to Development, adopted on 4 December 1986, Article 2.2.

27 See Iman Hashim 'Reconciling Islam and Feminism' in Caroline Sweetman (ed.), *Gender, Religion and Spirituality* (Oxford, 1998), p. 7.

28 Fatima L. Adamu, 'A Double Edged Sword: Challenging Women's Oppression within Muslim Society in Northern Nigeria', in Sweetman (ed.), p. 58.

29 See Morna Macleod, *Género y Diversidad Cultural: Algunos Conceptos y Pistas Metodológicas,* paper for Seminar on Gender and Cultural Diversity, organized by Hivos and Novib (Quito, 2003).

that if women are to 'believe in their own strength' they need to be able 'to see and to comprehend the power mechanisms that create inequality and gender discrimination'; Nahdlatul Ulama says that the reason for the formation of the Muslimat NU was to 'improve the well-being and status of Muslim women' within a male-oriented association; and the Bahá'ís chose to work with tribal women because 'the least valued among the tribal people are the women and girls'.

From their disadvantaged position, women are seeking to restore the right balance of a true partnership with men, the partnership to which they believe their faith points them. There is no intention of adopting the attitudes inimical to family life or to men which, rightly or wrongly, are often associated with Western feminist movements. Their sense of the need for cohesive communities is too strong for such an approach. Moreover such attitudes would not only run counter to the teaching of their faith but would also fly in the face of sheer common sense, since they need the support of the men in their communities.

Thus, when the male members of the tribal communities in Madhya Pradesh raised objections to their wives' and daughters' new-found assertiveness, the Institute responded by offering residential courses to include men in order to give them the opportunity to understand things differently and to change their attitudes as well. Recognizing that 'women's empowerment is highly dependent upon men's attitudes', the women of Nahdlatul Ulama and the AAMWC, too, have included men as a focus in their educational activities. A clear opposition between men and women on the issues of female genital mutilation has not, in any case, been the AAMWC's experience. According to Bedria Mohammed, the Council has been attacked by both women and men. [30]

In view of all this, it is understandable that gender and development programmes that are targeted only at women may create difficulties for many Muslim women. Moreover gender-awareness programmes promoted by Western development agencies for women alone can give rise to the suspicion that women are being singled out as the perceived 'victims' of Islam (and therefore open to changes from the West), with the idea of undermining Muslim values from within. There is thus a risk that the women who participate in them might find themselves socially isolated.

A further difficulty with gender and development programmes focused on women only is that they can divert attention from economic and social problems suffered by a Muslim community in general and thus avoid addressing some of the most crucial political issues that affect both women and men.

It seems that associations or movements such as the AAMWC and the women's movements within Nahdlatul Ulama are managing to combine the enormous value of women-only groups, associations and meetings as a space for encouragement, support, frank exchange and friendship, while keeping in mind the absolute need to work together with the men of their communities.

---

30 WFDD/VHS workshop, Delhi, February 2004.

Combating Injustice and Poverty

In answer to a comment that in the two stories about Muslim women's movements 'development' seems to be more about justice than poverty, Bedria Mohammed answered: 'This may mean that sometimes people can live with poverty but not with other kinds of injustice'.[31] For the AAMWC development means liberation from both poverty and injustice, which are anyway often inseparable.

In the light of the 'deep-rooted poverty' in Addis Ababa, and in accordance with the lesson learned by the AAMWC that Muslims should 'take care of the needs of those who are in poverty', the women carried out a fund-raising campaign for the poor among the more wealthy Muslims both in Ethiopia and abroad. That the money was used for the programme for orphans set up by the AAMWC is a testimony to the important place that children have as members of the Muslim community.

But poverty, says the AAMWC story, is a 'complex and multi-dimensional issue' that involves a lot more than a lack of material resources. At the WFDD/VSF workshop in 2004, Bedria Mohammed told how the aeroplane in which she had travelled to Delhi had been full of young Ethiopian girls who had all got out at Dubai, looking for jobs. 'This seemed to be a symbol of how we are degrading ourselves and losing self-respect through poverty', she said.[32]

The AAMWC women understand development in terms of liberation from the degradation and loss of self-respect poverty brings with it; but they also understand it as liberation from institutional injustice and oppression. Their struggle against the cultural practice of female genital mutilation on the one hand and the discriminatory application of family law by the Islamic courts on the other involves striving to bring about profound cultural and institutional changes. Only in this way will an environment be provided in which all the women in the community can feel free from these unjust practices.

The story we are told of the women of Nahdlatul Ulama makes a sharp contrast between the 'welfare' of families as encouraged by the Qur'an and Hadith and President Suharto's New Order based on the view that development means the economic growth of the nation – if necessary, at the cost of family welfare and particularly of the well-being of women. The focus of the story is on the liberation of women from the oppression of the most intrusive and intimate nature that was being carried out as an integral part of the state's 'development' programme.

Like the AAMWC the position of Muslimat NU and Fatayat NU is deeply rooted both in Islam and in humanitarian concerns: 'Those who do not care about the problems of others are as if they are not Muslim,' they say. They, too, see development as a matter of tackling both injustice and poverty. The nine departments at each of the five levels of Fatayat deal with a wide range of women's needs, including the ability to organize themselves autonomously. Economic and cooperative activities ensure that material poverty is addressed, but as just one of the elements.

---

31 Ibid.
32 Ibid.

The Bahá'ís' training courses started very simply, focusing on income-generating skills. Nevertheless right from the start it was considered important to help the women to 'develop confidence in their capacity to learn, to express their views and to take initiatives'. The Institute has always been about preparing the young women to overcome not only their material deprivation but also their position as the most downtrodden group in their society.

Technology

The Bahá'í vision of development is the transformation of society through the systematic application of spiritual principles. Since religion and science, or spiritual and material progress are interdependent, spiritual principles guide us in the right direction to find appropriate practical solutions to problems, and they 'induce the attitudes, the will and the dynamics that facilitate the implementation of those solutions'.

'There is no fear of technology' at the Barli Institute 'but there is a real concern that technology should be appropriate and sustainable.' Science itself is neither good nor bad but the way in which it is put to practical use is not value free. The work the Barli Institute has put into producing such high-quality solar cookers and water conservation techniques is in accordance with its concern for environmental conservation that is shown to be a priority throughout the story. The technology is put to the service of people but not at the expense of the natural environment.

The use of technology of a different sort plays a key role, too, in the Nahdlatul Ulama women's story. As in the case of the Bahá'ís, it was not the technology of family planning in itself that Muslimat NU and Fatayat NU regarded as anti-Islamic, but the abusive way in which it was used in the service of the government's economic development programme. If the same techniques are used for the well-being of the family, they can benefit everyone.

Both these women's organizations view technical or economic development as just one element that should contribute to the much wider aim of social transformation. For them this wider aim can only be achieved if the use of technology is firmly grounded on the principles of the propagation of human welfare and care for nature to be found in their religious traditions.

Ways of Working

Only for Their Own Religious Communities?

The AAMWC is working specifically with the Muslim community. The Qur'an (9:71) is quoted as saying that Muslims should be 'friends and protectors of one another'. But what about people outside the Muslim community? Does this focus indicate a sectarian attitude?

The AAMWC's exclusivity is explained well in the story. It is based on the long-standing exclusion of Muslims from the social, political and economic life of Ethiopia. This has left them with many disadvantages which they are still trying to overcome. The focus is thus on the most needy sector within Ethiopian society. Since within this group the women are even more disadvantaged than the men, they become the top priority of all, particularly in the campaign for justice within the family.

The AAMWC does in fact work with Christian groups on economic projects for women.[33] Moreover the grounding of their strategy in the local context, evoking 'some of the strongest values and practices of local culture', indicates that the AAMWC's aversion is not to traditional cultural beliefs as a whole but specifically to the practice of female genital mutilation.

Nahdlatul Ulama has explicitly adopted an inclusive philosophy to include the spiritual practices and principles of pre-Muslim Kejawen as well as an openness to people of other religions. The changes in the government's family planning strategy benefited Indonesian women in general as it was not only Muslim women who were being targeted. Non-Muslim women are cared for, too, by LKK maternity hospitals and health clinics. Indeed, these clinics often employ non-Muslim health practitioners. We are told that all Nahdlatul Ulama's activities 'are based on the recognition that Allah's blessings belong to everyone, without regard to their religion'. The purpose is to ensure that all women are freed from oppression in their married and family life. However, since this huge Muslim association works in the country with the largest Muslim population in the world it is primarily concerned with Muslims.

The situation of the Bahá'ís as a tiny minority in India is very different but we find no defensiveness in the Barli Development Institute. Since 'The principle of service underlies all the work', we are told, '... development projects are not conducted for the purpose of public relations or as a means of converting people.' The principles taught and practised at the Institute, such as 'love, respect and unity, work as a form of worship and service as prayer', belong to many other spiritual traditions too. Moreover we learn that in the personality and leadership training courses, emphasis is laid on the women's role in 'respecting and reinforcing the value of their culture'.

All these organizations are helping to change deeply engrained societal or religious attitudes. In the case of the AAMWC, Muslim women will be the prime beneficiaries of any changes in the way marriage and divorce laws are applied, since Sharia law only applies to them. The abolition of female genital mutilation for Muslim women, however, would be likely to set a pattern for similar changes for women outside the Muslim community. In Indonesia not only did the changed orientation of the government's family planning programme benefit all women but also, as with the Barli Institute, the efforts of Muslimat NU and Fatayat NU to bring about more autonomy for women in society will send ripples well beyond the confines of their own organization.

---

33 Ibid.

Consultation

We are told that within Nahdlatul Ulama, consultation is very important: the discussions and deliberations in which Muslimat NU and Fatayat NU women regularly engage lead to the 'satisfaction of the inner self'. This way of making decisions through discussion until a consensus is reached breaks down any division between beneficiaries and 'experts'.

In the light of its strategy to empower women, the AAMWC breaks down these divisions too. Resisting any centralized decision making, it 'leaves resolution and action up to the initiative of each community and its members'.

At the Barli Institute, the cycle of action–reflection–consultation ensures that all the women are given the opportunity to discuss the reasons for and ways of carrying out the activities, as well as to make suggestions for improvements. Moreover, when doubts about the programmes have arisen within the tribal communities Janak has personally gone out to spend time living with the people, listening and consulting. The result of this consultative method is that the women have gained self-confidence and trust has been built up in their villages. We are also told that one of the Bahá'í principles of development is that programmes should be locally controlled.

'Consultation' is a buzzword of development practice but because of time constraints or priorities set for the use of time – both by national and local NGOs as well as by the funding agencies – in reality consultation can often mean little more than the presentation of a programme on which the beneficiaries are asked to comment.

If people are to gain a better sense of their rights and 'who they are' (AAMWC), if women are to understand their right to use different methods of birth control and how to do so and if new dynamics within the family are to bear fruit in more harmonious, prosperous and happy ways of living together, there can be no superficial debate about an agenda that has been essentially brought from outside. A common faith but also spiritual principles common to all religions provide an invaluable basis for creating the trust necessary for true consultation that results in people being able to welcome changes in their lives.

Political Opportunism?

The women leaders of the AAMWC, Nahdlatul Ulama and the Barli Institute have been adept at taking advantage of opportunities to use their political context or relations with their governments for the good of the women of their communities.

The AAMWC's founders seized upon the opportunity for action provided by the change of the constitution in Ethiopia. Remaining faithful to their religion, they refused to ally with the NGOs who, with all good intentions, were decrying Islam as the oppressor of women; but at the same time they were determined to use the new law that allowed Sharia courts to function to end the injustices meted out by them.

To do this they showed strategic skills within their own community, preparing their arguments and looking for alliances among the leading clerics.

The women of Nahdlatul Ulama agreed to co-operate with the government on the question of family planning, but only on their own terms. The decision was not without risks but it was well calculated, based on a correct analysis of the movement's powerful position, given that the Ministry needed the support of the religious scholars to achieve its programme. At the same time, in a way not dissimilar to the AAMWC, Muslimat NU and Fatayat NU used the political context as a framework for bringing about changes within the Muslim community itself.

The Barli Institute collaborates with the Indian and other governments, not only receiving financial support but also exchanging information and methodologies. It teaches village women how to apply to the government for loans as well. In this way it has not only benefited from government support but has known how to use government institutions to replicate its good practice further afield.

The story of the Nahdlatul Ulama women warns that too close an alliance with institutional political power can undermine a religious movement. However, these stories show women being alert to political situations that could work in their favour and, in the case of Nahdlatul Ulama, being highly skilful in negotiating a good outcome. Their strength in all three cases has lain in the integrity of their intentions and their clarity about the religious principles on which their action is based, as well as about their final aims. While being, to use a Christian saying, 'as wise as serpents and as innocent as doves',[34] these women's organizations have staunchly upheld all they believe in.

Inner Spirituality

> Rarely is Islam approached for what it first and foremost is, a faith and a spirituality that does not cease to nourish hundreds and hundreds of millions of human beings, enabling them to live peacefully and in a peace-giving way. (Rachid Benzine)[35]

As with Christianity or Judaism or any strongly scripturally based religion, Islam can be – and no doubt in many cases is – experienced more as a set of moral codes for the way its followers should behave than as the generator of inner spiritual nourishment. But the stories of the women of Nahdlatul Ulama and the AAMWC show that it is both: the outward and the inward engage each other.

While following the precepts and the outward forms of worship of Islam, it is possible to attain inner strength, clarity and freedom. The Nahdlatul Ulama story tells us: 'The greatest resource of Muslimat NU is not material or financial, or even organizational, but spiritual. It is the commitment of Nahdlatul Ulama women to "to work to satisfy the inner self"'.

---

34 Matthew 10.16.

35 Rachid Benzine, *Les Nouveaux Penseurs de l'Islam* (Paris, 2004), p. 11. (Author's translation.)

'It is difficult to speak of a measure of inner transformation but in order to bring it about I have to practise what my religion tells me: to pray, to care for those around me and to make an effort to change their lives', says Bedria Mohammed. And she goes on:

> To bring about inner transformation it is necessary to teach religion and to give people a chance to know what their religion says but also to change their surroundings by providing skills and capacity training so that people can change their lives for themselves. By respecting social values we can bring about inner transformation as well.[36]

It is their inner experience of Islam that on the one hand makes the women of the AAMWC so very sure that the oppression of women has nothing to do with the Muslim faith and on the other convinces the women of Nahdlatul Ulama that family planning is in accordance with the teaching of the Prophet Mohammed.

Since Islam is about the whole of life, the attempts of some development agencies merely to avoid the whole question of religion when working with Muslim women can never really work. The yearning of many outsiders to 'free' women from Islam is based on a lack of appreciation of the meaning that their religion gives to the lives of 'hundreds of millions' of Muslim women: it provides them with a sense of belonging, with a large part of their identity and above all with emotional support through affording them a space of their own. Their struggle is shored up by their faith, even as they question aspects of the practice of their religious institutions and above all the disparities they see between what the Qur'an and Hadith actually say and the way they are interpreted.

For these women it is not a question of a 'mechanistic' following of the rules. Their focus on the need for consistency between what people say and do leads to a heightened awareness of situations where the rules do not match the spirit of the Prophet Mohammed's revelations from Allah. It is on the strength of this inner clarity or insight – 'a better sense of who I am', as Fatuma Abdi puts it – that the women challenge the way that the Qur'an has been applied to life.

Reading Scriptures

Indeed, one of the most important themes that arises from the two Muslim stories is a highly controversial issue in all religions with a scriptural base: how scriptures should be interpreted. The struggle of the women of the AAMWC has been to argue for a reading of the Qur'an 'from the standpoint of common sense and a more human understanding'[37] – particularly regarding women. Their method of achieving this is to find out for themselves what their religious texts say and then use argument and persuasion to convince others – be these men or women – that the texts should be interpreted sensibly and humanely.

---

36 WFDD/VHS workshop, 2004.
37 Ibid., Bedria Mohammed.

Is this merely an example of people manipulating religious texts in their own interest – reading into them what they want to find? The AAMWC would say it is not, that, on the contrary, unless religious texts are read with an understanding of their historical and cultural context as well as with openness to their spiritual meaning for the here and now, they become dead pieces of literature. The Qur'an reveals Allah as Merciful, Compassionate, Kind and Just; and the stories of the Prophet Mohammed's life as found in the Hadith demonstrate the same attitudes towards women. There is no suggestion in Islam that it could be the will of Allah for women to be treated with cruelty, injustice or disrespect.

The AAMWC approach is in some respects not dissimilar to that of Muslim scholars such as Nasr Hamid Abû Zayd who tells us that the Qur'an is a historical document, revealed in a certain historical context, in a specific place and in a specific language, so it is open to interpretation.[38] He is but one of many Muslims – and Christians too – who criticize scholars of their faith who are reluctant to allow their religious tradition to be open to the experience of common sense and human understanding. It is this obscurantism, they say, that has resulted in a failure to detect the true spirit of their scriptures and thus to deal with the problems of the present day – a failure that results in the kinds of obstacles that the Muslim women of these stories are trying to overcome.

The Nahdlatul Ulama women's story gives us an example of how certain Qur'anic verses have been used by opponents of family planning, even though their reference to the theme may be far from evident. Perhaps it is precisely because of the utmost importance of scriptures in very many – almost all – religious traditions as a source of guidance and inspiration that there will always be deep differences of opinion about what they mean. The willingness of the Indonesian Syafe'i School of Islamic Jurisprudence to consider the social context of the Hadith gives the 'kyai' of Nahdlatul Ulama the possibility of trying to understand the spirit of Islam in the context of the present-day debate about birth control. Nevertheless, there are some 'kyai' who are still unwilling to see another point of view.

Women of the AAMWC and Nahdlatul Ulama who have the courage to challenge stultifying rules are insisting that Islam is a liberating religious tradition that has been made oppressive only by male clerics who have built up rigid traditions in their own favour, sometimes even basing themselves on cultural traditions that have nothing to do with Islam. In this sense these two women's movements are sowing the seeds of religious reform which could help to bring about hugely important changes in the way Islam views women and their rights, even if less flexible Islamic sects seem at the moment to be holding sway.

---

38 Benzine, p. 26.

Chapter 5

Action for Justice and Freedom

These last three stories in the book tell of individuals, groups and movements who, in Thailand, India and Chile, have taken political action alongside persecuted, marginalized and outcast people, often seemingly against all odds and almost always at considerable risk to themselves. Their 'solidarity' has not merely been a slogan but a way of life that has both arisen from and transformed their Buddhist and Christian beliefs and practice. The stories highlight the theme of freedom: liberation from oppression both within and outside ourselves; they raise the issue of 'realism', showing on the one hand how carefully strategies are planned whilst on the other actions are taken on the basis of trust and hope; and they decry the notion that religion must be restricted to the private sphere.

Engaged Buddhism in Siam and South-East Asia

Pracha Hutanuwatr and Jane Rasbash, October 2003

Introduction

In Siam[1] and other parts of South-East Asia, development has taken a Western secular route, focusing on economic growth without adequate consideration for environmental sustainability, social justice, cultural diversity and spiritual well-being. This approach has created great suffering among the people in these countries, many of whose societies are traditionally Buddhist. Socially Engaged Buddhism emerged as a response to this suffering. It provides a frame of reference that critically embraces traditional values while cautiously and critically selecting and integrating appropriate values from modernization. It is an attempt to renew ancient wisdom using Buddhism as a guideline to confront contemporary suffering in an inclusive way. It advocates changing one's consciousness side-by-side with transforming structural violence in society.

---

1   We choose to use the old name Siam for our country instead of the anglicized, hybrid name of Thailand that it was given after the military coup d'état of 1947 because for us 'Thailand' has authoritarian connotations and stands for the crisis of traditional Siamese Buddhist values.

What Is the Suffering?

In Siam, after four decades of development, the gap between the rich and the poor has widened to an unprecedented scale. Subsistence farmers have lost their land to absentee landlords from the big cities and become indebted to government banks and private loan sharks as they move from subsistence agriculture to cash crops and from simple living to a consumer society. Desperate for cash and no longer able to provide for basic needs they join the huge migration from rural to urban environments, where massive numbers live in slums and poverty.

On top of this more obvious degradation is the sense of intellectual inferiority of the educated class, a much more subtle kind of colonization. With their Western education either abroad or within the country, these elites lose confidence in their own spiritual and cultural values or become obsessed with a catch-up mentality. Such an inferiority complex provides fertile soil for planting consumer monoculture in Thai society.

It seems ironic that the Thai 'sangha' [Buddhist monastic community] that is supposed to generate the Buddhist values of simplicity, generosity and compassion is now almost completely under the spell of consumerism. Many monks are competing with each other to possess consumer goods such as mobile phones, BMWs and portable computers; others are obsessed with raising money from their newly rich followers to build ever-bigger Buddha statues and rarely used halls and buildings.

Buddhism tells us that this is a basic form of alienation. The 'vibhava-tanha' [existential sense of not being good enough] has been stimulated by Western-dominated international and national media and advertising to the extent that today's young people reject the very basic facts of who they are.

What Is the Root Cause of the Suffering?

From a Buddhist perspective, the very core of the present development policy and resulting consumerism is the amplification of 'tanha' [craving]. According to Buddhist analysis craving is the root cause of all suffering. Traditionally craving is manifested in the three 'akusala-mula' [unwholesome roots] of 'lobha' [greed], 'dosa' [hatred] and 'moha' [delusion].

In the context of consumerism the maximization of the desire to acquire unlimited wealth, power, recognition and sensual pleasure can be classified as greed. The anxiety about acquiring these four worldly desires, the fear of losing them and the anger, sadness and depression (some of which can turn into physical violence) when they are lost or not attainable can be classified as hatred. Delusion is the individualism and competition involved in getting them, the pride when one has them and the defining of who you are according to what you have. It also includes the loss of self-esteem and the feelings that you are not good enough when you don't get them, and the jealousy when others get them and you do not.

However, in Siam we can see clearly that craving does not work only on the individual level: it manifests itself in accepted social values. It is also manifested in the form of 'vihimsa' [structural violence] such as the free market economy, the control of the media by transnational corporations and the state mechanisms that favour the rich over the poor. The unsustainable industrialization process that overuses natural resources for excessive human consumption without compassion for other beings is another form of structural violence. In short the present social structure produces social values that promote craving and perpetuate 'vihimsa'-violence, exploitation and oppression in society.

Of course craving has existed in all societies at all times since history has been recorded, but with the consumer monoculture, rooted in the capitalist mode of production and the European Enlightenment worldview, it has come to be eulogized as never before.

Consumerism assumes that human beings can be happy by satisfying craving, but the Buddha said: 'There is no river bigger than "tanha".' This implies that craving is something insatiable. Hence the endless circle of acquiring more and more and more but never satisfying the sense of lack within.

The Vision

The Buddha told us that to be contented is to be wealthy. Buddhism and other spiritual traditions have helped people to live a contented simple life close to nature but well advanced in the cultivation of human consciousness, relationships and community life.

The 'sangha' is a model for community life and individual growth. Many sets of teaching have been laid down for living a harmonious and fruitful community life. All of them have an emphasis on participatory decision-making and equality both for the lay community and monks.

The way the Buddha organized his 'sangha' showed that he preferred small and decentralized units of communities. According to his principles, the ideal society is a loose network of small non-centralized communities where the highest aim is individual enlightenment, but to achieve that one has to respect other members as equals and care for their well-being.

The Formation of Engaged Buddhism in Siam

When Buddhadasa Bhikkhu (1926–93), a renowned Buddhist monk and thinker, saw how the Buddhist 'sangha' was being degraded through the modernization process, he gave a theoretical framework for a very important Buddhist reform movement. But in 1932, he also began an experiment, creating and living in an alternative community for monks and nuns that became the famous 'Suan Mokh' [Garden of Liberation]. He proposed the use of the original 'sangha' model as an ideal for social reconstruction and coined the term 'Dhammic Socialism'[2] as an alternative to the present system. Unlike the Marxist concept of socialism, Dhammic Socialism sees human beings as part of the natural system not as the dominating agent. They thus have to live a materially very simple life and devote their energy to cultivating the Buddha potential within.

In the 1960s, Sulak Sivaraksa, a lay Buddhist and activist, also articulated an alternative to the mainstream American style of development adopted by the military junta and modern Thai technocrats. Instead of trying to be over-virtuous and avoid real issues, as many conventional Buddhists are prone to do, he felt that for Buddhists to be true to themselves they needed to confront the tremendous suffering in society with mindfulness.

This relates to the first Noble Truth of the Buddha, to see the truth of suffering. If we devote our lives to social change without taking care of and nourishing the healthy aspects within, such as compassion, generosity and wisdom, we will burn out and escape from dealing with our own baggage. If we meditate and calm our mind and inner qualities without looking at and tasting the suffering of our fellow beings, we are escaping from real issues and avoiding suffering. The two aspects need to be combined.

As an activist and organizer Sulak has risked jail several times in his life. As a social critic he has given a sharp warning to different authorities, including the monarchy. During his 40 years of committed engagement, with support from many colleagues he has built a network of small organizations based on Engaged Buddhist teachings working with different target groups. Sulak and friends have also organized numerous seminars and workshops among the progressive middle class, challenging the mainstream development discourse and arguing for Buddhist alternatives.

The Path

The following examples show how development is understood by some of the groups Sulak founded or co-founded and the efforts they have made both to confront negative measures and to come up with more sustainable solutions.

Thai Inter-Religious Commission for Development (TICD)

Traditionally, the Buddhist monastery was the centre of the Thai community. Monks were teachers, counsellors, artists, healers and so on. The modernization process has changed all this while at the same time creating new problems in rural communities. But some monks with natural leadership talents have stood up to try to work with village leaders to cope with the difficulties facing them.

---

2   'Dhamma' (Sanskrit '*Dharma*') is the teaching and practice of Buddhism, but it is more than this. It also means the nature of reality. Dhammic Socialism is socialism based on Dhamma.

TICD staff identify and visit these monks and bring them together to exchange their experiences. At the same time they provide them with a deeper analysis of the modern structures of violence that affect their community, as well as with other skills needed for community development work that are more empowering than relief type of work.

When TICD started 18 years ago, there were around 20 monks involved; now the network of monks and nuns active in community empowerment work numbers around 500 all over the country. Many have accomplished a certain level of sustainability in their communities which have become learning centres for both laity and clergy interested in holistic community development work.

Luang Pho Nan is a typically inspiring case. Once his village in Surin Province was self-reliant, with an abundance of natural resources. Villagers knew next to nothing about the cash economy. When modern development and consumerism came to the area, the villagers gradually became the victims of middlemen and loan sharks and got into heavy debt. Some even lost their land.

Luang Pho Nan started his campaign with community meditation, raising awareness of the dangers of consumerism and the cash crop economy where villagers have no control over the markets. He also encouraged the villagers to form rice banks, community co-operative shops and community savings groups all based on Buddhist principles of 'vajji-aparihayadhamm' [participatory democracy] that include collective decision making, the honouring of agreed principles, respect for elders and women and spiritual practice.

The work soon spread to nearby districts and provinces. It has shown a way for people to get out of poverty by working together. The meditation aspect has also made sure that wealth gained is not be used to buy unnecessary consumer goods.

International Network of Engaged Buddhists (INEB)

In 1989, with the encouragement of Sulak Sivaraksa, INEB was formed after an international meeting of around 30 Buddhist participants from more than 15 countries. During the initial five years INEB held several international meetings that clarified complex issues that modern Buddhists are facing, such as consumerism, Buddhism and the environment, meditation and social action, diversity and unity among different Buddhist denominations.

The INEB secretariat acts as a clearing-house for information about active Buddhist groups around the world and aids needy Buddhist communities with international and other assistance. Among others, it has supported the Chakma and other ethnic Buddhists in the Chittagong Hill Tracts in Bangladesh, the Singhalese-Tamil peacemakers in Sri Lanka, the peace walk in Cambodia, the Asian sex-related workers in Japan and Buddhist monks who are active in forest preservation in Siam. Engaged Buddhists are also active members of the Tibetan campaign. Later on the secretariat expanded into the areas of empowering Buddhist women in different countries in Asia, including promoting and supporting the higher ordination of 'Bhikkhuni' [Buddhist nuns].

The approach is decentralized to build a network, rather than another hierarchical institution. Even if an activity is initiated from an international meeting organized by the secretariat, country groups or other like-minded NGOs are encouraged to take over as active co-ordinators.

INEB also encourages like-minded members to get together and initiate activities of common interest. An offshoot of this was the 'Think Sangha', a group of INEB members and friends who like to think deeply to clarify complicated contemporary issues Buddhists are facing. They have done some good research and have several publications.

Wongsanit Ashram

In the mid 1970s, in the heat of fierce conflict between left-wing and right-wing political forces in Siam, a group called Ahimsa (roughly equivalent to non-violence) was formed by young activists around Sulak Sivaraksa. They were hated by the left and misunderstood by the right as they did not subscribe to the view of either. Inspired by Gandhi's vision of ashrams as places both for spiritual practice and political action, the Ahimsa group and Sulak dreamed of a place where activists can live a simple, contemplative life being active in society rather than following the usual commercial paths of the middle classes.

In the 1980s about 15 acres of abandoned land 70 kilometres from Bangkok was donated for this purpose. Hundreds of trees have been planted and simply constructed traditional houses built for around 25 residents and up to 50 visitors who come as volunteers or to join a variety of workshops. There is a large organic garden that supplies vegetables. Many people have been drawn to the ashram, all with a will to live simply, develop spiritually and cultivate a keen social conscience. Ashram residents and guests respect the five Buddhist precepts that have been reinterpreted by engaged Buddhist thinkers like the Vietnamese Thich Nhat Hanh and Sulak to make them relevant to contemporary issues (see Table 5.1).

Typical courses at the ashram include conflict resolution, community development, mud house building, yoga and meditation. Besides simple living in terms of material consumption, the ashram seriously experiments with participatory decision making so that all members have the same opportunity to grow together. It was, at the beginning, a painful process and took a lot of time and energy of the members, but eventually a new culture was established and members feel empowered and enjoy living with this collective decision making process.

Table 5.1 Traditional Buddhist precepts and contemporary considerations

Traditional precept	Contemporary version must consider
I shall train myself to abstain from taking life.	• Harming any living creature harms oneself • Taking life includes the arms industry, racial conflict, breeding animals to serve human markets, using harmful insecticides.
I shall train myself to abstain from stealing.	• Ensuring meaningful work for everyone • Challenging economic power structures and understanding that theft is implicit in our economic system and overconsumption is theft from society • Renouncing fame, profit and power as a way of life.
I shall train myself to abstain from sexual misconduct.	• Hurting or exploiting others in sexual relationships • Understanding the implications of the global structures of male dominance and working towards developing full and balanced human beings free from socially learned 'masculine' and 'feminine' patterns of thought and behaviour.
I shall train myself to abstain from false speech.	• Understanding that one should be grounded in a deep and critical doubt about all beliefs and prejudices and hold all views more loosely • Ecumenical tolerance • Being critical of the patterns of information in modern media • Speaking truth to power • Overcoming lies and exaggerations perpetuated in the name of national security and material well-being • Developing alternative media and education.
I shall train myself to abstain from intoxicants that cloud the mind.	• Overturning the forces that encourage the use of drugs, alcohol and other intoxicants • Understanding that an unequal distribution of wealth, unemployment and alienation from work are the causes of addiction.

Spirit in Education Movement

The Spirit in Education Movement is another Thai NGO under the leadership of Sulak Sivaraksa. It runs the Grassroots Leadership Training (GLT) programmes. Over the last ten years the efforts of the GLT initiative have underpinned a larger movement working for social justice in South-East Asia. Working with marginalized communities in Siam, Burma, Laos and Cambodia, the GLT initiative runs three-month courses and follow-up sessions to empower communities to be self-reliant in terms of basic needs whilst maintaining their cultural integrity and sustaining a healthy environment.

There are study tours visiting innovative projects, and introductions to appropriate solutions such as sustainable technology and micro-credit with an emphasis on complementing indigenous wisdom rather than overpowering it. The communities start to recognize the oppressive forces in society and how they are mirrored within themselves; but as they find renewed belief in traditional wisdom and regain their self-confidence and community confidence, they begin to manage to move beyond these trends. The outcome of these courses is that traditional communities move towards protecting themselves from the negative forces of consumer monoculture and learn critically to negotiate and make use of the positive elements of modernization in order to revitalize a healthy community life.

GLT works with participants of several faiths and encourages spiritual practice according to people's own beliefs. However, a large part of the training is to cultivate a Buddhist view of what development means for individuals and for communities. This requires one to see the nature of the inter-relatedness of the universe, and thus meditation, prayer and practice according to the individual faith of the alumni are essential.

Assembly of the Poor

The Assembly of the Poor is a wonderful example of a non-violent grassroots movement challenging the mindset of modernization and consumerism. Tens of thousands of ordinary people have worked together to confront the negative impacts on their lives caused by dams, the loss of land rights for hill tribe people, large-scale farming and fishing and the dire conditions for factory workers.

A high-profile initiative is Pak Moon Dam in north-east Siam, where for many years thousands of Assembly members have gathered on a rotational basis, latterly forming a large protest village. Up against the huge institutions of the World Bank and the Thai government whose policies have wreaked havoc on the lives of the rural poor, this is a real story of hope. The government went back on its first promises and the dam was built, changing beyond measure the lives of the local people, who were largely dependent on fishing and riverside gardens. However, they then started campaigning for the dam gates to be opened and the river to be returned to its previous ecological state to allow the fish to spawn and the local fishing communities to thrive. The gates were ceremoniously opened in June 2001, but once again the government reneged and now it plans to close the gates for eight months of the year. With support from local universities and the Thai NGO movement the villagers continue their protests.

Through workers from the Spirit in Education Movement, Engaged Buddhist monks and nuns began supporting the movement as educators and encouraged meditation and chanting. Under their influence the Assembly seriously adopted the Buddhist principles of non-violent action. This reduced the legitimacy of the government to use violent repression. The persistent and extremely difficult protests for many years have helped the authorities to rethink and delay building other dams around the country.

The Results

Buddhadasa and Sulak Sivaraksa are visionaries who saw the perils of modernization coming decades ago. They are lone voices among the elites of Siam and are often seen as eccentrics. However those suffering from the perils of modernization have begun to embrace their message.

It is three-quarters of a century since Buddhadasa started 'Suan Mokh'. The influence of Engaged Buddhism in Thai society is still limited, although it seems to be gradually increasing. Some compare the Buddhist approach to ripples in a pond that start small and slowly spread. In their work with the poor Buddhadasa and Sulak have helped build up examples of good practice in community development where, without policy change from above, people at the grassroots can create sustainable villages free from debt and poverty.

Intellectually, these two distinguished thinkers are very different from Buddhist thinkers of the previous generation who first encountered modernization. Instead of trying to explain how Buddhism can fit into the modernization ethos, Buddhadasa and Sulak use authentic Buddhist values as their basic criteria. Though adapting some aspects of modernization they are very critical of its process and values from a Buddhist perspective.

Buddhadasa's and Sulak's approach of gentle and non-violent anarchism that bypasses state power and creates self-reliant communities seems to be increasingly relevant in a world of rapid globalization where more and more people are pushed out from the mainstream. However, there is a lot of work to be done to make their vision more concrete and relevant to the future.

National Fish Workers Forum:
A Spiritually Inspired Movement for
Alternative Development

Wendy Tyndale, 2002/2005

This is the story of a movement of fisherfolk that was started in the 1970s by Christians in the southern Indian state of Kerala. The Christian perspective does not, however, mean a lack of recognition of the essential contribution of Muslims, Hindus and adherents of other religions and spiritual traditions who from early on have participated in the National Fish Workers Forum.

Background to Indian Fisheries

The Traditional Scenario

With its 3,750 miles of coast line and innumerable rivers and lakes, India has one of the largest populations of fisherfolk in the world. Estimates vary between 7 and 10 million, of whom one-third are marine fisherfolk and two-thirds depend on fishing in inland waters.

The fishing communities in India are generally very poor and have low social status and little political power. Among them are tribal people, animists, Dalits,[3] Hindus, Christians and Muslims. Traditionally they have lived as enclosed societies, gathered round the church, mosque or temple. Each community is socially stratified, particularly on a class (rather than caste) basis. Local merchants often hold positions of power.

Over the centuries, the fisher people have amassed a vast fund of knowledge about the resources in their immediate vicinity, and they have developed a variety of technologies tailored to the specific ecological niches along the coast. This accounts for the immense diversity of artisanal fishing techniques in the country, the hallmark of which has been their ecological sophistication rather than an orientation towards quick monetary gain.

Women have traditionally undertaken a number of land-based occupations in the fishing communities, such as net making, fish curing and vending. They are involved in fish harvesting in the inland waters and are particularly skilled at shrimp peeling, which is an important activity in a booming export trade.

---

3 Dalits are India's outcasts. They were formerly called 'untouchables' and then renamed 'Harijan' or Children of God by Mahatma Ghandi, but today they prefer the more militant term 'Dalit', meaning 'crushed' or 'broken'.

The Modernization Process

In the 1960s, outsiders began to arrive with mechanized trawlers that depleted the fish stocks by indiscriminately destroying larvae and young fish. By 1997, about 23,000 such trawlers were fishing in the seas around India. In the state of Kerala the government had set apart inshore waters up to a depth of 20 metres exclusively for traditional fish workers, but the trawlers never kept to the rules. As a result, the economy underwent a marked technological polarization with the traditional fisher people rapidly losing their hold on the livelihood which had kept them going for generations.

Since then matters have been made even worse by the huge industrial fishing vessels whose trade is sustained largely by the demand for fishmeal for farm animal feed and pet food in the United States and Europe. Even if these vessels were prevented from encroaching into coastal waters, the ecological damage caused by deep-sea industrial fishing would still mean the destruction of species essential to coastal fishing.

Inland Fishing

The plight of the inland fish workers is probably even worse than that of their marine-based colleagues. Problems caused by the construction of huge dams, water pollution and deforestation have been compounded by the government's push for industrial fishing and aquaculture. This involves large tracts of land being taken over for prawn farming by national élites and multinational investors, who export the prawns to the United States and Europe. After ten years or less, productivity declines, so the aquaculturists move on, taking over more land and leaving behind them saline and toxic wastelands.

Studies have revealed that if the traditional, small-scale, coastal aquaculture were upgraded, the supply of shrimp could be enhanced in an ecologically appropriate manner, which would bring benefits to coastal communities.[4]

Involvement of the Church

The state of Kerala has an ancient indigenous Christian tradition dating from the first century CE. Twelve per cent of Kerala's population is Christian (compared to about 2.5 per cent for the whole of India) and in the southern tip all the fishing villages are Christian. The Christian community in Kerala consists of Latin and Syrian Catholics, Orthodox and Protestants. The fisherfolk are almost all Latin Catholics but people from other denominations and different religious orders work among them.

In 1961, inspired by the Second Vatican Council's call for Catholics to adopt a 'preferential option for the poor' and become more socially and politically

---

4   John Kurien, *Industrial Fisheries and Aquaculture*, in NFF Annual Report (Thiruvananthapuram, 1995), pp. 37–47.

aware and active, the bishop of the Latin Catholic Church in Trivandrum (now Thiruvananthapuram), Bernard Pereira, founded a new village for needy fisher families. The village was called Marianad.

Strong and lively grassroots participation was fostered from the start in Marianad. However, the bishop and his co-workers were well ahead of their time in their approach. The more conservative clergy of the diocese did not always appreciate the increasing confidence of the fisher people. Conflicts arose when the fishermen began to discuss how to avoid paying such high interest on the money they borrowed from local merchants. They also questioned the collection of church taxes by the same merchants who, usually in alliance with the priests, kept a percentage of the money for themselves. Eventually, in 1971, challenging both the moneylenders and the priests in the local communities, the fish workers set up an independent co-operative, which they registered with the government.

Women

Even though the women had played an important role in getting the Marianad co-operative onto its feet, they were not included as members, so with the help of some professional community organizers, led by Nalini Nayak of the All India Catholic Student Federation, they began meeting on their own to read the Bible and have training sessions in matters ranging from hygiene to organizational skills. As their everyday concerns came to the fore, they soon began to veer away from the 'other-worldly' moralizing interpretations of the Bible made by the local priests towards the empowering insight that Christianity has to do with the here and now.

Fortified by this new vision of their faith, the women set up their own fair price shop and also ran pre-school and adult education programmes, preventive health work and cultural activities. In addition, they were the first women in Kerala to become members of a Church Committee.

The story ends sadly with the arrival in Marianad of a new priest who vehemently objected to the role the women were playing and marginalized their social programmes by crowding them out with religious activity, once again of an 'other-worldly' moralizing nature. Nevertheless, the process of empowerment which had begun with a new understanding of what the Christian faith is about later inspired many of the men as well as the women who were active in the fish workers' movement.

Fish Workers' Organizations

The First Trade Unions

In 1973, Father Thomas Kocherry, a Redemptorist priest, moved with two Redemptorist colleagues to Poothura, a little village north of Marianad. It was in Poothura that some nuns of the Medical Mission Order also settled. Their choice, in accordance with Jesus' own identification with the poor, was to live with the very poorest and most outcast communities.

Poothura happened to be the centre for a government project for the modernization of the small-scale fishing industry, but the local fishermen were being sold poor-quality boats for which they took out loans and were then cheated by the moneylenders. Tom Kocherry, a highly political thinker and an excellent mass organizer, took up their cause and in 1977, along with a fisherman called Joyachen Antony, he helped to found an informal trade union.

This was but one of many other initiatives which were going on at the same time, both for development programmes and unionization. Motivated by Christian teachings about justice and freedom for the poor, many priests and nuns of various religious orders played a leading role in bringing the fisherfolk together. It was not long before the (still unofficial) unions which had been set up in different villages joined forces and a federation was formed. This was the first step in what was to become a social, ecological and political movement to secure a livelihood for the fishing families.

Those who were committed to this work understood Christianity in much the same way as the women in Marianad had begun to: as a living faith concerned not only with spiritual matters but also with justice and peace in this world. For most of the people involved these were highly formative years spiritually as well as politically. It was then, for example, that Antonio Alibi, who today works on diversification issues for the National Fish Workers Forum (NFF), began to form the opinion he now holds. 'For me spirituality means that we do some good, and people become resurrected and establish their rights,' he explains.[5]

Sister Philomine Marie, one of the nuns from the Medical Mission Sisters, is very clear about the change that has occurred in her view of the meaning of Christianity: 'I was brought up as a very traditional Christian,' she says 'with the idea of saving myself to go to heaven. It was only when I started working with the fishing people that the meaning of Christianity started to evolve for me.'[6] Another fisherman from the NFF tells a similar story: 'Before, I just used to go to church to pray. Now I realize that I must work to liberate the fish workers.'[7]

This sharing of spiritual growth was evidently a strong ingredient of the solidarity which bound members of the movement together and gave them strength to keep going through periods of great difficulty.

Protest Action

By the early 1980s, the problem of the depletion of fish stocks through trawling was becoming acute. Because it was based in the southern district of Thiruvananthapuram, the leadership of the trade union federation was predominantly Christian; but the fact

---

5 Interview with Tyndale, Kerala, November 2001.
6 Ibid.
7 Ibid.

that they were all faced with the same threat united all the fishermen – Christians, Hindus and Muslims.

In 1981, the first real action began, when the fish workers asked the government of Kerala to establish a commission to study their problems. Picketing and blockades were accompanied by Gandhian-style hunger strikes by the nuns and priests, with the result that some of them were imprisoned. The participation of nuns and priests in such activities was a great novelty in Indian culture. It evoked bitter resentment among some people, including most of the local church leadership, but enthusiastic acclamation among others. The outcome was that the state of Kerala agreed to pass the Marine Fishing Regulation, which opened the way for the introduction of a ban on trawling during the monsoon season.

From then on, it became very clear to the Christians involved that if 'development' is to imply a long-term transformation in people's lives, it necessarily involves a stand-off against the powers that are preventing this – whether these are embodied in the clergy within the Church, in extortionate moneylenders at village level, in a state government or in the bodies regulating international trade. The Christians in the fishing communities have found inspiration for their action in the description in the gospels of Jesus' ministry as a sustained conflict against the authorities who oppressed and marginalized the poor and the disadvantaged.

Kerala Independent Fish Workers' Federation: The Movement Splits

By 1982, tensions within the fish workers' movement itself had arisen because of different perceptions about the religious nature of the federation. Some saw it as an organization of Latin Catholic fishermen, whereas others, including some of the priests, insisted that it should become the 'Kerala Swathathra Malsya Thozhilali Federation' [Kerala Independent Fish Workers Federation] and that Muslims and Hindus should be included. The latter view won the day. The independent federation was registered as a trade union and ever since then it has worked separately from any religious institutions. However, the decision was taken by only one vote and the movement split.

Christian Inspiration for a Movement Shared Equally by All

Christianity had been a vital inspiration for the fish workers' organization but there was a strong awareness among many of the Christians in Kerala of the importance of preserving the multi-faith, or what they now refer to as the 'secular', character of the movement ('secular' in the sense of the inclusion rather than exclusion of all religions). They favoured this option partly on political grounds, as they wanted to strengthen the movement. However their main reason was that they genuinely wanted to include everyone.

Sister Patricia, one of the Medical Mission Sisters who settled in Poothura, explains that they always had an inclusive attitude:

Our idea was to work together creatively for a new society of justice, love and peace. Different people bring a commitment from their own faith. Development cannot be one-sided. If Christians alone develop, then that is only one side of the face of God. ... God has created the whole world and would not want anyone to be lost.[8]

Fr Tom Kocherry goes even further when he speaks of 'secular spirituality' as the sustaining power available to all human beings. 'Social change based on a prophetic approach needs the same sustaining power whatever religion or non-religion you belong to', he says.[9]

For the members of religious orders working with the fisher people, their 'option for the poor' meant a commitment to live physically and economically at the level of the people they sought to serve, sharing not only their knowledge and their time but also their reputation. There was no 'top-down' charity here, nor was there a relationship of 'experts' on one side and 'target group' on the other. The movement was one and they were all in it together. They saw their ministry as embracing the social and economic as well as the spiritual aspects of people's lives.

National Fish Workers Forum (NFF)

In 1978, under the leadership of Matanhy S. Aldanha of the All India Catholic Student Federation, the National Fish Workers Forum was set up, based in Goa. Fish workers of all kinds, women and men from both the marine and inland sectors, are entitled to belong to the Forum, which acts in many ways more as a mass movement than as a trade union. The membership of the NFF has now reached about 4 million, but its religiously and politically inclusive nature has meant that whenever it organizes actions it is able to mobilize support far beyond its membership.

In 1995, for example, the Forum succeeded in mobilizing 8 million fish workers who went on strike against fishing licences being granted to foreign trawlers in Indian waters. Protests continued until 1997, when the Indian government finally supported the fish workers' position – a great victory for the fishing population.

The NFF aims to be an inclusive body in all senses. In 1985, it was decided that the priests and nuns should hand over leadership to the fisher people themselves, though Tom Kocherry was asked to stay on for several more years as president, and he is still permanently invited to the National Executive Committee. Sister Philomine Marie stayed on too and has been faithfully working as secretary and treasurer to the movement in its small office in Thiruvananthapuram ever since.

One-third of the members of the NFF's national decision-making body are women and concerted efforts are being made, also by many male members, to include at least the same percentage at district level. Since the average literacy level in the fishing communities is very low, training has been of the utmost importance in order to ensure that the Forum is genuinely an organization of the fish workers themselves. The NFF has been helped in this work by the International Collective

---

8   Interview with Tyndale, Kerala, November 2001.
9   Ibid., September 2002.

in Support of Fish Workers, formed in 1986 by a group of social activists who have been vital to the movement in supplying economic and technical research to back up its demands.

World Forum of Fish Harvesters and Fish Workers (WFF)

Where the NFF has shown extraordinary leadership and vision is in the work carried out beyond India itself. In 1997, in New Delhi, men and women fish workers from 33 countries created the World Forum of Fish Harvesters and Fish Workers to defend and promote the interests of fisherfolk whose livelihood depends on traditional small-scale fishing. Fr Tom Kocherry was elected General Coordinator of this new international body that today has 37 member organizations from 27 countries, from Malaysia to Canada, Senegal to Honduras, Thailand to Madagascar. Fish workers are now aware as never before of the similarity of the problems all over the world posed by factory fishing ships, shrimp farms and the destruction of the environment. They make their voice heard at gatherings such as the World Social Forum and have played a prominent role in lobbying the World Trade Organization.

Conclusion: All Inclusive Spirituality

The story of the National Fish Workers Forum shows how a certain group of Christian fisher people, accompanied by committed priests and nuns, has made a highly significant contribution to development. The way they chose to do this was by acting as a catalyst for the formation of a movement of fish workers that has managed to bring about some important improvements for the fishing communities.

Their commitment led them to challenge the kinds of priorities usually set for Christian action by the churches. That their option for the poor has also transformed the way in which they understand and live their own faith only goes to show how intimately their spirituality and their everyday lives are intertwined.

Nevertheless, the recognition early on that many of the values highlighted in this study as hallmarks of a Christian contribution to a process of development are widely shared by people of other religions has led these Christians to adopt a genuinely open attitude that has enriched their own spiritual life as well as making the NFF a body to which all can fully belong. The members of the NFF are inspired by an all-embracing spirituality: an empowering energy whose source, they say, is not confined to any one spiritual tradition. Today the Forum is led by Harekrishna Debnath, an enthusiastic follower of Tagorean religiosity. The General Secretary, N.D. Koli, is a Hindu.

Sebastián Acevedo Movement against Torture: A Project for the Dignity of Life

Rosa Parissi, May 2005[10]

Introduction

The largely Catholic region of Latin America was and has been the scene of religious and cultural encounter, but also of cruelty, wars and human rights abuses. Human rights violations are not a thing of the past. The pressures exerted today by the globalized world in search of the region's valuable natural resources incorporate elements of structural injustice. 'Because of its logic of competition rather than co-operation, globalization constantly generates inequality, injustice and violence' says the Brazilian theologian Leonardo Boff. 'Its forces are structurally linked so as to consolidate the culture of violence that dehumanizes all of us.'[11]

Alongside the inequalities and injustices there have always been non-violent responses for survival and development. At the centre of these is the human being, with his/her capacity to build up solidarity networks in the defence of life. Perhaps it is intrinsic to human culture that resistance and respect for life spring up in the face of threat.

In the 1970s and 80s, the logic of war and high levels of violence created a reign of terror in various countries of Latin America, Chile among them. But the imposition of a single model of government and the efforts of dictatorships to keep people gagged and immobilized did not prevent the appearance of countless strategies of resistance. The civilizing processes of denunciation, started off by small groups, made such an impact on society that they opened up paths that would later lead to more humane ways of living together.

In the midst of the turmoil many Base Christian Communities[12] came into being, providing room for the persecuted as well as for those who 'hungered and thirsted after justice' – those whom Jesus named as 'blessed' (Matthew 5:6 and 10). It was in this spirit that Christian communities and organizations of the poor were able

---

10 Translated from the original Spanish by the author.

11 Leonardo Boff, 'Cultura de Paz' in *Tópicos 90, No. 10, Panorama de Teología y Cultura de Paz* (Santiago de Chile, January 2003), p. 9.

12 Base Christian (or Ecclesial) Communities arose as part of the movement of Liberation Theology in Latin America. They combined social and political engagement for more just societies, the inspiration of biblical faith, a critical stance towards institutional religion and prayerful celebration. Structurally they provided an alternative to the normal Catholic parish, gathering believers into close-knit communities brought together by reflection and action. Because of the changed political situation, but also because of opposition from the Vatican, these communities have now declined in number. (See Simon Barrow, *Christian Communities Challenge Exclusion in Europe*, http://www.simonbarrow.net/article61.html (accessed 16 September 2005). (Author's note.)

to build up structures for their survival, in defence of their life and their rights. These were times when the Christian gospel was made flesh and action. The ultra-conservative hierarchy of later years had not yet robbed the Church of its social and liberating dimension – a process set in motion by the Vatican in Rome, fearful of losing control in Latin America.

For the Base Christian Communities 'development' meant the construction of a culture of peace and the realization of a worldview within the framework of that culture – a vision far removed from the concept of economic development as the main pillar of life.

The most powerful value underlying their action was solidarity, a value completely alien to political realism measured against its potential for war and state security. For believers and non-believers, solidarity was the supreme value that not only enabled people to get their daily bread but also to inspire actions of denunciation. These actions – none the less heroic for being non-violent – kept alive the hope of attaining the positive peace that people longed for. They began to show that powerlessness and despair can be transformed. The sensitivity of these Christians to the will of God made them able to respond to the demands of the situation in the face of abuse carried out according to unjust laws and distorted truths used to justify horrendous crimes.

For the Jesuit theologian and ethicist, José Aldunate: 'Truth is not in the clouds nor in absolute universal principles but in the different circumstances of reality itself.'[13] This was one of the thoughts that motivated him, together with a Christian community, to undertake the difficult task of opening up a space to denounce the practice of torture in Chile.

The Birth of a Movement against Torture

Following the military coup that overthrew the government of Salvador Allende in 1973, there was a considerable growth of Base Christian Communities in Chile. Within them were not only men and women from religious orders, priests and laypeople, but also people who had belonged to different social organizations, especially from the sectors that were most impoverished and repressed by the dictatorship. These communities generated small initiatives that in the course of time became large networks. They carried out tasks that were indispensable for people's survival and above all for obtaining social justice.

The popular protests against the military dictatorship that began on 11 May 1983 had provoked an increase in violence and the systematic practice of torture as a way of immobilizing the population and keeping terror alive.

Clandestine torture centres, such as the sadly notorious Villa Grimaldi, were not functioning at first. Torture was carried out in police stations, marginal residential areas, slums or simply in the streets of the cities. People were beaten and there were

---

13 Conversation with Parissi at that time.

mass raids and detentions. Many people died; others were obliged to put out the bonfires – the expression of protest – with their bare feet and bodies.

This story is about the Christian community to which both José Aldunate and Roberto Bolton, priest and rector of the Catholic Seminary, belonged. The group would meet in the city of Santiago for reflection and to share out the work required by the persecuted: prisoners and the families of people who had disappeared after their arrest. For security reasons they always met in different places and many of the members did not even know the others' names. The priests – both of whom were well known in Chile – appeared as the public faces and voices of the group, but although they gave strategic and moral guidance, they did not impose their views. All decisions were taken democratically.

Roberto Bolton tells how in the month of September 1983, this Christian community met in the parish of the Sacred Heart in the centre of Santiago. Those present listened to a hair-raising report given by a psychiatrist who had received direct testimonies from the victims of the cruellest aberrations and torture carried out by specialized trained groups of the military regime. The reflection that followed led the people to ask themselves how long they could peacefully talk about what was happening in the country while violence was tearing bodies apart and leaving deep scars on people's minds. 'People are being tortured in Chile and what are we doing? What are we doing? People are being systematically tortured. What should we do?' Their heightened awareness of their moral responsibility and of the complicity implied by silence was to give rise to actions of denunciation against torture.

Since systematic torture had been introduced into the country, everyone had kept silent. It was a theme that was only commented on in whispers. No one dared to publicize the situation. The media were censored but stronger still were fear and self-censorship. Torture was the most effective way of instilling terror and keeping organizations scattered. In such a climate it was difficult to undertake any action that might develop initiatives for the common good.

The group's idea was to counteract the effect of torture on society with non-violent action. They had to cause an impact, to jolt people's consciences. They should get the idea off the ground by overcoming their own gut terror. Their actions had to be influential at a national and international level to lead to a climate of disgust. The small community would thus be leaven in the dough of a great movement against torture.[14]

At the Side of the Tortured

The group, made up of 70 people – members of the Christian community with friends from other sectors – took courage and stepped into the very jaws of the repressive regime. On 14 September 1983, they put up a banner in front of the doorway of No. 1470 in the street called Borgoño, a secret prison of the National

14 A reference to Jesus' likening of the Kingdom of Heaven to yeast that makes the whole loaf of bread rise (Matthew 13:33). (Author's note).

Centre for Information (CNI, the secret police). The banner read: 'Here someone is being tortured'. Each participant stood with their arm stretched out, pointing at the place, while they sang at the tops of their voices so that the victims incarcerated in the cellars would be able to hear their solidarity.

The silence of complicity had been broken. The people being tortured were not alone. From that day on the group sang a song that became the Hymn of Freedom of the Sebastián Acevedo Movement against Torture:

> For the bird in the cage
> For the fish in the bowl
> For my friend imprisoned
> For saying what s/he thinks
> For the flowers pulled up
> For the grass trodden down
> For the trees with lopped off branches
> For the people being tortured
> I name you Freedom[15]

This first non-violent action was greeted by police repression: 28 people were detained in a police station, most of them nuns and priests. José Aldunate was wounded by a missile – his 'baptism of blood', as he was to say later on. For the first time the main media felt obliged to publicize pictures and report on what had happened.

The impact of the action provoked reactions from the hierarchy of the Catholic Church as well. Statements by the Archbishop of Santiago, who was not convinced by the group's methods, motivated its members to write a letter in which they quoted Pope Paul VI's [1963–78] papal encyclical 'Gaudium et Spes':

> Whatever violates the integrity of the human person, such as mutilation, torments inflicted on body or mind, attempts to coerce the will itself ... All these things and others of their like are infamies indeed. They poison human society, but they do more harm to those who practise them than to those who suffer from the injury. Moreover, they are a supreme dishonour to the Creator.

During these years the bishops of some dioceses excommunicated those who practised or permitted torture.

Sebastián Acevedo

On 11 November 1983, a workman called Sebastián Acevedo set himself alight in front of the cathedral of the southern city of Concepción. Two of his sons had been arrested and were being tortured in the quarters of the secret police, the CNI. This father's sacrifice was a desperate act to attract people's attention and to save his sons from torture. Having sought help from all sides, Sebastián Acevedo felt he had no

---

15 This poem by the French poet Paul Eluard (1895–1952) was turned into a song by the Argentine Nacha Guevara.

alternative but to offer his own life in a supreme act of love, turning himself into a flaming firebrand.

From that moment on, the Movement against Torture took on the name of Sebastián Acevedo. By 1990, the date on which they gave their evidence to the Truth and Reconciliation Commission, they had carried out 180 actions in the course of seven years. Hundreds of people had taken part, bearing witness to their beliefs in the streets of Santiago and other Chilean cities.

The community that started the Sebastián Acevedo Movement against Torture (MCTSA) welcomed all who accepted the method of active non-violence and denunciation. This led to some of the street actions involving more than 400 people. Overcoming their fear, they returned several times to the CNI's premises in Borgoño Street and to other detention and torture centres (see Plate 6). They made complaints to the most important newspapers, such as *El Mercurio* and *Diario la Nación*, and they denounced the lack of justice in the courts. 'Torture is practised in Chile and the courts are silent', said one banner unfurled in front of the Supreme Court of Justice.

The Spirit of the Actions

The members of the movement were borne up by the belief that things that humans deem impossible can happen. Their actions were imbued with an energizing spirit of commitment and faith ['una mística'] that went far beyond the material or the objective.

The initial idea was to set up a movement that would make denunciation possible and act as a channel for people's indignation in the face of the abuse and fundamental inhumanity of the use of torture as an instrument of control.

For the Christians committed to the movement, to take part was a minimal ethical requirement in accordance with the gospel of love and life. They trusted that God was with them and that God would give them the courage to face the risk of each denunciation. But for Christians and non-Christians alike, the strength that kept them together and on their feet came from their feeling of solidarity with their brothers and sisters. This feeling strengthened their will to remain firm, with their heads held high, and to put up with blows, detention and aggression every time they went out into the street.

The group felt the pain of their wounded brother or sister as their own. More than once, on hearing the crunch of a bone broken by the blow of a policeman's baton they were enraged by the unbearable aggression. But, clenching their teeth, with great discipline they remained loyal to their collective commitment to respond to violence with an attitude of non-violence.

On some occasions, when the police aggression grew more severe, they showed unusual fervour, calling upon God with a throaty 'Our Father'. At other times the Hymn of Freedom broke out spontaneously and again and again the verse 'For the people being tortured, I name you Freedom' came out with ever more force and conviction.

The group always made a great impact on the passers-by in the streets where they carried out their actions. Sometimes their firm determination to be there in the face of violence disconcerted the police, making them hesitate to respond aggressively. At other times the violence turned the place into a battlefield whose sole protagonist was the police contingent, while the members of the MCTSA protected themselves by linking their arms and turning their bodies into a single human mass which the police beat unmercifully in the midst of tear gas and water cannon. The group never failed in its non-violent approach. Not once did it respond with violence of any sort, whatever the circumstances.

'We are Witnesses'

When the process of transition to democracy began in Chile, the MCTSA believed its mission had ended and that the task it had assigned to itself should be taken up by the authorities elected to restore democracy to the country. The social movements had gathered strength through their struggle against the military dictatorship. Since they had mostly adopted non-violent forms of struggle, they were in a good position to contribute to the new situation.

Nevertheless, the restoration of justice has been a long process and is still going on. First, the Truth and Reconciliation Commission undertook an investigation to give some elements of the truth to Chilean society and to confirm the most flagrant cases of human rights violations, especially the cases of people who had been executed and of those who, having been detained, had disappeared. A long time passed before the torture systematically carried out by agents of the state was officially recognized. The National Commission on Political Imprisonment and Torture set up on 13 August 2003 received testimonies of those Chileans who had the courage to remember the dramatic facts of the past. In 1990, the MCTSA had given a report to the Truth and Reconciliation Commission pointing out:

> We are witnesses that during the years of the military regime in Chile, the official bodies practised torture systematically and on a massive scale. They did so in a refined and scientific manner with infrastructure and trained personnel, among whom were medical professionals. We have been told that, as far as torture is concerned, the Commission wishes to restrict itself to the cases that resulted in death. We would like to comment that in any civilized country abuses can happen, even to the point of death. What was particularly serious in Chile and what the Commission should report on is the systematic torture which was instituted in our country and of which we are witnesses.

Rather than seeking to achieve quantitative achievements and recognition, the MCTSA was able to point to a way, a method and an attitude in search of peace and respect for life: the fundamental starting point for development.

From Active Non-Violence to Non-Violence as a Strategy for Life

Over the last 15 years, the former members of the Sebastián Acevedo Movement against Torture have continued to meet each other now and then when anything scandalous has occurred in Chile that must be publicly denounced. One such occasion was in 1998, when General Pinochet was sworn in as Senator for Life in the National Congress in the city of Valparaíso. The group held up a banner saying 'Do not swear by his Holy Name in vain'. Even though the democratic government had replaced the military dictatorship by then, the police vented their anger on the demonstrators as they had in times past.

Today the lives of the MCTSA's former members bear witness to just as much commitment as when they were all protesting together for the first time in front of the doorway of the secret police in 1983. The principles put into practice through the movement's methods and the kinds of actions it took made clear that development cannot be constructed on a foundation of violence, domination, religious alienation, or a single way of thinking with the demonization of those who think differently. The MCTSA's principles were deeply engrained in each of the members, and they continue to share them in their experiences with other people and other groups.

Claudio Escobar Cáceres, who was one of the youngest and most active members of the movement, says: 'The movement led me on from tactical non-violence to a non-violent strategy for life. This is a path that I try to follow in my private life as well.'[16] Claudio has made a very important contribution to movements demanding justice in court cases concerning torture as well as in the Movement for Conscientious Objection to repeal the law that obliges young men to do military service. He was also tireless in his accompaniment of two indigenous Pehuenche leaders, Nicolasa and Berta Quintreman, as they struggled in the mountains of southern Chile to prevent their lands from being flooded by a hydroelectric dam being built by one of the huge transnational companies.

The young students who gave their energy to the MCTSA were unaware of the impact it would have on their lives. Today these young people, men and women, are fathers and mothers of families, lawyers, social workers, anthropologists. They all continue to recognize the strength of solidarity and they work to put the principle of respect for life into practice.

Erika Espinoza Allende, now an anthropology graduate, says: 'What I learned gave me hope and has given me strength for solidarity work today.' Erika participated as a very young girl in the MCTSA along with a group of extremely impoverished women.

Ana Cristina Torrealba was a schoolgirl who participated in the street actions in her blue uniform. Today she is an architect. 'Non-violence was a unique lesson: to learn to face up to fear, to be brave and to trust in others, to tolerate differences', she says. 'The fight for human rights was an exercise in incorporating respect, trust,

---

16 This and all the following quotations are from conversations with Parissi, Chile, May 2005.

courage and faith into our lives.' At the Catholic University, Ana Cristina's subject was symbolic architecture. Her academic work led her to rebuild the former torture house of Villa Grimaldi in the east of Santiago. Today it is the Park for Peace. For Ana Cristina the project for her final qualification:

> was like a long action of Sebastián Acevedo that had to be created and lived through – an action that will remain for ever in tangible form, with its corridors and its trees that saw so many tortured men and women passing by. This action will ensure that the young people of today are able to know about and relive our struggle for human rights.

In November 2004, the meeting of the Asia-Pacific Economic Co-operation (APEC) – one more symbol of neo-liberal globalization – was held in Chile. At the same time a Chilean Social Forum had been organized, similar to the forums that have been held in Porto Alegré, Brazil and in India with the slogan 'Another world is possible'. Starting from the standpoint of diversity and pluralism, the Chilean Social Forum provided space for discussions and solidarity actions, where people could dream that 'Another Chile is possible'. The faces of the former members of the MCTSA who took part in it reflected their silent emotion as they witnessed the strength of the non-violence, the desire for peace and the signs of solidarity that were present in each of the activities.

Signs of the Times: Courage to Take Action

> Daring to do what is right, not what fancy may tell you,
> valiantly grasping occasions, not cravenly doubting –
> freedom comes only through deeds, not through thoughts taking wing.
> Faint not nor fear, but go out to the storm and the action,
> trusting in God whose commandments you faithfully follow.
> Freedom, exultant, will welcome your spirit with joy.
> *Dietrich Bonhoeffer*[17]

Solidarity: Living Spirituality

A common characteristic of the three movements in this chapter is that they were founded by groups of people who allowed themselves to become fully aware of uncomfortable truths. Their willingness to feel 'the pain of their wounded brother or sister as their own' (Sebastián Acevedo Movement) compelled them to speak out for justice in situations in which it would have been far safer, more comfortable and less conflictive to keep quiet.

It is this compassion for (feeling with) others that transforms 'solidarity' from a rhetorical slogan into a truly uniting force, following the total commitment that Jesus showed to the poor and oppressed as well as to his friends and disciples. Solidarity of this sort is what the International Network of Engaged Buddhists, as well as movements such as Sarvodaya, are bringing to Buddhism, not as a new concept – for compassion has always been an important Buddhist value – but as an expression of compassion that includes the idea of taking action for social justice.

When solidarity means to step into other people's shoes, putting their interests above one's own, it becomes indeed a 'powerful value' that is certainly alien, as the Chileans noted, to political or any other kind of 'realism'. Here there is no room for weighing up the costs to oneself or for being certain of success before 'going out to the storm and the action'. Members of all these three movements have spent time in prison on account of their public denunciations of wrong-doing and demands for reform.

Wholehearted, loyal commitment to others is not the prerogative of religious people. There are many examples of people from secular trades unions or even from staunchly atheist political groups who have shown this kind of self-sacrifice in standing up for the oppressed. Nevertheless the stories show how the effort to live one's life according to the true spirit of one's religious or spiritual tradition

---

17 'Stations in the Road to Freedom: Action', in *Letters and Papers from Prison* (New York, 1953), pp. 228–9. Bonhoeffer was imprisoned by the Nazi regime in Germany in 1943 and executed in 1945 for his part in the small Christian movement of resistance to National Socialism.

can provide the sustaining power of which Father Tom Kocherry talks. We see how the protagonists of these stories are constantly meeting for prayer, meditation and reflection. For them it is their spiritual life together that helps them to be mindful, keeps them going, prevents the 'burnout' and disillusionment from which so many social activists suffer, and that inspires their action with new creativity and boldness.

The stories show, too, how social action can in its turn strengthen people's religious practice. It is striking that it was precisely their openness to sharing in the suffering of others that led the individuals involved in these struggles towards the deeper spiritual understanding which sustained their action against injustice. Buddhadasa Bhikkhu and Sulak Sivaraksa were motivated to include social action in their Buddhist practice through identifying with the people whose lives were being damaged by the modernization process in their country, and the involvement of the nuns, priests and fisherfolk in Kerala in the struggle of the fishing communities led them to change their understanding of Christianity. For the Christian community of the Sebastián Acevedo Movement it was the psychiatrist's report of the testimonies of tortured people that jolted them into reflecting upon what true Christian witness meant in those years of the military dictatorship.

In the same way as the people in all the other chapters, the members of these movements experience spirituality as an integral part of daily life. Their religious practice goes far deeper than the prayer, chanting, singing and observance of rituals on which it is based. It involves letting go of preconceived ideas and being open to opportunities that present themselves. The decision of the nuns and priests in Kerala to go and live with impoverished fisher people, for instance, launched them into a process they had not foreseen at all. Once again we are presented with the dynamic between individual inner transformation and outer social change.

This dynamic is not, however, an easy one. The Engaged Buddhists tell us that part of their training courses consists in enabling people to see how what they want to fight against outside them is in fact mirrored within them – a painful as well as a challenging recognition. The resolve of the Wongsanit Ashram's inhabitants to train themselves to live according to Buddhist precepts interpreted with relevance to the world today shows the strict personal discipline that would-be social activists are required to undergo. Similar discipline was demanded of the members of the Sebastián Acevedo Movement in their determination never to respond with violence, even in the face of untold provocation.

To try to act with personal and collective integrity in movements calling for social, political and economic change requires constant reflection and a great deal of effort. Sulak Sivaraksa suggested that Buddhists should 'confront the tremendous suffering in society with mindfulness'. It is this 'mindfulness', being fully aware of what one is doing, that is needed as a safeguard to prevent activists of any cause marching under the banner of solidarity while their own needs, interests or concern for status and power are uppermost in their minds.

Was it their prayer and spiritual reflection that also gave members of the Sebastián Acevedo Movement the necessary detachment and clarity to decide to disband when the dictatorship had ended? Just as they had come together, so they left each other, each to continue on his or her way, taking with them the lessons they had learned from their movement and a firm commitment to human rights, solidarity and justice. They had no vested interests in the organization they had founded, it had offered them no positions of power or security, their friendships did not need it, their feeling of self-worth was not dependent on it. Its time had come; it had served its purpose. They knew how to let go.

Illusory Struggles?

We need to return to the theme of realism. When these movements are accused of being 'unrealistic', their critics are usually referring to the need, as they see it, to guide one's actions – and one's life? – according to what is apparently possible. This is the framework of the whole development scene. Plans are made, outcomes measured and more plans made (which may contradict the first set of plans if these have proved to be unworkable) according to criteria set within a narrow set of analyses, measurable rules and controlled outcomes. There is much talk of thinking 'outside the box', but such thinking is rarely accepted as feasible grounds for action.

Members of movements such as the ones in this chapter are well aware of their relative weakness in the face of the enormous power of those they are trying to influence. Their persistence in acting seemingly against all odds arises from their admission of the limitations of human understanding; from their willingness to acknowledge that 'things that humans deem impossible can happen', as the Chileans say. While using political and economic analysis and the study of history and sociology to help them to form an opinion and build up a strategy, they are not bound by a mindset that leaves no room for the immeasurable ingredients of hope and faith. Their judgment of the 'rightness' of their actions includes pragmatic considerations but is not restricted to them.

The idea that the tiny Christian community in Santiago would be 'leaven in the dough of a great movement against torture' could have seemed illusory, even absurd, to any impartial observer. Nevertheless, together with all the other protest groups, human rights organizations, religious leaders, individual lawyers and politicians of integrity, the movement made an important contribution to awakening the public conscience about the barbarities that were going on. It was part of the groundswell that led to the public denunciation of the violations of human rights committed by the dictatorship in Chile, and eventually to its demise. Furthermore, those who formed part of it are still acting in the same spirit of solidarity and non-violence as leaven in other lumps of dough to change attitudes and policies about the rights of young men to refuse military service, of indigenous people to keep their land and of people all over the world to economic justice.

We could equally well ask whether it was 'realistic' to dream that a small group of nuns and priests and largely illiterate and socially despised fisher people could influence the Indian government's fishery policies, let alone the policies of the World

Trade Organization. Of course, as Tom Kocherry himself says: 'No movement is "pure".'[18] Political and financial interests from outside always encroach, distrust arises and conflicts occur, particularly as fish workers do not all have identical interests even within India, let alone the world over. All the same, in spite of conflicts and difficulties, the fish workers' movement has achieved significant successes and now it has millions of adherents from all over the world.

The group that began with a handful of monks and lay Buddhists in Thailand has likewise grown and become an international network. They acknowledge that there is still 'a lot of work to be done to make their vision more concrete and relevant to the future', but if the dough is well kneaded, the yeast will make it rise!

Strategies of Inclusion

Each of these three movements has worked according to carefully thought-out strategies. The strategy of the Christian community in Santiago was, through seeking alliances and building up a movement, 'to exert influence at a national and international level to lead to a climate of disgust'. The fish workers' strategy has been to mobilize a maximum number of people to protest about specific policies and, with the help of intellectuals and experts, to make proposals for specific changes at a local, national and international level. The Engaged Buddhists are working to bring about change by way of example through small concrete actions as well as by contributing to worldwide debates on development at the highest level.

One of the main strengths of all of them has been their willingness to act together with people of other religions or of no religion at all who in general share their outlook, aims and principles, both by including them within their own movements and by forming alliances with them. As the fish workers' story tells us, this is not only a political strategy in order to gather strength; it is also an acknowledgement that spirituality is not 'owned' by any religious tradition. Is it possible that one day these movements will be remembered for the prophetic spiritual insights that inspired their ways of working just as much as for the social, political and economic transformations that they helped to bring about?

Movements for Freedom

The movements in this chapter inspire people to seek alternative ways of living with creativity and hope that will bring well-being and freedom to all. The theme of freedom arises continually throughout these stories: freedom from economic oppression, freedom from the imposition of an alien culture and consumerist values, freedom from oppressive religious hierarchies and rigid laws, freedom from discrimination and political repression and freedom from prison and torture. But the stories are also about freeing oneself inwardly from a sense of inferiority based on

---

18 Conversation with Tyndale, June 2005.

criteria of wealth and status, from social prejudice (the nuns and priests also shared the *reputation* of the fisherpeople), from false idols within one's own religion and from fear. Buddhadasa Bhikkhu's Garden of Liberation was a symbol of the freedom to be who we really are.

All religious traditions talk about making people free. Sometimes this is difficult to equate with the way that religious institutions exert control and impose burdens on their members but the Buddhist notion of contentment residing in freedom from greed, hatred and delusion is, expressed in other ways, common to all. 'And you shall know the truth, and the truth shall make you free,' says Jesus (John 8:32). The struggle of the fish workers was first inspired above all by the belief that when the Christian gospel speaks of 'good news for the poor' it means setting people free.

It may not be illuminating nowadays to label the interpretation given to Christianity by the erstwhile members of the Sebastián Acevedo Movement or by many of the leading fish workers of Kerala as 'Liberation Theology'. Nevertheless, whatever its name, it is a theology that sees 'development' as the liberation of the poor and the oppressed from structural relationships which serve to perpetuate their poverty and their oppression. The 'exaltation of the humble and the meek' may be concerned with removing power from mighty individuals (Luke 1:52) –among whom one could certainly count Augusto Pinochet, the Chilean dictator – but it has equally to do with changing the way the world is ordered in the interests of the powerful as a whole.

The proponents of this interpretation of the gospel of Jesus Christ believe in the power of God, working through people, to transform the world into a place in which no one is excluded but where everyone is invited to the banquet (Luke 14:12–24). It would thus be contradictory to their deepest held convictions to accept the inevitability, much less the desirability, of an economic model which essentially involves the accumulation of wealth and power in the hands of a few to the exclusion of the large majority. Moreover, they see the destruction of the environment this model has brought with it not only as detrimental to the lives of the poorest people in the world but also as running counter to any idea of respecting the earth entrusted to us by God.

The notion of freedom has influenced the way these movements work as well as their aims. For people to be free, they need to be able fully to participate in decisions that concern them. We hear how Luang Pho Nan has encouraged villagers to carry out their initiatives along the lines of Buddhist principles of participation and democracy, and how the Wongsanit Ashram overcame some painful situations in its determination to work on the same basis.

Despite budgetary limitations, the Engaged Buddhists and the fish workers have both given high priority to training in order to ensure that as many people as possible can participate equally. And, flying in the face of their prevailing cultures – perpetuated partly by their own religious institutions – both movements have also made great efforts to include women in decision-making positions. In fact the International Network of Engaged Buddhists is at present run by a woman. Moreover the way all three movements work through networks gives maximum space for grassroots participation.

Religion and Politics

All the stories in this chapter are about political conflicts with state authorities, but they are also about conflicts within religious institutions. Although their own religious orders have by and large supported the priests and nuns in Kerala, this has not been the case with members of the local church hierarchy who, especially at the beginning, were appalled at the public identification of religious leaders with the fish workers' movement, especially when they began to demonstrate in the streets. The Sebastián Acevedo Movement experienced the same rejection of their 'methods' by the archbishop and other Chilean clergy, who were unwilling to get involved in a highly political (and highly risky) conflict.

Throughout the ages, there has always been a minority of Christians who have taken up the cause of the poor or oppressed against emperors, kings and governors and who have been persecuted by their own Church in consequence.[19] but this has not been generally true of the Buddhist tradition. With its overt and active concern for social justice, the International Network of Engaged Buddhists is to a large extent charting unknown waters and has inevitably aroused suspicion and hostility among many leading Buddhists for doing so, not least because of its critique of the consumerist values that have taken hold in many monasteries.

Diverse political views within the same religious community arise from the different ways in which people understand and live out their spiritual tradition. It is probably true to say that a great many people form their political opinions first and foremost on the basis of their social situation, their experience and the opinions of people who influence them. Only then, if at all, do they attempt to match them up with their religious beliefs. This does not, however, appear to be the case of the people in these stories. Although they are clearly influenced by the social and political conditions of the societies they live in, they allow the vision inspiring their actions to arise from their spirituality rather than squeezing their spirituality into a preconceived political position.

There are many who say that religion and politics should be kept separate, that religion is a purely private matter and that the role of religious people should be limited to doing 'good works' for the relief of suffering. This is problematic in a situation such as the one faced by the Christian community in Santiago where prison visiting, for example, was out of the question. But a much more fundamental problem is the one that Sulak Sivaraksa discerned: that however necessary and virtuous it might be to administer to the poor and the oppressed, to fail to take action to transform their situation brings the danger of avoiding the 'real issues'.

If we acknowledge that religion is part of every aspect of human life, it actually makes no sense to say that it is separate from politics. Indeed, to 'stay out of politics' is just as much a political action as to enter them. It is precisely because religion has to do with the whole of life that religious leaders are so influential. They can,

---

19 See Andrew Bradstock and Christopher Rowland (eds), *Radical Christian Writings* (Oxford, 2002).

as in these stories, inspire people to speak out and take action for those suffering from injustice. But they can also give misguided leadership into religious–political power conflicts or keep silent in the face of the ill-treatment of human beings and the devastation of the environment.

Membership of a religious institution in itself is certainly no guarantee against mistaken judgments or even fanaticism. But is it not here that Buddhist 'mindfulness' comes in? Once again we return to the theme found in so many of these stories of the vital importance of motivation, of detachment, of letting go and of constantly checking what we are doing or failing to do, and how and why we are acting as we are.

We return too to the importance shown by the Muslim women in Chapter 4 of grounding political or social action firmly on the essential principles and values of one's faith tradition. Both Christianity and Buddhism teach us that we are all as intimately related to each other as are the members of one family or the parts of one body. If we ignore the suffering of others, we are not only letting them down but doing harm to ourselves. As the Brazilian theologian Leonardo Boff, quoted in the Chilean story, says: 'The culture of violence dehumanizes us all'.

The violations of the human rights of political prisoners in Chile were evident and grotesquely brutal. Moreover the people responsible for them were identifiable individuals who lived close at hand. Political and economic institutions that deprive human beings of a dignified life may be less visible and seem more distant but they are no less violent than those Chilean torturers.

It is on the grounds of their experience of what is going on in the villages of South-East Asia that the Engaged Buddhists are defending the rights of peasant farmers not to be forced into debt, exploited by loan sharks and driven to live in the cities. And it is the devastation of the economy of their own villages that motivates the members of the National Fish Workers Forum to demand the right of millions of fish workers to keep their traditional livelihoods. In both cases they are coming up with alternative proposals for viable livelihoods based on initiatives such as rice banks, community co-operative shops and savings groups in Thailand and the upgrading of small-scale coastal agriculture in India.

Are these movements and individuals such as Claudio Escóbar, who stood alongside the Pehuenches in their struggle to keep their land, to be dismissed as politically naïve? Should they not be taking a more positive way forward and encouraging people to find their place within the modernized economy of the global market? These questions are being asked again and again, but we should look at what such questions imply.

As Sulak Sivaraksa has often said: the promise of economic prosperity in the future can never justify the prostitution of anyone's daughter in Bangkok today. The Engaged Buddhists are at pains to point out that they are happy to train people to take advantage of the aspects of modernization useful to them, but they would see nothing 'positive' in encouraging people to support policies that mean losing their land, their homes and their livelihoods in order, at best, to swell the mass of underpaid labour that produces cheap goods for export.

The fish workers, the Engaged Buddhists and the former members of the Sebastián Acevedo Movement who now work in solidarity with the economically oppressed are daring to listen attentively to the testimonies of the victims of the structural violence in which we all, in some way, participate. And, on the grounds of the essential principles of their faith, they have made a conscious decision to take political action by speaking out for those whom the world would rather not know about.

Chapter 6

Some Final Reflections

> We are like those who stare into an abyss
> so deep that we cannot find its bottom,
> but who also raise our eyes
> to mountain tops that are unreachable.
> And we stand between them,
> wavering, unsettled and uncommitted.
> *Hildegard of Bingen (1098–1179)*

The stories collected here have been chosen as examples of the contribution spiritual insights and practice can make to the debate about what development consists of and ways in which it can be carried out. As all who have had anything to do with the subject will be very well aware, these examples in no way represent a cross-section of the very many faith-based organizations that are working on 'development' issues. There are many such organizations whose outlook and practice is very little different from that of secular NGOs, while others prioritize a religious agenda that can imply the manipulation of power, proselytism, exclusivity and/or attitudes leading to dependence and passivity. There are plenty of all sorts around!

Nevertheless, even though they do not pretend to prove anything definitive, these stories do raise many questions – questions that warrant serious thought if spiritually inspired organizations such as the ones featured here are to feel assured that 'development' is likely to bring fulfilment to individuals, harmony to communities and flourishing to their natural surroundings. It is hoped that the stories provide some insights, too, into where co-operation can be fruitful between such groups and movements as these and Western NGOs or governmental development agencies. They might also serve to point out what can make such co-operation problematic or even undesirable.

Before reflecting on these issues, however, we should take a closer look at the concepts of 'religion' and 'development' themselves.

Religion and Spirituality

Religion is most commonly understood as a phenomenon embracing a metaphysical, transcendent dimension of life that can be experienced but not seen. But, as the stories show again and again, religion is not to be separated from everyday life. 'We are not meant to live either disembodied, purely spiritual lives, like the angels, or purely physical and sensual lives, like animals and plants; we are meant to inhabit both worlds, both "lower" and "higher", and maintain the flow of energy between them', says the Benedictine monk, Cyprian Smith.[1]

Religion is practised by a community of believers through rituals, symbols and practices that are usually forms of communication with the divine (thanksgiving, petition, penitence), as well as through more contemplative or meditative practices that are means of heightening one's awareness of the presence of God (or of the dimension of the essential self or 'no-self').

Religion can lead to violence or peacemaking, tolerance or exclusiveness, the abuse of power or resistance to the abuse of power.[2] The reasons for these contradictory expressions of religion are highly complex; some explanations may be sociological, others are rooted in what people think religion is, or particularly what religious scriptures really are. Many of the negative manifestations of religion have to do with the use, or abuse, of scriptures, traditions and belief to gain power and control over other people.

Where religious fundamentalism – or rigid adherence to orthodox beliefs and a literal interpretation of creeds and scriptures – arises in the countries of the global South it is often as a reaction against secularization and the processes of economic, political and cultural globalization. In the industrialized North, too, it is usually a defensive response to perceived threats from political and social attitudes. However, fundamentalism is not, of course, an exclusively religious phenomenon. It is not unknown among economists either!

Most religions are anchored in institutions created to give guidance and coherence to the community of believers and to keep the spirit of the religious tradition alive. In the best of cases, their leaders provide a courageous and discerning example of how to live out their faith, even at the cost of their own safety. But religious institutions are human and they have their flaws. Some are caught up in power struggles or are obsessed with their own growth in status, size and wealth, and some even appear to have lost sight of the essential meaning of the tradition they are supposed to represent.

The stories in this book demonstrate again and again that no religion can be monopolized by any single group; nor can any number of repressive laws, dogmas and practices control the irrepressible freedom, creativity and love that is at the heart of every spiritual experience. Spirituality is used here in the sense of the dynamic, life-giving energy that can arise both collectively and individually in connection with a personal quest for the true purpose, meaning or reality of life. It refers to an existential experience that is described in many of the stories as 'personal

---

1   Cyprian Smith, *The Way of Paradox: Spiritual Life as Taught by Meister Eckart* (London, 1987), p. 125.

2   See Ann-Marie Holenstein, *Role and Significance of Religion and Spirituality in Development Co-operation* (Berne, 2005), p. 10.

transformation'. Spiritual experience cannot be counted or measured. It is intuitive rather than rational and is thus difficult – or indeed impossible – to describe through purely rational language. This is why symbolism and poetry are so often the media of religious scriptures and why their interpretation in only literal rational terms leads to their meaning being reduced or even flattened out.

Spirituality is not the same as the religious framework within which people usually (though not necessarily) become aware of it, but without it that framework will become ossified as merely a tradition handed down by our ancestors with no living relation to our lives today. When this happens, all too often religion can become little more than tedious repetition encased in moral laws. Such laws may be oppressive and have a hollow echo to them, as it is not the ordering of society that is the centre of the spiritual search but rather to develop an awareness of our unity with God and with each other and all beings.

It is vital for secular aid agencies (many of whose staff are, of course, deeply spiritual people) to understand the nature of religion if they want to work with faith-based organizations. Attempts intellectually to control the phenomenon by focusing only on its sociological dimension and boxing it into theories such as 'identity politics' or 'clashes of civilization', or even by reducing it to a set of rules that justify social justice, cannot fail to fall wide of the mark. Religion has to do with all dimensions of life. Without the inner dimension, the outer dimension withers or stagnates.

Are all Religions Basically the Same?

If religious traditions are indeed 'deposits: distillations of the cumulative wisdom of the human race',[3] does this mean all religions are? Underneath their differences do they all open the gate to the same shared wisdom?

At one level different religions have common ethical features. In their various ways they all teach the Golden Rule that you should behave to others as you would like them to behave to you, which implies behaving with respect, kindliness, loyalty, non-violence, honesty and so on in relation to other people.

In other regards they have developed differently. One of the key differences with direct relevance to the development debate is the cyclical understanding of the process of life found in Hinduism and Buddhism, referred to in Chapter 1 – an understanding that contrasts to the linear view of the Abrahamic religions (Judaism, Christianity and Islam). Pracha Hutunawatr explains: 'In Buddhism we don't talk about "the First Cause". We see all things as the flow of causes and conditions. No beginning and no ending. Everything changes all the time and there is no solid permanent individual self', though he adds that 'in popular Buddhism there is also

---

3   Huston Smith, 'Is there a Perennial Philosophy?', *Journal of American Academy of Religion* vol. LV, 3, Fall 1987, p. 554, quoted by James Burnell Robinson in Arvind Sharma (ed.), *Fragments of Infinity: Essays in Religion and Philosophy* (Bridport, 1991), p. 218.

a concept of the coming of the era of the future Buddha, "Ariyamettri", the ideal society and ideal human being will be here on earth.'[4]

The teaching of Christianity and other religions is that human history not only had a beginning created by God but also has a point and a direction and is moving towards a culmination or a goal. In the Christian case this is the second coming of Christ or the coming of the Kingdom of God, though there are very many diverse interpretations of the meaning of this. This is but one of the many differences that can be found among the religious traditions – differences that include different conceptions of God or even, in the case of Buddhism, remaining agnostic about the very existence of a personal God.

Nevertheless, as Huston Smith points out,[5] all religions give us glimpses of the fact that reality is much more of an integrated whole than we are able to discern, and also that things are better than we normally perceive them to be through our senses: that in some way that we cannot fully grasp 'all things will be well'. On the other hand all religious traditions attest to the mystery of life, a mystery the human mind will never be able even partially to penetrate unless it is cultivated to the extent that it can perceive things beyond the narrow sense of self as well as beyond the normal sense of perception.

Candomblé and Mayan spirituality (the Awakatán story, see Chapter 2) are included in this book in order to demonstrate that indigenous spirituality is just as influential in many communities as are the religious traditions usually classed as 'world religions'. Indeed, in very many places of the world people practise religions such as Christianity and Islam simultaneously with their own older traditions.

In fact all religions are inherently syncretic, that is they are an amalgamation of their own received wisdom and their own beliefs with those of indigenous cultures, beliefs and spiritual practices as well as with the practices of other religions. Since all religions, too, have a social, political and historical context, the way in which they are practised involves a variety of different influences. This is why the same religions are often interpreted and practised differently, even within the same cultural contexts; and it is one reason for the wide variation of faith-based development programmes referred to above.

Development

What Is Development and What Are Its Aims?

Even when carried out by secular organizations, development is often spoken of as a quasi-religious mission: as the moral duty of the Western industrialized countries to take active steps to help those who are more backward technically (and culturally) to advance along the road of progress, which usually means, at least to some extent, imitating the United States and Europe. Development is thus understood to be the

---

4   Correspondence with Tyndale, September 2005.
5   Huston Smith, *The World's Religions* (New York, 1991), pp. 387–89.

process by which people move from their traditional way of being into 'modernity' and it is grounded on the belief that economic growth is vital to achieve this. The agenda in general terms is rarely justified. It is assumed that everyone in the world wants their societies to be 'developed'.

This agenda contains within it many sub-agendas which may even contradict each other. They include a desire to alleviate the suffering of materially poor people, to remove the causes of civil unrest, mass migration and the spread of disease and also to build up a flourishing world market. When it comes to the details, these sub-agendas can include anything from improving schools and health systems to promoting Western-style democratic governance.

People Deciding for Themselves?

Within the framework of this overall vision of development, there have been many different approaches and today, in some circles at least, there is an increasing emphasis on the need to allow people to make their own decisions about how they want to live. The former Chief Economist of the World Bank, Joseph Stiglitz, talks about development providing people with more control over their own destiny,[6] and the Nobel Prize winning economist, Amartya Sen, and others emphasize development as freedom for people to develop their capabilities 'to lead the kinds of life they value – and have reason to value'.[7] Sen is prepared to accept the possibility that people might not necessarily regard economic development as their first preference. 'If a traditional way of life has to be sacrificed to escape grinding poverty or minuscule longevity', he writes, 'then it is the people directly involved who must have the opportunity to participate in deciding what should be chosen.'[8]

Latterly, in step with the idea of 'development as freedom', an increasing number of organizations, both governmental and non-governmental, have been turning their attention to a rights-based approach to development. Using the UN Declaration on the Right to Development (December 1986) as its guide, this approach sees development as

> a comprehensive economic, social, cultural and political process whose object is the constant improvement of the well-being of the entire population and of all individuals, on the basis of their active, free and meaningful participation in development and in the fair distribution of the resulting benefits. The human rights approach to development is therefore integrated and multidisciplinary.[9]

Despite the theory, however, when it comes to the right to development, it is still not clear that this extends to the right to seek an alternative beyond the concept of a

---

6   Joseph Stiglitz, *Globalization and its Discontents* (London, 2002).

7   Amartya Sen, *Development as Freedom* (Oxford, 1999), p.18.

8   Ibid., p.31.

9   http://www.unhchr.ch/development/approaches-02.html (accessed 26 September 2005).

'modern' society and the free market model. [10] There are still very many examples of aid being given both at government level and at the grassroots with explicit or implicit conditions attached. These include governmental impositions of measures like the privatization of state services such as water; but they can also consist of a more subtle insistence on people adopting certain notions and ways of doing things as though they were the universal norm without regard for – or indeed often in ignorance of – the fact that they may run counter to particular deeply held beliefs, values and practices.

Changes in points of view and ways of doing things can be both desirable and necessary to bring about improvements in people's quality of living. However, unless the right to development is genuinely understood as including the right to find one's own purpose and meaning for life, we are in danger of continuing to witness the development agenda 'transmogrifying people's very perception of change' in order to substitute it with its own. [11] The suspicion still lingers that for many of the larger development agencies, development ultimately means altering what does not fit in well with market globalization so that it will fit in better.

These are crucial issues for debate even in connection with the UN Millennium Development Goals (MDGs), with whose immediate aims of poverty reduction and improvements in education, health and environmental protection few would disagree. But it is the long-term agenda behind them that will invest these quantitative, numerical targets with qualitative content and also determine how they are met. If the MDGs are about achieving the global common good, they must be seen to be driving the macro-economic agenda rather than being merely an instrument to achieve it.

For a long time there has been substantial disagreement among development theorists and practitioners, not all of them from NGOs, about economic issues such as whether the integration of all into competitive global markets should be promoted in preference to selective integration based on local or regional endogenous development, or whether economic growth should take precedence over environmental and social sustainability. But as development ethicists such as Denis Goulet have long been stressing, the way in which development is carried out is equally as crucial as its aims and strategies. Development is, after all, not primarily about allocating resources, upgrading technology or making administrative procedures more efficient. It is far more importantly about attitudes and values, about priorities and about deciding whether the costs of change are worth it.

When he was President of the World Bank, James D. Wolfensohn made many calls for a more inclusive world, and Wolfensohn is not the only one who has often spoken of the need for a change in human consciousness if these goals are to be achieved: 'Ultimately it will be the honesty of introspection that will lead to compassion for

10 See, for example, Yao Graham, 'The Commission Must End the Monoculture of a Single Development Model ... Only if We Stay in the Market', *Guardian* (12 March 2005).

11 Rahnema, Majid, 'A Development Worker's Second Thought: Preparing for the Post-Development Era', *Compass* (Toronto, Nov/Dec 1995).

the Other's experience,' writes UNESCO, 'and it will be compassion that will lead us to a future in which the pursuit of individual freedom will be balanced with a need for common well-being, and in which our agenda includes empathy and respect for the entire spectrum of human differences.'[12]

Western Development NGOs

Since the beginning of the 1990s, worldwide campaigns for more just financial and commercial dealings between the rich nations and the poor ones have been a firm part of the international development agenda of many Western NGOs. As members of the most powerful nations, they are driven by a sense of responsibility to use their position to put pressure on their governments to bring about changes in areas such as terms of trade and debt repayments. And, in alliance with movements from the global South, they have had some successes, both in influencing policy changes on debt relief and trade and in mobilizing public opinion on many issues worldwide.

There are now thousands of groups and movements all over the world that are advocating more environmentally friendly technologies, institutions that work in favour of the poor, a just and responsible distribution of the earth's resources, an end to the monopoly of transnational corporations and so on. These changes 'from the top' are crucially necessary to provide a favourable environment for the poor to be able to take charge of their own lives. However, they are not sufficient in themselves to bring about the kind of social transformation that the people in the stories in this book are striving to achieve.

For this, as we have seen all along, no outside agenda can be imposed. But it is not clear to what extent the growing dependence of Western non-governmental development agencies on government funding, the seemingly inexorable slide of many of them into the managerial 'business' culture and their now more and more openly recognized identity as part of the 'aid industry' is making it difficult for them to pursue a course of development as 'accompaniment' rather than prescription. Despite deep commitment on the part of many of their staff to contributing to changes for the better in a spirit of solidarity and sharing, the non-governmental development agencies seem to be being torn in two directions. Will they be able to resist being drawn in their practice into an increasingly 'de-politicized' process that in the end is designed to achieve goals that have been largely determined by technocratic modes of thought?

---

12 UNESCO, *Our Creative Diversity* (1995), p. 12.

Contributions of Religion and Spirituality to Development

Different Layers of Perception: Different Ways of Comprehending

'Mere logic never moves us on', says the Zen Buddhist, D.T. Suzuki. 'There must be something that transcends the intellect.'[13] Throughout the ages, two ways of 'knowing' have been recognized: the rational and the intuitive. In the stories these two ways of knowing are talked about in terms of 'inner' and 'outer' transformation, in terms of the relationship of the spiritual to the material and in terms of the 'oneness' of everything.

We see the world around us within the bounds of what we presume to be possible. For thinkers trained only in scientific rationalism this is a one-dimensional understanding of terrestrial reality, limited to what can be quantified and 'proved'. But reality has another layer, a world of the spirit or of 'being-itself' which, though not visible, is charged with power and energy. Since rational knowledge depends on abstraction through which reality is reduced to representations that we can easily grasp, it is only through intuitive knowledge that we can glimpse the multidimensional world that is beyond our rational comprehension, a world in which everything is at one, interrelated to everything else.

One of the most important but also most challenging contributions that spiritually inspired movements have to make to development is to remind people of this particular form of intellectual activity that in the post-Enlightenment age we have been inclined to forget. The intuitive or imaginative way of knowing or 'seeing' is as necessary an ingredient of development thinking as is scientific rationality. This way of knowing is not, as the British psychologist Guy Claxton points out, the prerogative of poets or mystics, but is 'accessible, and of value, to anyone':[14]

> As a culture we are … very good at solving analytic and technological problems. The trouble is that we tend, increasingly, to treat all human predicaments as if they were of this type … We meet with cleverness, focus and deliberation those challenges that can only properly be handled with patience, intuition and relaxation.[15]

Yet even the term 'intuitive knowledge' is an inadequate description of the insight of spirituality. For the Jesuit, Bill Ryan:

> the eyes of faith are closer to intuition than to reason but the vision of faith is at a deeper and richer level than intuition. At its best it means a direct experience of God in our lives – seeing and finding God in all things and it leads to commitment and a change of mindset.[16]

---

13 William Barrett (ed.), *Zen Buddhism: Selected Writings of D.T. Suzuki* (New York, 1966), p. 32.

14 Guy Claxton, *Hare Brain, Tortoise Mind* (London, 1997), p. 14.

15 Ibid., p. 6.

16 Correspondence with Tyndale, August 2005.

On the other hand, it is equally true that rational understanding is essential to religion. 'Knowledge is one;' a tenet of Islam tells us, 'only the ignorant have divided it.'[17] This is a focus of a new generation of Muslim scholars with whom 'one leaves the dualistic framework of knowledge where reason is opposed to imagination, history to myth, true to false, good to evil, reason to faith etc' and 'one assumes a plural, changing, welcoming rationality'.[18]

It is only when faith is combined with the practical wisdom of ordinary people that religious traditions are able to make a relevant contribution to life as we are experiencing it in the twenty-first century. 'Truth is not in the clouds nor in absolute universal principles but in the different circumstances of reality itself', says José Aldunate in the story of the Chilean movement against torture (see Chapter 5). In all the stories we see how important the melding of spirituality and common sense is for people who believe that development is about human flourishing in all its dimensions.

So what does all this mean in practice for development? Hanspeter Finger of Swissaid sums it up:

> Although intellectual discipline and expert knowledge remain the foundation for practical action, they are enriched by intuitive knowledge about the limits of the possible and open to a more all-embracing reality. This enables us to act with a combination of efficiency and 'soft' qualities such as patience, wisdom, love and openness. It also puts into perspective the over-powerful orientation towards outcomes from which development co-operation suffers today and by which it is often hindered from doing the right thing in the here and now. Moreover it strengthens our motivation and ability to clear away the slag from our methodological tools. 'Be spiritual – act rationally.'[19]

Understanding Poverty

Since development has to do with creating a good life for people, it is a metaphysical question. All of us, whether we are 'religious' or not, harbour some notions about the meaning of life and death, and these notions directly affect how we understand 'progress' or 'human flourishing' or any other definition we might find for development. They also affect our understanding of what poverty means.

In these stories, people whom development agencies might well describe as 'the poorest of the poor' actually turn out to have a wealth of resources. One of the most important of these is the dignity they gain from the knowledge of their own self-worth which their own culture and spirituality give them. The knowledge of 'who they are' gives them the confidence to get organized, to take on leadership roles, to think up new initiatives and to challenge oppressive power structures.

---

17 Report on a conference on 'Spirituality, Culture and Economic Development' (Quebec, 1995), p. 5.

18 Mohammed Arkoun, 'Penser de l'islam Aujourd'hui', quoted in Rachid Benzine, *Les nouveaux penseurs de l'islam* (Paris, 2004), p. 282 (Author's translation).

19 Holenstein, p. 33.

We see before us the paradox of the wealth of the poor, the power of the powerless and the wisdom of the uneducated. That development agencies have difficulty in apprehending these multiple dimensions of the same reality is borne out by a recent report on indigenous peoples in Latin America written by two development economists from the World Bank. The authors acknowledge that they have been unable to 'reflect the totality of the needs and the values of the indigenous people of Latin America' precisely because they have defined poverty only in quantifiable and material terms, ignoring the cultural and spiritual wealth so highly valued by indigenous people themselves. They claim that this quantitative approach was necessary so that the people responsible for formulating national and international development policies would find it 'familiar and meaningful'.[20] But will this not lead to still more programmes being planned almost exclusively in terms of what people lack or need as seen through the eyes of Western-trained experts?

We have seen that the protagonists of the stories in this book give no hint of an acceptance of destitution and indigence, nor of approval of a world in which a rich minority lives in luxury and a handful of multinational corporations control most of the wealth. Since the groups and movements featured here are working to improve the material situation of impoverished and marginalized people in their countries, they clearly equate poverty with physical deprivation that has to be removed.

But they also equate it with another kind of deprivation that is at the same time a cause of the extreme material impoverishment of such large numbers of people in the world. This poverty is the lack of awareness of the wealth that every human being already possesses. It is the poverty of alienation from who we really are that results in our hectically seeking an identity through 'success' or achievement and through the shallow culture of consumerism, with its emphasis on money, material possessions and the status they bring with them. It is the poverty that comes from emptying our lives of meaning.

Values of Development

Assumptions about the nature of human beings help to shape the values underlying development policies and practice. The view, promoted by some Christian (especially Protestant) theologians – that human beings are intrinsically self-centred and aggressive – has served to justify the supposition of economics that the most rational way to live is in pursuit of private gain.[21] Christian views of the dominance of humankind over nature have also been blamed for justifying the thoughtless destruction of the environment by people for their own profit.

Within Christianity, however, as we see in the stories of Tokombéré, Awakatán, the Indian fish workers and the Sebastián Acevedo Movement, many others emphasize that it is possible for people to open themselves up to their true nature in the image

---

20 Gillette Hall and Harry Anthony Patrinos, *Pueblos Indígenas, Pobreza y Desarrollo Humano en América Latina: 1994–2000* (Washington, 2005), pp. 2–3.

21 See Herman Daly and John Cobb, Jr, *For the Common Good* (Boston, 1990), p. 5.

of God and to change their relationship to others and to their natural environment despite their constant failings. Islam, too, highlights the fundamental goodness of human beings, even though they are prone to 'forgetting' their divine origin. And we see in the Hindu and Buddhist stories how self-knowledge or 'awakening' leads to compassionate behaviour. It is only a firm belief in the possibility of people behaving well towards each other and towards the earth and other living creatures that gives an authentic ring to a call for development policies and processes to be grounded in values such as generosity, kindness, mercy, honesty, respect, justice, restraint and humility.

Basing themselves on this belief, a major contribution that faith-based groups can make to the development debate is to urge that the values embedded in development processes, at the macro- as well as the micro-level, should be made explicit, as they are in the stories in this book. The imbalance of wealth, the existence of people living in misery and the relentless depletion of the earth's resources that the 'development' model seems to have brought about, or at least been unable to prevent, can only be put right by a determination to transform the values underlying it. But, as Amartya Sen points out, these values are seldom, if ever, explicitly addressed in development agencies' plans or evaluations.

Sen emphasizes the importance of making values explicit as a way to democratize the development process. He observes that 'those who prefer a mechanical index, without the need to be explicit about what values are being used and why' complain about this approach. 'But explicitness', he goes on to say, '... is an important asset for a valuation exercise, especially for it to be open to public scrutiny and criticism.'[22]

It is important to differentiate between 'moralizing' and ethics in this context. 'Somehow ethics must get inside the value dynamisms of the instruments utilized by development agents and become, as it were, 'a "means of the means"', says Denis Goulet.[23] We cannot expect to be able successfully to graft a few humanitarian values onto a system which fundamentally undermines them. What is needed is a wholesale reconsideration of the values of the framework into which development programmes and projects are supposed to fit.

Struggles for Structural and Political Change

Many religious organizations all over the world – up to now mostly, but by no means exclusively Christian – have taken part in calls for a change in the values underlying social and economic policies and practices that ignore or are harmful to vulnerable and impoverished people. Government departments and international institutions have been lobbied and picketed and countless rallies and demonstrations have been held. Among the stories in this book we have many examples of groups and movements which have been ready to challenge those in power. One of the most

---

22 Sen, p. 30.

23 Denis Goulet, 'Confronting Social Upheaval' in Thomas. M. McFadden (ed.),· *Theology Confronts a Changing World* (Connecticut, 1977), p. 19.

encouraging features of these activities has been the alliances made between people of many different beliefs and ideologies who all share a common commitment to acting in solidarity with those who have been wronged or abandoned.

Although Buddhism and Hinduism have traditionally focused more on Being rather than Doing, the Vivekananda Girijana Kalyana Kendra (VGKK), Sarvodaya and the International Network of Engaged Buddhists show us that while the concepts of compassion and social justice cannot be equated with each other, they are certainly not contradictory. The people of VGKK do not hesitate to take action to defend the Soligas' land rights in India (and go to prison for it), and the Engaged Buddhists in Thailand have been supporting popular protests at the site of the Pak Moon Dam for years.

In our day pressures to conform to the dominant social values and to put personal interests first are very great. Moreover there are still very many countries in which those who mobilize opposition to unjust laws and practices are in danger of losing their liberty and even their lives. In such situations, people of faith who show courageous leadership or are willing to 'stand up and be counted' alongside others of different religions or none are making an immeasurable contribution to development, that is if development entails ensuring a fair deal for all.

At a Professional Distance?

It is more or less ten years since the academic and development practitioner Robert Chambers first called for more self-questioning among development experts. The primacy of personal actions and non-actions in development, he said, required 'critical self-awareness, thinking through the effects of actions and enabling those with power and wealth to experience being better off with less.'[24] This is not very far removed from the injunctions of Swami Vivekananda by which the VGKK lays so much store.

As things stand, it is usually impossible for practical reasons for development agency or NGO staff to go and live in the communities they are working to support, as the Tokombéré story so strongly recommends (see Chapter 3). But the Agency for Development Co-operation of the Swiss government (SDC) suggests that there is room to analyze whether such busy schedules for the people in charge of programmes are necessary. 'Why do we not take the necessary time?' they ask. 'Why do our travel programmes hinder us from patiently drawing nearer? Has this got to do with quasi-religious value concepts of efficiency-oriented development co-operation?'[25]

It has often been pointed out how difficult it is for development experts to trust as much in the experience of the beneficiaries of their programmes as in their own technical superiority. But then how easy it is to fall into what Tokombéré describes as a 'master–slave' attitude! Getting to know people like the actors of the stories

24 Robert Chambers, Editorial, 'Responsible Well-Being – A Personal Agenda for Development', *World Development*, 25/11 (1997): 1743–44.

25 Holenstein, p. 24.

in this book, who have had little or no formal schooling, is one way to dispel these prejudices. In his latest book, Chambers commends the gradual move among development agencies towards closer personal contact between their staff and the people they wish to help. 'The testimonies of those who have lived, however briefly, with poor and marginalized hosts indicate how this can be a source of deeper change and, some would say, transformation', he writes. And he goes on to comment that personal meetings can not only give us new insights but also challenge our values and beliefs and even 'raise questions about the sort of people we are and want to be, and what we do'.[26]

The SDC urges people responsible for projects to become more aware of the mental and spiritual ideas of the beneficiaries and to integrate them into co-operation projects. But they are aware of the risks too. '... how do we do this without instrumentalising religion and spirituality and diverting them from their real purpose for the sake of our programme objectives?' they ask.[27]

It is not only secular agencies that are open to the danger of 'harnessing' religious beliefs and values in order to promote their agenda and mobilize local people's support for it. It is even easier for faith-based NGOs, whether consciously or not, to 'match' the beliefs of a local community of the same religious tradition with the agenda they wish to impose. A search through the Bible or the Qur'an will provide them with an abundant supply of texts that meet almost any purpose! As a way of trying to avoid this sort of manipulation, the SDC suggests that 'The question: What nourishes your soul? What nourishes us? can be helpful. Needs assessments should not only take material needs into consideration but also consider the interests and needs of the soul.'[28]

Paradoxically, this more personal approach might well lead to the 'detachment' from the results of our labour that the VGKK calls for. This does not, of course, mean irresponsible nonchalance about the outcome of what we do but of looking carefully at our motivation and trying not to equate our own ego with success or failure. We would all do well to learn here from the more contemplative religious traditions that it is not a 'waste of time' to stop our incessant activity for a while in order to try to get to know ourselves a little better – a challenging but not necessarily uninteresting pursuit!

Modernity

'Modern man has burned his hands in the fire which he himself kindled when he allowed himself to forget who he is.'[29] The attitude to modernization of many faith-based groups working at the grassroots is, at best, ambivalent. Even though they have incorporated many aspects of 'modernity', such as equal opportunities for

26 Chambers, *Ideas for Development* (London, 2005), p. 181.
27 Holenstein, p. 24.
28 Ibid.
29 Seyyed Hossein Nasr, *Islam and the Plight of Modern Man* (Cambridge, 2002), p. 4.

women, into their own cultures, their experience of modernization as brought by the globalization of the market, the media and communications systems has all too often been a negative one: the depletion of their coastal fishing grounds, the destruction of their habitat in forests, the use of more and more land to grow export crops rather than local food, and the mass migration of youth, either lured or driven into city slums. And, as the story of the Engaged Buddhists points out (see Chapter 5), it has meant Western culture taking over with its consumerism and technological progress and its self-proclaimed superiority.

Small wonder that the education programmes of VGKK and Tokombéré include the aim of rooting tribal people firmly in their own culture so that they will be able to use their own principles to evaluate the modernity that has come to be equated with Westernization! And yet – the Swadhyayee fisher people are diversifying their activities and even running cybercafés, the people of Tokombéré are learning to eat new kinds of food and are introducing modern forms of transport and farming methods; the Barli Institute in India has a highly up to date solar powered energy supply and the women of Nahdlatul Ulama in Indonesia are using modern family planning techniques.

We return to the point that it is not modern technology and science in themselves that are the problem. The crisis is a spiritual one. Science and technology will only help humankind to flourish if they are consciously used to promote the all-round development of the individual, social harmony and care of the environment. But modernity seems to have no time to build upon the accumulated wisdom of the ages.

Religious groups and movements such as the ones in these stories are opening themselves up to opportunities offered by modernization while resisting the ideology of the globalized market that is out to destroy all traditions, thought patterns and ways of life that are an obstacle to its relentless penetration of every corner of the world. By doing so, are the people of these groups proving themselves to be more 'enlightened' than the children of the European Enlightenment, now trapped in 'totalitarian rationalism'[30] and blind to wisdom? 'Modernity may end up being devoured by the inflexible, inhuman logic of its own creations', says José Casanova. 'It would be profoundly ironic if ... religion could somehow unintentionally help modernity to save itself.'[31]

Views of Development Agencies

Grounds for Ignoring Religion in Development

Until very recently only the Western development agencies with religious connections themselves have focused their attention on Southern religious organizations working on development. The secular agencies' reluctance to relate to religious groups can

---

30 Ibid., p. 16.
31 José Casanova, *Public Religions in the Modern World* (Chicago, 1994), p. 234.

be accounted for partly by the still widely held view that development is above all a scientific discipline based on economics, technology and the social and political sciences. Seen from this standpoint, religion, which many regard as a private affair anyway, has little or nothing to contribute and will in any case become progressively less relevant as modernity advances.

Indeed, if religion has been considered at all, it has been as part of the problem rather than the solution. Among mainstream development agencies, religious institutions and groups are not uncommonly regarded as a divisive rather than a cohesive force – irrational and given to fanaticism, intrinsically hostile to modernization, or indeed change of any sort, inimical to women's rights, fatalistic, deeply anti-democratic and a severe menace when they enter the political arena. There is, of course, no lack of examples in every country of the world to give backing to those who hold such views, though many of these attributes and types of behaviour often have as much to do with culture as with religion.

If the social and political philosopher, Govert Buijs, is right, another of the underlying reasons why Western development workers have so consistently overlooked religion is because religion and spirituality seem to lie beyond the sphere of influence of development interventions. Referring to the 'utterly unmanageable' nature of religion, Buijs sees the central issue as being 'the paradox of religious change: for religions can and do change and yet, they cannot be "tailored"'.[32] In other words it is improbable that outside agents will be able to bring about the changes in religious institutions that they perceive to be necessary for development to take place.

At a more personal level, development experts may fear that they will be drawn into 'unscientific' debates about sensitive issues such as family planning or the prohibition of work on holy days which they do not know how to handle. The sociologist Kurt Alan Ver Beek suggests that many experts avoid the issue of religion out of 'respect' for the local culture and a fear of imposing their views. However Ver Beek sees a 'certain degree of condescension implicit in withholding what one believes to be a superior understanding of reality so as not to offend or impose'[33]. His argument is taken up by the SDC: 'The dialogue fails to take place', they write, 'but there is also an unspoken conviction that science and development will in the end persuade the people to leave their unscientific perceptions behind.'[34]

It is encouraging that in the midst of all these difficulties there are government agencies that are calling upon their staff to try to draw nearer to the culture and spirituality of those they are claiming to help. 'As staff in charge of programmes we should again and again have the possibility of immersing ourselves in the reality of

---

32 Govert J. Buijs, 'Religion and Development' in Oscar Salemink, Anton van Harskamp and Ananta Kumar Giri (eds), *The Development of Religion/The Religion of Development* (Delft, 2004), pp. 106–7.

33 Kurt Alan Ver Beek, 'Spirituality: a Development Taboo' in Eade (ed.) *Development and Culture* (Oxford, 2002), pp. 71–2.

34 Holenstein, p. 20.

the lives of the actors/beneficiaries, of taking part in rituals and of trying to understand their farming and eating culture with its material and spiritual dimensions', suggests the SDC.[35]

What Hopes for a Rapprochement?

Why are secular development institutions now beginning to take steps to build up relationships with both religious leaders and religious communities/faith-based NGOs that are working with the poor? In addition to the World Faiths Development Dialogue, the United Nations Population Fund (UNFPA) has been co-operating for some time with religious leaders in Senegal and various other countries in Africa; UNESCO and, more recently, the Commonwealth Foundation, have shown interest in gathering together inter-religious advisory groups; the International Labour Organization regularly consults religious leaders on work ethics; the Inter-American Development Bank has held various consultations about ethics with Jewish and Christian leaders in many Latin American countries and the UK government's Department for International Development (DFID) has commissioned a five-year study on religion and development. Moreover development NGOs such as Oxfam now have relationships with religious leaders and groups on their agenda, and since its meeting in Porto Alegre, Brazil in 2003, spirituality has been a theme at meetings of the World Social Forum.

The reasons for this unprecedented interest are numerous and complex and the same reasons are not, of course, shared by all development bodies. One set of reasons, underlined by the Israeli-Palestinian conflict as well as the attacks on the twin towers in New York and subsequent acts of terrorism in European cities, has to do with the political need to address the risk of terrorist movements gathering support among economically underprivileged Muslim communities.

At another level the search for partnerships with religious groups is the result of the realization by both multilateral and bilateral government agencies, as well as the NGO sector, that they need to work jointly with other organizations to achieve the reduction of poverty that is their aim. Although some highly worthwhile advances have been made, in the fields of health and education for instance, despite the effort and resources dedicated to it, the development process up to now has been marked by many failures: UN goals not met, billions of dollars wasted, unfinished or abandoned projects of all types and sizes strewn all over the planet and strategies constantly falling apart and having to be 're-thought'. For a long time now, realizing the need for different approaches, government development agencies have been seeking co-operation from academic institutions, NGOs and the private sector and NGOs too have sought partnerships with government authorities and private bodies, so the addition of the religious sector could seem merely like a logical extension of the list.

---

35 Ibid., p. 24.

Some agencies, such as the Inter-American Development Bank (IDB), have approached religious leaders to try to win the backing of their moral authority: in the case of the IDB for its campaign in Latin America against corruption. Since most world political leaders are also members of a religious community, religious institutions have an important role to play here. However, in general it is probably true to say that development agencies are hoping above all that collaboration with religious bodies will be a way of making their programmes more effective at grassroots level, with a particular focus on the UN's Millennium Development Goals (MDGs).

Development agencies, including NGOs in the South, are aware that it is difficult for outside development workers to achieve the same kind of intimate relations with grassroots communities that many faith-based groups enjoy. This is because the latter are *part* of the communities, they belong there, live there and they do not move on. The support of the local priest, monk or nun, imam or swami for a development programme is often the key to ensuring people's full co-operation with it. Conversely, if religious leaders oppose a plan, it can mean that it is never given a chance to work.

Since the adherents of all religions gather for worship and other rituals, in many cases as often as once a week, their leaders have a unique opportunity to communicate with large numbers of people on a regular basis. They can use these opportunities to inform people about the dangers of HIV and AIDS or to encourage them to go to literacy classes just as well as to exhort them to avoid or even to protest against development schemes whose values seem to be opposed to those of the religious tradition in question. Moreover the far-reaching local, regional and international networks of all faith-based communities allow information and guidance to spread well beyond the gathering in a particular temple, church or mosque.

In countries suffering under repressive governments, it is also the case that religious bodies are sometimes the only functioning part of civil society where people are able to meet and discuss together. This has been the case under Latin American dictatorships and in the Philippines for instance. In this role, religious organizations can be valuable partners in helping to encourage participation and create a democratic culture.

With the MDGs in view, however, it is towards religious communities as the deliverers of social services that development agencies feel most drawn in their efforts for dialogue and co-operation. Religious institutions run innumerable hospitals, clinics, health programmes, schools, universities and kindergartens the world over. The fact that most of them have never heard of the MDGs does not mean that they are not making a significant contribution to achieving them. A study called 'Working for God?' published by the World Bank in 2003,[36] concludes that religious non-profit organizations working on primary health care in Uganda provide a better quality of care and charge less for it than other non-governmental and state institutions working

---

36 Ritva Reinikka and Jakob Svensson, *Working for God? Evaluating Service Delivery of Religious Not-for-Profit Health Care Providers in Uganda* (Washington, 2003).

in the same field. Countless more examples of the same phenomenon could be cited, among them VGKK, Tokombéré and Nahdlatul Ulama.

Nevertheless, development agencies will encounter serious difficulties if they are tempted merely to regard faith-based organizations as the providers of cheap, good-quality services, disregarding the fact that they have an agenda of their own. We have seen this in the case of the co-operative and AIDS prevention programmes run by Sarkan Zoumountsi and in Nahdlatul Ulama's concept of family planning. Can development agencies use religions as a source rather than merely a resource? Do they really want to enter into the kind of dialogue that raises very different ideas about development? Some do.

Within many agencies there is an increasing awareness that when development projects fail to resonate with the religious beliefs (and cultural attitudes) of the would-be beneficiaries, their chance of success is greatly reduced. This has been experienced in cases such as Mayan parents in Guatemala refusing to send their children to schools whose values are alien to their own world view, or Haitians rejecting modern medicine in favour of traditional healers who treat their patients as spiritual as well as physical beings.

To ignore the spiritual dimension of life is to ignore the main driving force of many of the materially poorest people in the world. It is to ignore the logic behind their agricultural practices, the strength of their bonds to certain places, the importance they give to their community, and their relation to nature. As James Wolfensohn said when he was President of the World Bank: 'Over and over again, we have found that when we ignore the way of life of the poor, their values, relationships and culture, we cannot improve even their material condition.'[37]

Challenges for Working Together

'Different Worlds'

However strongly motivated they are and however open their attitude, development agencies that want to enter into a relationship of co-operation with faith-based organizations will inevitably encounter some serious obstacles. In many respects, in our age which is still so strongly influenced by Cartesian dualism, the widely held view that religion and development belong to 'two different worlds' is all too real.

One of the reasons for this is the difficulty of communication. There have been many occasions on which people from faith-based communities have felt unable to take full advantage of opportunities to voice their opinions, whether at formal meetings on issues relating to their government's policies or in conversations with individual development workers. Sometimes this is because experts make little effort to make jargon-filled technical discussions comprehensible, but equally as often it

---

37 Martin Brown, Joan (Task Manager), *Culture Counts: Financing, Resources and the Economics of Culture in Sustainable Development*, Proceedings of the Conference in Florence, 1999 (Washington, 2000), p. 11.

may be because the same experts simply cannot see how what they are hearing from faith-based organizations has anything to do with 'development' as they know it.

This is not just a question of the use of language but of concepts, logic and ways of perceiving reality. Katherine Marshall and Lucy Keough of the World Bank tackle a major problem arising from such a difference in understanding when they ask: 'How can development agencies and governments constructively integrate faith groups' perspectives on "poverty reduction" into their programs and polices, when many faith groups do not view poverty reduction as the central question in the creation of more fulfilling, sustainable lifestyles?' '... Without a clear consensus about the causes and nature of poverty,' they observe, 'it is hardly surprising that there is less agreement still about what should be done about it and by whom.'[38]

Many on the religious side would agree with the Indian social activist, Swami Agnivesh, who sees the blockage as lying in the resistance of the 'secular material discourse' to a required paradigm shift.[39] But such a shift is far from easy to bring about. If it were to incorporate elements such as the Buddhist view that personal fulfilment is equated with contentment rather than material wealth, Jewish and Islamic views that the very meaning of 'charity' (or aid) incorporates social justice or the means to set to right the causes of people's poverty and Christian insights into the real meaning of poverty and of power and powerlessness, the whole development agenda would be radically changed, if not turned upside down. Such radical aspirations seem to many committed development workers hopelessly idealistic, but to harbour them does not mean being incapable or unwilling to get on with the job in hand and work on poverty reduction within the limitations imposed upon us by the historical context in which we find ourselves.

There are others who regard coercion as the only realistic way of setting the world to rights. The idea that spirituality might have the power to embrace and 'awaken' those with power to a new way of understanding the reality of the world and their role in it seems to them misguided. This may reflect the state of the religious institutions, each of which claims the membership of very many of the richest and most powerful people of our time. But such scepticism may be founded, too, on the misconception that those who believe that a spiritual 'awakening' of the powerful is possible shun all forms of confrontation. Our stories show that this is not the case.

Inadequate Development Theories and Strategies?

Those who are looking for the possibility of partnerships between development agencies and faith-based organizations face problems of a different kind as well. These concern the way in which the latter carry out that very part of their work that falls within the remit of 'development' as it is commonly understood.

---

38 Katherine Marshall and Lucy Keough, *Mind, Heart and Soul in the Fight against Poverty* (Washington, 2004), pp. 23 and 15.

39 Swami Agnivesh, 'Religious Conscience and the Global Economy' in Paul F. Knitter and Chandra Muzaffar (eds), *Subverting Greed* (New York, 2002), p. 51.

In Chapters 1 and 2, references have already been made to criticisms levelled at faith-based groups: on the one hand about their lack of effort to fit their projects and programmes into any regional, let alone national development plans, and on the other for being too small and local ever to make a real difference. Not only the story of Sarvodaya, but also VGKK and Nahdlatul Ulama tell us that it is not necessarily the case at all that faith-based organisations ignore government development programmes; but they also highlight why co-operation with governments is often not easy and indeed why it is sometimes impossible.

As for programmes being too small, we saw how, if 'scaling up' were undertaken as a result of outside pressure, it might end in changing the very identity of some grassroots communities. The options of scaling up and replicating small faith-based programmes should be positively considered but sensitivity will be required if the scope of the work is to be increased without some of its essential qualities being lost.

It is often said, too, that, lacking any development theory of their own, faith-based organizations merely follow the latest trends of secular agencies and NGOs (which implies that they have no clear vision or strategy). This is certainly true in some cases (and it is true of very many secular NGOs as well!). But the criticism puts religious groups into a no-win situation, as most of the problems for the development agencies actually tend to arise in the areas in which faith-based organizations' vision and strategy differ from their own.

David Korten suggests that a development theory implies making 'explicit assumptions about the forces that maintain the problems being addressed' and about the vulnerable points of the system at which 'intervention will create a new and more desirable equilibrium of forces.'[40] We are thus concerned with theories about what causes change.

Most of the groups described in this book would subscribe to one or several of the development theories described by Korten as belonging to different 'generations' of NGOs. They would agree that an outside change agent can help a community to realize its dormant potential through education, awareness raising, small loans and simple new technologies; some of them seek to change specific policies at a local, regional or national level; and some, such as the Engaged Buddhists and the National Forum of Fish Workers, are movements for global change. Since faith-based organizations and secular NGOs are, after all, living in the same world, these overlaps should be reassuring!

Nevertheless, as we have seen, the groups and movements in these stories have a more all-embracing view, since their theories about change do not only concern outward, social but also inner and personal transformation. Moreover, though many of the policies on which they focus and the strategies they pursue to achieve their goals are the same as those of secular NGOs, initiatives such as the Addis Ababa Muslim Women's Council (AAMWC) seeking to reform the Sharia courts rather

---

40 David C. Korten, *Getting to the 21ˢᵗ Century: Voluntary Action and the Global Agenda* (Bloomfield, 1990), p. 113.

than to abolish them point to differences in motivation. And while the analysis of the current development model made by the Network of Engaged Buddhists is not dissimilar to that of many secular NGOs, the reasoning behind it is different.

One of the areas in which development agencies' theory of what brings about change differs most radically from that of many faith-based organizations is the area of family planning and the prevention of HIV and AIDS. Highly complex issues are involved here.

On the one hand, there are Christians, Muslims, Hindus and Buddhists who view the distribution of condoms as a purely pragmatic and even simplistic solution that will achieve little apart from the degeneration of family life and social mores. In the eyes of many of these people, the leaders of Sarkan Zoumountsi among them, the principle change needed is a cultural one, a change in the way that men regard women and relate to them, and often a concomitant change in the attitudes of women themselves. Their main problem is that in many cases their own religious institutions – institutions that have more influence over these matters than any others – have done and are still doing little or nothing to help.

At the same time there are many religious leaders who work closely with materially poor communities, who are already advocating the use of condoms to stop the spread of HIV and AIDS. Their reasoning is that this is a measure to prevent death against which there are no sound theological arguments.

There are yet other religious leaders who allow the use of condoms and other forms of artificial birth control, not only to combat AIDS but also to protect women from giving birth year after year and families from having more children than they can feed. These are people who may well be continuing to work for a change of attitude in their religious institutions as well, but who feel that the crisis warrants the use of all measures that might make even a partial contribution towards solving it. This is the approach of many of the 'kyai' of Nadhdlatul Ulama and it is probably the one that is nearest to that of most development agencies.

It is not a question here of saying who is right or wrong. However, it is worth noting that if it is true that religious institutions can only be changed from within, the work of their members to overcome the entrenched views about the inferiority of women that are to be found in the institutions of all the major world religions should not be undervalued. A change in the attitudes of religious leaders could be the single change most needed in order to put an end to the sexual exploitation that is a major contributor to the AIDS epidemic, to untrammelled population growth, to prostitution and the trading of women on such a huge scale, to domestic violence and to women being deprived of education as well as of influence in public life.

Evaluation

Religiously inspired groups are often criticized by development agencies too – and perhaps this is the most serious criticism of all – on the grounds that a great deal of their work (not only in the area of AIDS prevention and population control) is suspected of being largely ineffectual. Marshall and Keough grasp this nettle: 'A principle difficulty of these initiatives is weak evaluation with practitioners hard-pressed to "show results"', they write. 'Progress on this front will be indispensable to making the initiatives more broadly appealing and to clarifying their strengths and weaknesses'.[41]

At the WFDD/VSF workshop in 2004 to which various references have already been made, people from the groups described in this book discussed the topic of evaluation at some length. They felt strongly that it was undesirable to create a dichotomy between faith-based and secular groups working on development issues; but they recognized that, given the different visions of what 'development' consists of, the criteria used for assessing success would not necessarily be identical.

There was general agreement on the prime importance of evaluating sustainability from the point of view of continuing life: 'God has given us this world where people, animals and insects live. Our criteria should be life-based and based on life for future generations as well as for our own. Sustainability is vital and so the irresponsible exploitation of resources and greed are unacceptable', said one participant. But it was recognized that within this overall criterion, it was not easy to find ways of evaluating specific aspects of their work.

Many questions arose about the extent to which faith-based organizations should mesh their education, health and other work into existing systems, and how widespread the results of their work needed to be in order to constitute success. While rejecting a passive acceptance of the criteria of outside evaluators – 'Evaluations are often a question of putting people's feet into shoes other people make for them' – they considered indicators such as the United Nations Development Programme's deprivation measures and gender disparity measures potentially useful tools.

The participants recognized the need for quantitative evaluations and critical assessments but rejected numbers, particularly as aggregates, and quantitative criteria on their own as an indication of development. The crunch question was whether faith-based movements could come up with any complementary or alternative criteria. In spite of efforts being made by various groups, there is still no clear answer to questions such as how we measure the transformation of human relationships, for example.

A final conclusion implicitly rejected the idea that evaluation of development work should be carried out according to predetermined decisions about what the results should be. This reflects the belief that development workers should do their best while realizing that they cannot totally control the outcome of their efforts: 'We can do results related assessments but the work of spiritual movements can have many aspects and it is difficult to plan and quantify the results. We should do the best we can and the results will come,' they said; but they did add that they needed criteria to measure the quality of what they were doing. There is clearly room for a lot more work to be done on the area of evaluation in the future!

---

41 Marshall and Keough, *Mind, Heart and Soul*, p. 10.

Partnerships

Although the challenges for secular development agencies that are seeking co-operation among faith-based communities, groups, movements and NGOs are multiple, broad areas of agreement can be found and partnerships are possible: indeed many such partnerships have already been in existence for some time and have often been found to be enriching for both sides. These are mostly with NGOs, but individual governments and the World Bank have also given support to various religious organizations. However, Marshall and Keough are well aware that such partnerships, however rich, do not mean that the 'many layers of misunderstanding, differing perceptions and outright disagreements over development priorities and work that have separated faith and development institutions' have been dissolved.[42]

Dialogue Must Take Place, But How?

Dialogue has been described as 'the embracing of different points of view – literally the art of thinking together.'[43] A prerequisite for such a process is the acceptance by people from mainstream development agencies that while a largely economistic, analytic, technical approach to development makes a vital contribution, in the eyes of most people in the world it is not in itself sufficient to bring about human fulfilment. For some development workers it may be quite natural to move from acknowledging this to taking seriously the prime importance of religion in the lives and work of people such as the actors in these stories. However, others, especially those from the increasingly secular cultures of many of the European countries, may find that such a move raises more questions than it answers.

Is all this not an illusion? What are the people in the stories in this book really talking about? What do Allah or God or the Enchanted Ones stand for in psychological terms? Are the inspiration and commitment of these people any different from the inspiration and commitment of dedicated activists to any cause? Some might even be tempted to dismiss the idea of people drawing power from a spiritual source as a result of poverty and lack of education – a sign that they have not yet entered the modern world. Why can't they just stick to the more rational explanation that they are humanly moved by the plight of the people around them? There are plenty of people who toil day and night in the service of others who do not seem to have the need to call upon a deity or to become aware of any spirituality in the depth of their being (and there are plenty of people who declare themselves to be religious who do nothing to serve others).

Such questions probably go through everyone's mind at one time or another but they leave out the other half of the argument. It could equally well be asked why so many people are content to reduce the reality of life merely to what can be proved,

---

42 Ibid., pp. 2–3.

43 William Isaacs, quoted in Joan Anderson, 'Successful Dialogue', *Soka Gakkai International Quqrterly Review* (2002): 1.

counted, measured and perceived by the senses, or why people deny themselves the inner regeneration that is a source of freedom and spontaneous action, of equanimity when things 'go wrong' and of energy to overcome exhaustion and disillusionment. 'The sense of the sacred leads to letting go and regaining strength', says Thierry Verhelst, who also alleges that, on his death bed, Vladimir Lenin is purported to have said 'What was lacking in our revolution was a Francis of Assisi'![44]

The opening of a dialogue depends, then, on genuine acceptance that the others' starting point for the way they live and thus their vision of the nature of development may be very different from one's own. It depends too, says the Swiss Agency for Development Co-operation, on each side making clear where they stand on the topic so that the rest of the conversation can take place in a comprehensible context.[45] Only then will religion and spirituality take their rightful place as important elements of the discussion rather than merely being tolerated or ignored by the mainstream as long as they do not get in the way of 'good' development practice.

It is only then, too, that sufficient understanding and openness will be generated for constructive discussions on the most sensitive of issues such as gender roles and the use of contraceptives. If a dialogue is truly open and understanding is shown for different strategies arising from different beliefs and values, dialogue can help the process of change in a way that the imposition of outside criteria never will.

The agenda of faith-based groups and movements will always be different in some respects from that of secular development agencies, but there are large overlapping areas where both sides can learn a great deal from the experience of the other. Dialogue is probably most fruitful when it is carried out in the context of specific programmes or plans, preferably in the place of action. This allows for conversations and debates about what is most important to the people whom development programmes will affect most directly. But dialogue requires time if it is to provide a space for a real exchange of ideas and learning on either side.

At the other end of the dialogue spectrum are round-table discussions held between the leaders of religious institutions and development agencies. There is certainly a place for these. It is important that decision-makers and people with influence at the highest level should listen to each other in order to reconsider where they stand. However, the risk of regularly held international gatherings is that they may start to be regarded as an end in themselves.

At whatever level, dialogue isn't easy. Perhaps if it were, it would not be so necessary. But experience shows that it can be a very enriching (as well as frustrating) experience. Probably the most encouraging thought to bear in mind is that no one can fully predict what forces genuine dialogue might unleash or how it might result in unexpected ways of bringing about long-term changes.

---

44 Thierry Verhelst and Patrice Sauvage, *Ailes et Racines* (Nantes, 2001) pp. 23–5.
45 Holenstein, p. 26.

Beyond Pragmatism

In our world today hundreds of millions of people go to bed hungry every night, more than 10 million children die each year from largely preventable causes, nearly 40 million people, including 2 million children are living with HIV/AIDS, over a billion people lack clean water, more than 3 billion lack access to sanitation, at least 100 million children of primary school age do not attend school. In addition to this human suffering, forests are shrinking, water sources are drying up, the air is becoming increasingly polluted and climate change is causing more and more havoc.[46]

In such a situation we need economists, scientists, technicians, development planners, environmentalists and so on to help to solve the problems; but we also need prophets – people who have the insight that enables them to read the 'signs of the times', people who have the courage to speak out on the side of the oppressed. Although strictly speaking the prophetic tradition belongs to the Abrahamic religions, we can find plenty of 'prophets' among the actors of all our stories.

It is because of their insights and their commitment to those who suffer that the people in these stories act in unconventional ways: breaking with their church in order to serve families torn apart by war in Guatemala; recognizing the value and ingenuity of despised tribal people in Cameroon and India; opposing the widely welcomed consumer culture in Thailand; demonstrating in front of torture centres in Chile and re-reading the Qur'an in a different light to find out what it says about women. They see opportunities opening up through their spirituality: opportunities for equality in caste-ridden India through the notion of the indwelling God; opportunities to include husbands and fathers in new ways of looking at family power-relations in Madhya Pradesh; and opportunities to transform a horrible government birth-control programme into a family welfare scheme in Indonesia.

Their hope and their faith empower the people in these stories to act without calculating what the results of their action will be. This does not mean that they refuse to plan in a rational way or to use tools such as market research, but rather that they are free to pursue their work as an open-ended endeavour, guided by deep ties of solidarity with those in need. They do not stand back with an 'objective' view, weighing up the pros and cons; they take sides and find out what is practicable along the way. Their way is not to tweak situations at the edges but to try to inaugurate new patterns of human relationships and behaviour.

Spiritual motivation is not the only kind of motivation that leads people to take risks and inspires them with the kind of hope that leads to innovation, but it seems that true spiritual motivation must necessarily be a radical force. Compassion is a radical form of criticism because it means that suffering must be taken seriously.[47] Hope is a radical discernment of what can be done if there is the will to do it. The message of these movements – a message given by their example – challenges all who have

---

46 http://www.millenniumdevelopmentgoals.org (accessed 20 September 2004).

47 See Walter Brueggeman, *The Prophetic Imagination* (Minneapolis, 2001), p. 88

become attached to the way things are, to the safety of theoretical frameworks or to exterior forms of values, culture or religious observation whose content has long since decayed. It is a message of thorough-going personal, institutional and social transformation.

References and Further Reading

`Abdu'l-Bahá, *Paris Talks* (London: Bahá'í Publishing Trust, 11th edn, 1972).

`Abdu'l-Bahá, *Japan Will Turn Ablaze: Tablets of `Abdu'l-Bahá, Letters of Shoghi Effendi and Historical Notes About Japan* (Osaka: Bahá'í Publishing Trust, 1974).

`Abdu'l-Bahá, *Promulgation of Universal Peace* (Wilmette, IL: Bahá'í Publishing Trust, 1982).

Agnivesh, Swami, *Religion, Spirituality and Social Action* (India: Hope, 2001).

Ahmed, Durre S. (ed.), *Gendering the Spirit: Women, Religion and the Post-Colonial Response* (London/New York: Zed Books, 2002).

Aldunate Lyon, José et al., *Crónicas de una Iglesia Liberadora* (Santiago de Chile: LOM Ediciones, 2000).

Alkire, Sabina, *Valuing Freedoms* (Oxford: Oxford University Press, 2005).

Alkire, Sabina and Newell, Edmund, *What Can One Person Do? Faith to Heal a Broken World?* (London: Darton, Longman and Todd, 2005).

Anderson, Joan, 'Successful Dialogue', *Soka Gakkai International [SGI] Quarterly Review* (Tokyo: Soka Gakkai International, 2002): 1.

Armstrong, Karen, *The Battle for God: Fundamentalism in Judaism, Christianity and Islam* (London: HarperCollins, 2000).

Aurobindo, Sri, *The Future Evolution of Man* (Pondicherry: Sri Aurobindo Ashram, 1995).

Bahá'u'lláh, *Gleanings from the Writings of* Bahá'u'lláh (Wilmette, IL: *Bahá'í Publishing Trust,* 1976).

Balchin, C., 'With her Feet on the Ground: Women, Religion and Development in Muslim Communities' in *Development*, 46/4 (London: Sage Publications, December 2003): 39–49.

Barber, Benjamin R., *Jihad vs. McWorld* (New York: Ballantine Books, 1996).

Barrett, William (ed.), *Zen Buddhism: Selected Writings of D.T. Suzuki* (New York: Doubleday, 1966 [repr. 1996]).

Baskouda, J.B., *Baba Simon, le Père des Kirdis* (Paris: Le Cerf, 1988).

Bell, Daniel, 'The Return of the Sacred?', *British Journal of Sociology*, 28/4 (December 1977): 419–48.

Benzine, Rachid, *Les Nouveaux Penseurs d'islam* (Paris: Albin Michel, 2004).

Bond, George D., *Buddhism at Work* (Bloomfield, CT: Kumarian Press, 2004).

Bradstock, Andrew and Rowland, Christopher (eds), *Radical Christian Writings: A Reader* (Oxford: Blackwell, 2002).

Brueggeman, Walter, *The Prophetic Imagination* (Minneapolis: Fortress Press, 2001).

Buddhadasa Bhikkhu, *Dhammic Socialism* (Bangkok: Thai Inter-Religious Commission for Development, 1993).

Camilleri, Joseph A. and Muzaffar, Chandra (eds), *Globalisation: The Perspectives and Experiences of the Religious Traditions of Asia Pacific* (Petaling Jaya: International Movement for a Just World, 1998).

Capra, Fritjof, *The Tao of Physics* (London: Flamingo, 1982).

Casanova, José, *Public Religions in the Modern World* (Chicago: University of Chicago, 1994).

Chambers, Robert, *Whose Reality Counts? Putting the First Last* (London: Intermediate Technology Publications, 1997).

Chambers, Robert, Editorial, 'Responsible Well-Being – A Personal Agenda for Development', *World Development*, 25/11 (Oxford: Pergamon Press, 1997): 1743–44.

Chambers, Robert, *Ideas for Development* (London • Stirling, VA: Earthscan, 2005).

Chaplin, Ann, *Metodología para la Medición de Impacto de Trabajos que Buscan el Fortalecimiento de la Sociedad Civil*, Manual for NOVIB and its Counterparts in Bolivia (La Paz: achaplin@megalink.com, 2005).

Claxton, Guy, *Hare Brain, Tortoise Mind: Why Intelligence Increases When You Think Less* (London: Fourth Estate, 1997).

Coleman, John A., SJ and Ryan, William, F., SJ (eds), *Globalization and Catholic Social Thought: Present Crisis, Future Hope* (Toronto: Novalis, 2005).

Collier, Paul and Dollar, David, *Globalization, Growth and Poverty: Building an Inclusive World Economy*, World Bank Policy Research Report (Washington: The World Bank • Oxford: Oxford University Press, 2002).

Cragg, Kenneth, *The House of Islam* (Belmont, CA: Wadsworth, 1988).

Crush, Jonathan, *Power of Development* (London • New York: Routledge, 1995).

Daly, Herman and Cobb, John, Jr, *For the Common Good: Redirecting the Economy toward Community, the Environment, and a Sustainable Future* (Boston: Beacon Press, 1990).

Daneel, M.L. *Old and New in Southern Shona Independent Churches*, vol.2, *Church Growth: Causative Factors and Recruitment Techniques* (The Hague: Mouton, 1974).

Dunning, John (ed.), *Making Globalisation Good* (Oxford: Oxford University Press, 2003).

Eade, Deborah (ed.), *Development and Culture*, Development in Practice Reader (Oxford: Oxfam, 2002).

Edwards, Michael, *Future Positive: International Co-operation in the 21st Century* (London: Earthscan, 1999).

Effendi, Shoghi, *The World Order of Bahá'u'lláh Selected Letters* (Wilmette, IL: Bahá'í Publishing Trust, 1974).

Ela, Jean Marc, *Ma Foi d'Africain* (Paris: Monograph M0000482, Call Number 230 E37m, 1985).

Feillard, Andrée, *NU vis-à-vis Negara* (Yogyakarta: LkiS, 1999).

Gardner, Gary, *Invoking the Spirit: Religion and Spirituality in the Quest for a Sustainable World*, Worldwatch Paper 164 (Washington: Worldwatch Institute, 2002).

Goulet, Denis, 'Confronting Social Upheaval', in Thomas. M. McFadden (ed.), *Theology Confronts a Changing World*, Annual Publication of the College Theology Society (West Mystic, CT: Twenty-Third Publications, 1977).

Goulet, Denis, 'Development Experts: The One-Eyed Giants', *World Development*, 7/8 (1980): 481–9.

Goulet, Denis, 'Development Indicators: A Research Problem, a Policy Problem', *The Journal of Socio-Economics*, vol. 21, No. 3 (1992): 245–60.

Goulet, Denis, *Development Ethics: A Guide to Theory and Practice* (New York: Apex Press • London: Zed Books, 1995).

Goulet, Denis, 'Développement: L'Epée à Double Tranchant', in *Foi et Développement*, No. 245 (Paris: Centre Lebret, 1996): pp. 1–6.

Gupta, Pawan K., *Swadhyaya, The Alternative Paradigm* (Mussoorie: SIDH, 1999); www.swaraj.org/shikshantar/resources_gupta2.html.

Hall, Gillette and Patrinos, Harry Anthony, *Pueblos Indígenas, Pobreza y Desarrollo Humano en América Latina: 1994–2000* (Washington: The World Bank, 2005).

Harcourt, Wendy (ed.), 'Development', *The Journal of the Society for International Development*, 46/4 (December 2003).

Harper, Sharon M.P. (ed.), *The Lab, the Temple and the Market*: *Reflections at the Intersection of Science, Religion and Development* (Ottawa: International Development Research Centre • Bloomfield, CT: Kumarian Press, 2000).

Harrison, Lawrence E. and Huntingdon, Samuel P. (eds), *Culture Matters: How Values Shape Human Progress* (New York: Basic Books, 2000).

Haverkort, Bertus and Hiemstra Wim (eds), *Food for Thought: Ancient Visions and New Experiments of Rural People* (Leusden: ETC/Compas • Bangalore: Books for Change • London: Zed Books, 1999).

Haverkort, Bertus, van't Hooft, Katrien and Hiemstra Wim (eds), *Ancient Roots, New Shoots: Endogenous Development in Practice* (Leusden: ETC/Compas • London: Zed Books, 2003).

Hogan, John P., *Credible Signs of Christ Alive: Case Studies from the Catholic Campaign for Human Development* (Lanham, MD • Oxford: Rowman & Littlefield, 2003).

Holenstein, Anne-Marie, *Role and Significance of Religion and Spirituality in Development Co-operation: A Reflection and Working Paper* (Berne: Swiss Agency for Development and Co-operation, 2005).

Huntingdon, Samuel P., *The Clash of Civilizations and the Remaking of World Order* (New York: Simon and Schuster, 1996).

Hutanuwatr, Pracha and Manivannan, Ramu, *The Asian Future: Dialogues for Change* (2 vols, London: Zed Books, 2005).

Jayapal, Pramila, 'Swadhyaya: Toward a New Order', ICWA *Letters* (India, September 1996).

Jayapal, Pramila, 'A crisis of imagination – IV, Creating something different', *Michigan Citizen*, 2–8 June 2002; www.boggscenter.org/mc6-8-02.htm.

Kapur, Promilla and Tribhuwan (eds), *Science, Religion and Development: An Interface* (New Delhi: Har-Anand Publications, 2001).

Knitter Paul F. and Muzaffar Chandra (eds), *Subverting Greed: Religious Perspectives on the Global Economy* (New York: Orbis Books, 2002).

Korten, David, *Getting to the 21ˢᵗ Century: Voluntary Action and the Global Agenda* (Bloomfield, CT: Kumarian Press, 1990).

Küng, Hans, *Yes to a Global Ethic* (London: SCM Press, 1995).

Leech, Kenneth, *The Sky is Red* (London: Darton, Longman and Todd, 2003).

Loy, David, *The Great Awakening; A Buddhist Social Theory* (Boston: Wisdom Publications, 2003).

Macleod, Morna, 'Mayan Dress as Text: Contested Meanings', *Development and Practice* 14/5 (August 2004): 680–9.

Macleod, Morna, *Espiritualidad, Movilización Política y Reparación Social: Recursos del Movimiento Maya en Guatemala*, Ponencia presentada en el X Congreso Latinoamericano sobre Religión y Etnicidad, Pluralismo Religioso y Transformaciones Sociales (Mexico, 5–9 July 2004).

Macleod, Morna, *Género y Diversidad Cultural: Algunos Conceptos y Pistas Metodológicas*, Paper for Seminar on Gender and Cultural Diversity, organized by Hivos and Novib (Quito, November 2003).

Macy, Joanna, *Dharma and Development: Religion as a Resource in the Sarvodaya Self-help Movement* (West Hartford, CT: Kumarian Press, 1983 [repr. 1985]).

Marshall, Katherine and Keough, Lucy, *Mind, Heart and Soul in the Fight against Poverty* (Washington: The World Bank, 2004).

Marshall, Katherine and Keough, Lucy, *Finding Global Balance: Common Ground between the Worlds of Development and Faith* (Washington: The World Bank, 2005).

Marshall, Katherine and Marsh, Richard (eds), *Millennium Challenges for Development and Faith Institutions* (Washington: The World Bank, 2003).

Martin Brown, Joan (Task Manager), *Culture Counts: Financing, Resources and the Economics of Culture in Sustainable Development*, Proceedings of the Conference in Florence, 1999 (Washington: The World Bank, 2000).

McMichael, Philip, *Development and Social Change: A Global Perspective* (Thousand Oaks, CA: Pine Forge Press, 2000).

Mernissi, Fatima, *Dreams of Trespass: Tales of a Harem Girlhood* (New York: Basic Books, 1995).

Narayan, Deepa with Patel, Raj, Schafft, Kai, Rademacher Anne and Koch-Schulte, Sarah, *Voices of the Poor*, vol. 1, *Can Anyone Hear Us?* (Oxford: Oxford University Press, 2000).

Narayan, Deepa with Chambers, Robert, Shah, Meera K. and Petesch, Patti, *Voices of the Poor*, vol. 2, *Crying out for Change* (Oxford: Oxford University Press, 2000).

Narayan, Deepa and Petesch, Patti (eds), *Voices of the Poor*, vol. 3, *From Many Lands* (Oxford: Oxford University Press, 2002).

Nasr Seyyed, Hossein, *Ideals and Realities of Islam*, (London: Aquarian Press, 1994).

Nasr Seyyed, Hossein, *Islam and the Plight of Modern Man* (Cambridge: Islamic Texts Society, 2002).

Norberg Hodge, Helena, *Ancient Futures* (London: Rider, 2000).

Paranjape, Makarand (ed.), *Dharma and Development: The Future of Survival* (New Delhi: Samvad India Foundation, 2005).

Payutto, Ven P.A., *Buddhist Economics: A Middle Way for the Market Place* (Bangkok: Buddhadhamma Foundation, 1994).

Peccoud, Dominique, *Philosophical and Spiritual Perspectives on Decent Work* (Geneva: International Labour Organization, 2004).

Rahnema, Majid with Bawtree, Victoria (eds), *The Post-Development Reader* (London: Zed Books • Dhaka: University Press Ltd. • Halifax: Fernwood Publishing • Cape Town: David Philip, 1997).

Reed, Charles (ed.), *Development Matters: Christian Perspectives on Globalisation* (London: Church House Publishing, 2001).

Reinikka, Ritva and Svensson, Jakob, *Working for God? Evaluating Service Delivery of Religious Not-for-Profit Health Care Providers in Uganda*, Policy Research Working Paper 3058 (Washington: World Bank, 2003).

de Rivero, Oswaldo, *Myth of Development* (London: Zed Books, 2001).

Rukmani, T.S., *Turmoil, Hope and the Swadhyaya*, Presentation at CASA conference, Montreal 1999; www.infinityfoundation.com/mandala/s_es/s_es_rukma_hope.htm.

Sachs, Wolfgang (ed.), *The Development Dictionary* (London • New Jersey: Zed Books, 1996).

Sacks, Jonathan, *The Dignity of Difference: How to Avoid the Clash of Civilisations* (London • New York: Continuum, 2003).

Salemink, Oscar, van Harskamp, Anton and Kumar Giri, Ananta (eds), *The Development of Religion/The Religion of Development* (Delft: Eburon, 2004).

Sen, Amartya, *Development as Freedom* (Oxford: Oxford University Press, 1999).

Sharma, Arvind (ed.), *Fragments of Infinity: Essays in Religion and Philosophy, Festschrift in Honour of Huston Smith* (Bridport: Prism, 1991).

Sharma, Arvind, *Hinduism and Human Rights: A Conceptual Approach* (Oxford: Oxford University Press, 2004).

Siebers, Hans, *Tradición, Modernidad e Identidad en los Q'eqchi'es*, Textos Ak' Kutan 10 (Cobán, Guatemala: Ak' Kutan, 1998).

Sivaraksa, Sulak, *A Buddhist Vision for Renewing Society* (Bangkok: Thai Inter-Religious Commission for Development, 1994).

Sivaraksa, Sulak, *Global Healing* (Bangkok: Thai Inter-Religious Commission for Development, 1999).

Smith, Cyprian, *The Way of Paradox: Spiritual Life as Taught by Meister Eckhart* (London: Darton, Longman and Todd, 1987).

Smith, Huston, *The World's Religions* (New York: Harper, 1991).

Soros, George, *Open Society*, (London: Little, Brown and Company, 2000).

Srivastava, R.K., *Vital Connections – Self, Society, God: Perspectives on Swadhyaya* (New York: Weatherhill, 1998).

Stiglitz, Joseph, *Globalization and its Discontents* (London: Penguin, 2002).

Sweetman, Caroline (ed.), *Gender, Religion and Spirituality* (Oxford: Oxfam, 1998).

Taylor, Michael, *Poverty and Christianity* (London: SCM Press, 2000).

Taylor, Michael, *Christianity, Poverty and Wealth* (London: SPCK, 2003).

Taylor, Michael, *Eat, Drink and Be Merry for Tomorrow We Live* (London: Continuum, 2005).

Tucker, Mary Evelyn, *Worldly Wonder: Religions Enter their Ecological Phase* (Chicago: Open Court • Illinois: La Salle, 2003).

Verhelst, Thierry, *No Life Without Roots* (London: Zed Books, 1990).

Verhelst, Thierry and Sauvage, Patrice, *Ailes et Racines* (Nantes • Laval: Siloë, 2001).

Wolfensohn, James, D., *The Other Crisis*, Address to the Board of Governors (Washington: The World Bank, 1998).

Wolfensohn, James, D., *Coalitions for Change*, Address to the Board of Governors (Washington: The World Bank, 1999).

The World Bank, *Attacking Poverty*, World Development Report 2000/2001 (Washington: The World Bank, 2001).

The World Bank, *Sustainable Development in a Dynamic World: Transforming Institutions, Growth, and Quality of Life*, World Development Report 2003 (Washington: The World Bank, 2003).

The World Bank, *Making Services Work for Poor People*, World Development Report 2004 (Washington: The World Bank, 2003).

Zuhri, Saifuddin et al., *Fatwa: Keluarga Berencana Ditinjau dari Segi Syari'at Islam*, [Religious Opinion: Reflections on Family Planning from the Perspective of Muslim Law] (Jombang, Indonesia: Lembag Kemaslahatan Keluarga Nahdlatul Ulama, 1979).

Index

agriculture, 46–7, 73
Aldunate, José, 138–40, 161
All India Catholic Student Federation, 132, 135
Allende, Erika Espinoza, 143
Allende, Salvador, 138
APEC (Asia-Pacific Economic Cooperation), 144
Ariyaratne, A.T., 9, 13–15, 17f, 21f
Ariyaratne, Neetha, 21
Ariyaratne, Vinya, 15f, 21
Ashram, Wongsanit, 126, 146, 149
Assembly of the Poor, 128
Aurenche, Christian, 70, 83
awakening, 9, 17

Bahá'í(s), 87, 102–4, 107–10, 112, 114–16
Bahá'u'lláh, 102, 110
Bangladesh, 125
banks,11f
Barber, Benjamin, 83
Base Christian Communities, 137f
Bhagavad Gita, 1, 3f, 20, 63
bhakti, 1f
Bible, 4, 72, 132, 165
Boff, Leonardo, 137, 151
Bolton, Robert, 139
Bonhoeffer, Dietrich, 145
Brazil, 144, 168
Buddhadasa, Bhikkhu, 123, 129, 146, 149
Buddhism, Buddhists, 9f, 13, 15–17, 20–23, 26f, 94, 121–5, 128f, 145f, 148–51, 155f, l60, 163f, 171, 173
Burma, 128

Cambodia, 125, 128
Cameroon, 29f, 33, 69, 73, 177
Canada, 136
Candomblé, 37–9, 50, 52, 54, 57, 156
Carey, George, xv
CASS (Centre of Social and Sanitary Promotion,Yaounde), 35

Castro, Pedro and Juan, 45, and Rosalinda, 46
Chambers, Robert, 14, 164f
charity, 1, 4
Chile, 137–9, 141–7, 150, 161, 177
Christian(s), Christianity, 18, 33, 36, 44f, 48, 153, 56f, 77, 88, 94, 115, 117, 119, 130–38, 141, 146, 148f, 151, 155f, 162f, 171, 173
  Baptist, 33, 57
  Catholic, 44, 57, 69, 81, 131, 140
  Pentecostal, 57
  Presbyterian, 45
  Orthodox, 87f, 131
CIEDEG (Conference of Evangelical Churches of Gautemala), 46
Commonwealth Foundation, 168
community, 81–3
condoms, 34, 42f, 51f, 173
Confucians, 94
consumerism, xviii, 85, 122f, 125, 128
craving, 122f
culture, 3, 52, 61, 72, 80, 83f, 166

Dada (Pandurang Vaijnath Athavale Shastri), 1, 5, 7
Dalits, 20, 27, 130
Didi (Dhanashree Talwalkar), 21, 26
DFID (Department for International Development, UK), 168
donor agencies (see funding), 14f, 36, 51
dualism, xviii, 2, 161, 170

education, 7f, 19f, 39f, 45, 64f, 72, 91
Ela, Jean Marc, 70f, 80
Enlightenment, xviii, 123, 160
environment, 25f, 66, 107f, 136, 149
EPRDF (Ethiopian People's Revolutionary Democratic Front), 88
Escobar, Claudio, 151
Ethiopia, Ethiopians, 87f, 110, 113, 115f
Europe, 131

evaluation, 174
exploitation, 56, 173

faith, 69
family planning, 97–100, 119, 170, 173
female genital mutilation, 91f, 112f, 115
Finger, Hanspeter, 161
Francis of Assisi, 176
freedom, 148f
funding, 23–5, 36, 41, 56, 75, 108

Gaudium et Spes, 140
Gautemala, xvi, 44f, 57, 170, 177
gender, 53f, 93, 112
Ghandi, Ghandian, xv, 9, 16, 22, 55, 126,
        130, 134
Ghandi Peace Prize, 28
Al Ghazali, Imam, 95
giving, 10, 18, 26, 53
Goulet, Denis, xv, 83, 158, 163
Gowda, Jadeya, 65, 84 and Shivane, 67
Gupta, Pawan, 20, 23

Haitians, 170
Hall, Gillett and Patrinos H.A., 162
hand-outs, 1
health, 47f, 65f, 70f, 91, 106
        reproductive, 98–100, 110
Hildegard of Bingen, 153
Hindu(s), Hinduism, 4, 14, 17, 26f, 63, 77f,
        82, 94, 130, 134, 136, 155, 163f, 173
HIV and AIDS, 34, 51f, 55, 65, 70, 169f,
        173, 177
Honduras, 136
Hutunawatr, Pracha, 155

ILO (International Labour Organisation),
        168
India, Indian, xvi, 1, 21–3, 27f, 61f, 82,
        102–4, 108, 115, 117, 130f, 134–6,
        144, 148, 151, 155, 166, 171, 177
Indonesia, 87, 94f, 97, 100, 115, 166
INEB (International Network of Engaged
        Buddhists), 125f
Inter-American Development Bank, 168f
interest, *see* usury
intuition, 160
Iran, 102
Islam, Islamic, 31, 34–6, 51–5, 69, 77,
        87–96, 99f, 111–19, 156, 161, 163,
        171
Ismaila, Sheik, 32

Japan, 125
Jayapal, Pramila, 25
Jesus, 57, 69, 134, 137, 145, 149
Jews, Jewish, Judaism, 117, 155, 171

Karma Yoga, 63
Kejawen, 94f, 115
Keough, Lucy, 171, 173f, 175
Kirdi, 69f, 78, 80–84
Kocherry, Thomas, 132f, 135f, 146, 148
Koinonia, 42, 57
Koli, N.D. 136
Komoch, Agnieska, 11
Korton, David, 172

Laos, 128
leadership, 20–22, 54f, 78
Liberation Theology, 149
literacy, 107
loans, 4, 11, 73
Loyola, Ignatius, 79

Madagascar, 136
Malaysia, 136
Marie, Philomine, 133, 135
Marshall, Katherine, xxi, 171, 173f, 175
Mayan, 22, 44f, 48, 50, 53, 57, 156, 170
MDGs (Millennium Development Goals),
        158, 169
Medical Mission Order, 132–4
Mexico, 22
mindfulness, 151
modernisation, modernity, xviii, 1, 14, 61, 72,
        83f, 121, 123f, 128f, 151, 157, 165f
Mohammed, 99, 118
Mohammed, Bedria, 112f, 118
monks, 13, 21
motivation, 79, 151, 177
Mpeke, Simon, 69–71, 76–8, 80
Muslim(s), 33, 35f, 75, 87–93, 96–8, 100,
        110–19, 130, 134, 161, 168, 173

National Commission on Political
        Imprisonment and Torture (Chile),
        142

nature worship, 62f
Nasr, Seyyed Houssein, 165
Nayak, Nalim, 132
needs, 12, 19
NGOs (non–government organisations), xv,
    14f, 21, 36, 45f, 54f, 80, 89, 116,
    129, 153, 158f, 168f, 172f, 175
non-violence, 129, 140–43

organisation, 11f, 20–22, 67

Pak Moon Dam, 128, 164
Palta, Janak Dulari (also Janak Palta
    McGilligan), 103f, 116
Pancasila, 94f
partnership, 24, 168, 175
Patrinos, H.A., *see* Hall
Paul, 81
peace, 13f, 33, 56f
Pehuenches, 151
Pereira, Bernard, 132
Philippines, 169
Pinochet, Augusto, 143, 149
politics, 22f, 35, 42, 95f, 116f, 150
poor, poverty, 1, 14, 18f, 91f, 113, 128f,
    161f, 171
Pope Paul VI, 140
population control, 97f
Porto Alegre, 144
professional distance, 164f
progress, 25
proselytizing, 3

Qur'an (and Hadith), 4, 31f, 34, 54, 89–93,
    95, 98–100, 110, 118f, 165, 177

Rahnema, Majid, 158
Ramakrishna Mission, 63
realism, 121, 147
Redemptorists, 132
religion, 77f, 153f, 166f
rights (human, women's), 14, 87, 89f, 92f,
    95, 102, 110, 151, 157f
Rosa, Mae, 39–41, 52–4
Rukmani, T.S., 20
Ryan, Bill, 160

Salvador, 37
SAP (Structural Adjustment Programme), 36

scaling up, 51, 58, 172
scriptures, 118f
SDC (Agency for Development Cooperation
    of the Swiss Government), 164f,
    167f, 176
Senegal, 136, 168
Selassie, Haile, 88
Sen, Amartya, 157, 163
Sharia, Islamic courts, 88–90, 92, 113, 115f,
    172
Siam (Thailand), 121f, 125f, 128f, 136, 148,
    177
Sivaraksa, Sulak, 124, 126, 128f, 146, 150f
Smith, Cyprian, 154
Smith, Huston, 156
socialism, 1, 5, 124
solidarity, 31f, 138, 141, 145
Soligas, 62–8, 78–81, 83f, 164
Soros, George, 82
Spirit in Education Movement, 128f
spirituality, 17f, 44, 48–51, 78, 117f, 133,
    135f, 146, 148, 154, 175
Sri Lanka, 1, 9, 11, 14, 22f, 25, 27, 125
Stanford University, 108
state, 80f
Stiglitz, Joseph, 157
Sudarshan, H, 61f, 66, 68, 78–82
suffering, 122, 124
Suharto, 94, 96f, 113
Sukarno, 97
sustainability, 174
Suzuki, D.T., 160
Swedish International Development Agency,
    108

Tagore, 136
technology, 114
temples, 4–6, 12, 27
Templeton Prize, 27
Thailand, *see* Siam
Thatcher, Margaret, 82
TICD (Thai Inter–Religious Commission
    for Development), 124f
Torrealba, Ana Cristina, 143f
torture, 138f
trade unions, 132f
transformation, 17, 79, 155, 165
    inner, 1, 8, 10, 18, 117f, 146, 160, 172
trees, 6f

Truth and Reconciliation Commission
        (Chile), 141f

Uganda, 169
United Nations Declaration of the Right to
        Development, 111, 157
UNDP (United Nations Development
        Programme), 174
UNESCO (United Nations Educational,
        Scientific and Cultural
        Organisation), 159, 168
UNICEF (United Nations Children's Fund),
        38, 108
UNFPA (United Nations Population Fund),
        168
United States, 131
Upanishads, 3, 63, 82
urbanisation, 59
usury, 34f, 52

values, 162f
Vatican, 138
Ver Beek, Kurt Alan, 167

Verhelst, Thierry, 176
Vivekananda, Swami, 63f, 67, 77–9
VSF (Vikram Sarabhai Foundation), xvii,
        113, 174

Wahid, Abdurrahman, 95f
water, 6, 12, 158
wealth, 2, 18f
    impersonal, 3–5
welfarism, 1
WFDD (World Faiths Development
        Dialogue), xv, xvii, 113, 168, 174
Wolfensohn, James, xv, 58, 158, 170
women, 11, 19f, 46–9, 74, chapter 4, 130,
        132, 173
World Bank, xv, 55, 58, 128, 157, 162,
        169–71, 175
World Social Forum, 136, 168
WTO (World Trade Organisation), 136, 147f

youth, 31, 71f, 84

Zayd, Nasr Hamid Abn, 119